HEIDEGGE

INTENSITIES: CONTEMPORARY CONTINENTAL PHILOSOPHY OF RELIGION

Series Editors:
Patrice Haynes and Steven Shakespeare,
both at Liverpool Hope University, UK

This series sits at the forefront of contemporary developments in Continental philosophy of religion, engaging particularly with radical reinterpretations and applications of the Continental canon from Kant to Derrida and beyond but also with significant departures from that tradition. A key area of focus is the emergence of new realist and materialist schools of thought whose potential contribution to philosophy of religion is at an early stage. Rooted in a vibrant tradition of thinking about religion, whilst positioning itself at the cutting edge of emerging agendas, this series has a clear focus on Continental and post-Continental philosophy of religion and complements Ashgate's British Society for Philosophy of Religion series with its more analytic approach.

Other titles in the series:

Intensities
Philosophy, Religion and the Affirmation of Life
Edited by Katharine Sarah Moody and Steven Shakespeare

Re-visioning Gender in Philosophy of Religion
Reason, Love and Epistemic Locatedness
Pamela Sue Anderson

Heidegger on Death
A Critical Theological Essay

GEORGE PATTISON
University of Oxford, UK

ASHGATE

Published by
Ashgate Publishing Limited
Wey Court East
Union Road
Farnham
Surrey, GU9 7PT
England

Ashgate Publishing Company
110 Cherry Street
Suite 3-1
Burlington
VT 05401-3818
USA

www.ashgate.com

British Library Cataloguing in Publication Data
Pattison, George, 1950–
   Heidegger on death: a critical theological essay. – (Intensities)
   1. Heidegger, Martin, 1889–1976. 2. Heidegger, Martin, 1889–1976. Sein und Zeit.
   3. Death. 4. Death – Religious aspects. 5. Philosophical theology.
   I. Title II. Series
   193-dc23

The Library of Congress has cataloged the printed edition as follows:
Pattison, George, 1950–
Heidegger on death: a critical theological essay / By George Pattison.
      pages cm. — (Intensities)
   Includes bibliographical references and index.
   ISBN 978-1-4094-6694-9 (hardcover: alk. paper) — ISBN 978-1-4094-6695-6 (pbk.: alk. paper)—ISBN 978-1-4094-6696-3 (ebook)—ISBN 978-1-4094-6697-0 (epub)
1. Heidegger, Martin, 1889-1976. 2. Death. 3. Heidegger, Martin, 1889–1976. Sein und Zeit. 4. Death—Religious aspects. I. Pattison, George, 1950– Running towards death. II. Title.
   B3279.H49P385 2013
   128'.5092—dc23

2012040652

ISBN 9781409466949 (hbk)
ISBN 9781409466956 (pbk)
ISBN 9781409466963 (ebk – PDF)
ISBN 9781409466970 (ebk – ePUB)

Printed and bound in Great Britain
by MPG PRINTGROUP

Dedicated to you, Adam,
who went towards death
with a clarity reserved for those who, seeing the world, see God.

Contents

Acknowledgements

Several of the chapters in this book took shape through seminar and conference presentations. Chapter 2 is a much expanded and revised version of a paper presented at the Post-Kantian Seminar at the Philosophy Faculty of Oxford University in 2011. Chapter 3 largely reflects a paper given at the 2008 Oxford Centre for Theology and Modern European Thought seminar 'Heidegger on Language, the Holy, and Poetry', itself part of a series of seminars and conferences on 'Heidegger and Religion' funded by Oxford University's John Fell Fund. Chapter 4 is largely based on a paper presented at the Department of Philosophy at Essex University in 2011 in the context of the British Academy funded series on 'Selfhood, Authenticity and Method in Heidegger's *Being and Time*, Division Two' convened by Denis McManus. It also includes material from a paper given at the conference 'The Ethical Demand in the Philosophies of Løgstrup, Kierkegaard and Levinas' held at Århus University in 2011. Chapter 5 started off as a paper to the Woodroffe Society Dinner at Worcester College, Oxford also in 2011. Chapters 1, 2, and 3 formed the basis of a study-day in the department of Religion and Theology at the University of Manchester (2012). Teaching courses on *Being and Time* at the University of Århus and Løgum Kloster Teaching Centre also played an important role in the genesis of this work. All of these occasions involved extensive and constructive comment and criticism, both formally and, in many cases, informally. At many points such comment and criticism has been incorporated into the reworking of the material, although there will doubtless remain several points at which agreement has not yet been reached.

In any case, I am grateful to all colleagues who gave me the opportunity to develop these arguments through such conversations and I am particularly indebted in this regard to Clare Carlisle, Taylor Carman, Daniel Dahlstrom, Theodore Kisiel, Denis McManus, Stephen Mulhall, Joseph Schear, Tom Sheehan, Judith Wolfe, Mark Wrathall, and many students who have all significantly helped me deepen my understanding of the relevant aspects of Heidegger's thought. Melissa Raphael provided helpful reassurance regarding Rosenzweig. Gilly McKie is owed thanks for references to current medical literature on dying. As always, Hilary has lived with the conception and genesis of this book for some time and, for much longer, with the existential questioning out of which it has grown. In addition to the usual trials and tribulations of living with a writing project, this has involved bearing with and helping make sense of questions that have been and that continue to be of sometimes overpowering human importance. I am, finally, grateful to Steve Shakespeare for inviting contributions to this series, an invitation that provided the opportunity to work these various papers together into book form.

I am grateful to Faber Ltd for permission to reproduce selections from Edwin Muir's *Collected Poems*.

The dedication indicates that, as must be the case, we will always learn more about death and about any other decisive existential question from existence or life itself than from the studious labour of sourcing, organizing, and arguing through what life is always and everywhere teaching us. The coming into existence of the book, however, testifies my belief that such work also has its own modest value.

George Pattison
Oxford, September 1, 2012

References

References to *Being and Time* are to the 1962 translation by John Macquarrie and Edward Robinson. They are given without further reference in brackets in the text, giving first the page number in Heidegger's first edition (also valid for the edition in the *Gesamtausgabe* [GA] or Collected Works) and then the page number in the English edition, e.g., 20/41. Other references are given in footnotes to works from the *Gesamtausgabe*. Where I have relied on an English-language version, details of this will be given first, followed by a reference to the *Gesamtausgabe* with volume and page number.

Similarly in the case of Kierkegaard, references are to the now complete new standard edition of his works, *Søren Kierkegaards Skrifter* (SKS), followed by references to relevant available English translations.

Occasionally, where I have cited a single source extensively over a number of pages, I have used a short reference included in the main text, providing details on first quotation.

Introduction

This is, in the first instance, a book about death. In writing it, I have been mindful of the philosopher Vladimir Jankélévitch's teasing and self-critical remark that writing a book about death might be a good antidote to thinking about it. Why? Because the process of writing creates a distance between author and topic that minimizes the existential impact of what is being written about. Writing, that is to say, removes the conditions that make it possible *really* to *think* (in this case) death.[1] Perhaps that is a warning that all who set out to write a book about death should bear in mind, and it might well be extended to their readers. As we shall learn from Heidegger, whose own writing about death provides the more particular focus of this study, there is already something suspect in wanting to talk too much about our relation to death. The more we talk, the less we say. And yet it would be strange to place any kind of embargo on death as a topic of human reflection and discussion, since death has been a pervasive theme of religion, art, literature, and philosophy from the beginning of recorded history and it would be historically and culturally ruinous to ignore it.[2] It is certainly the case that it has been a defining focus not only of much Christian religious practice but also of Christian theology and, more broadly, of the Western philosophical tradition.

Yet it is no less true that the issue of death has been very differently thematized in different eras. In the so-called Christian centuries human responses to death were, at least officially, contextualized by faith in immortality, even if the Stoic, Platonic, and biblical elements that contributed to this faith were ultimately too disparate to be fully harmonized. In the early modern period, a combination of increasing scientific knowledge and new approaches to the Bible rendered these assumptions about the immortality of the human soul increasingly questionable.[3] Nevertheless (or perhaps just for this reason), insistence on the immortality of the soul had by the later eighteenth century become one of the lynchpins of Christian apologetics. Joseph Butler declared that 'whether we are to live in a future state … is the most important question which can possibly be asked'.[4] Kant seemed to give it similar importance when he grouped immortality with God and freedom as one of

---

[1]   V. Jankélévitch, *Penser la Mort* (Paris: Liana Levi, 1994), p. 9.

[2]   On the foundational role of death in human culture, see J. Assmann, *Der Tod als Thema der Kulturtheorie* (Frankfurt am Main: Suhrkamp, 2000).

[3]   See A. Thomson, *Bodies of Thought: Science, Religion, and the Soul in the Early Enlightenment* (Oxford: Oxford University Press, 2008).

[4]   J. Butler, *The Analogy of Religion, Natural and Revealed* (London: Dent Dutton, 1906), p. 257.

the three metaphysical assumptions that were needed in order to underwrite belief in the sovereignty of practical reason.

In the decades following the French Revolution this began to change and to change rapidly. In 1828, David Friedrich Strauss wrote a prize essay on the resurrection of the flesh of which he later said that 'as soon as I made the last full-stop, it was clear to me that there was nothing in the whole idea of resurrection'.[5] The Danish theologian H.L. Martensen (often the target of Kierkegaard's attacks on an overly philosophical kind of theology) reported Strauss as saying, 'I had scarcely finished reading Hegel's *Phenomenology of Spirit*, before that belief [immortality] fell away from me like a dead leaf'.[6] That the *Phenomenology* did indeed internalize a radical sense of the finitude and unqualified mortality of the human subject and that this was both absolutely integral to Hegel's whole philosophical programme as well as being a point at which Hegel distanced himself from the Judaeo-Christian tradition would be forcefully argued in the twentieth century by Alexandre Kojève. According to Kojève, Hegel's conception of the life of Spirit is precisely that of a life that has incorporated the consciousness of its mortality into its self-understanding.[7] Whether this is a correct interpretation of the *Phenomenology*, Hegelianism certainly provided a powerful impetus to those younger thinkers minded to deny the possibility of any future life. Ludwig Feuerbach's *Thoughts on Death and Immortality* (1830), according to a recent translator, 'is a straightforward denial of the Christian belief in personal immortality, a plea for recognition of the inexhaustible quality of the only life we have, and a derisive assault on the posturing and hypocrisies of the professional theologians of nineteenth-century Germany'.[8] In *The Essence of Christianity* (1841), Feuerbach sums up: 'Faith in a future life is therefore only faith in the true life of the present ... faith in a future life is not faith in another unknown life; but in the truth and infinitude, and consequently in the perpetuity, of that life which already here below is regarded as the authentic life'.[9] Later, in *The Essence of Faith according to Luther*, he will say that 'death ... is the only ultimate basis of religion. And the abolition of death, immortality, is the only ultimate goal of religion, at least of the Christian religion, and the means of this abolition is God'.[10]

---

    [5]   H. Harris, *David Friedrich Strauss and His Theology* (Cambridge: Cambridge University Press, 1973), p. 19.

    [6]   H.L. Martensen, *Af mit Levnet*, vol. 1 (Copenhagen: Gyldendal, 1882), p. 131.

    [7]   See A. Kojève, *Introduction à la lecture de Hegel; leçons sur la phénoménologie de l'esprit* (Paris: Gallimard, 1947). For further discussion see Chapters 2 and 6 below.

    [8]   L. Feuerbach, *Thoughts on Death and Immortality: From the Papers of a Thinker, along with an Appendix of Theological-Satirical Epigrams, Edited by One of His Friends*, ed. and trans. J. Massey (Berkeley: University of California Press, 1980), p. ix.

    [9]   L. Feuerbach, *The Essence of Christianity*, trans. M. Evans (New York: Prometheus, 1989), p. 181.

    [10]   L. Feuerbach, *The Essence of Faith According to Luther*, trans. M. Cherno (New York: Harper and Row, 1967), p. 126.

Even before Feuerbach religious apologists such as Schleiermacher (whose lectures Feuerbach himself attended) were in fact already turning away from articulating the Christian response to death in terms of a promised hereafter. In his *Speeches on Religion*, Schleiermacher laments how 'most people' understand immortality in an essentially 'irreligious' manner:

> [T]hey resist the infinite and do not wish to get beyond themselves and they are anxiously concerned about their individuality ... they do not want to seize the sole opportunity death affords them to transcend humanity; they are anxious about how they will take it with them beyond this world, and their highest endeavour is for further sight and better limbs. But the universe speaks to them, as it stands written: "Whoever loses his life for my sake, will find it, and whoever would save it will lose it" ... In search of an immortality, which is none, and over which they are not masters, they lose the immortality that they could have, and in addition their mortal life with thoughts that vainly distress and torment them. But try to yield up your life out of love for the universe. Strive here already to annihilate your individuality and to live in the one and all ....[11]

As Schleiermacher sums up, 'To be one with the infinite in the midst of the finite and to be eternal in a moment, that is the immortality of religion'.[12]

Such views became widespread in the nineteenth century and everything we shall read in Heidegger regarding death and the possibility of affirming human meaning in the face of death presupposes but also radicalizes this new understanding. There is no afterlife. Human existence comes to an entire end in death. Yet life is, nevertheless, meaningful and to be affirmed as the ground and context of all possible meaning. Of course, Heidegger will largely abandon religious or consolatory references to God, infinity, or eternity that have by his time become merely rhetorical. Authentic existence does not aspire to be a life divine.

If the ground for Heidegger's view was remotely prepared by these nineteenth-century revisions of earlier belief systems,[13] it is very plausible that the experience of the First World War called for just the kind of further radicalization that we find in Heidegger. Paul Tillich, who had served as an army chaplain in the war, saw it as bringing to an end a period in which death had largely been ignored. It was the moment when, as he put it in one of his sermons, 'the lid was torn off' and 'the picture of Death appeared, unveiled, in a thousand forms. As in the late Middle Ages the figure of Death appeared in pictures and poetry, and the Dance of Death

---

[11] F.D.E. Schleiermacher, *Speeches on Religion*, trans. R. Crouter (Cambridge: Cambridge University Press, 1988), p. 139.

[12] Ibid., p. 140.

[13] Heidegger himself was, incidentally, an astute reader of Schleiermacher's *Speeches*. See, e.g., T. Kisiel and T. Sheehan (eds.), *Becoming Heidegger* (Evanston: Northwestern University Press, 2007), pp. 86–91.

with every living being was painted and sung, so our generation – the generation of world wars, revolutions, and mass migrations – rediscovered the reality of death'.[14]

This is not to say that Heidegger's thought is a mere reflection of a moment of intense cultural anxiety about death. He himself robustly rejected the view that the philosophy of *Being and Time* was a 'philosophy of death', as some claimed. And even if the crisis of the 1920s provided the immediate occasion for his re-envisioning of human beings' relation to their death, there is little doubt that what Heidegger offered must be contextualized in the larger paradigm shift that can be traced back to the generation after Hegel or even to Hegel himself.[15] In this larger perspective, Heidegger articulated the implications of the new paradigm with a depth, energy, and consistency that was and that remains unrivalled. How he did this was, in large part, due to the way in which (as we shall see) he deliberately applied new intellectual resources to ancient philosophical problems, but it would be historically naïve and in some respects alien to his own conception of philosophy to think of him as doing so outside the context of his own cultural moment. Even the new resources on which he drew – a rediscovered Luther, Kierkegaard, and the poetry of Trakl, Rilke, and Hölderlin – were very much of the moment and are shared with many of his contemporaries.

With these comments we have already introduced Heidegger, whose work, especially *Being and Time*, provides this study with its line of approach to the question of death. The potential service that a Heideggerian approach might offer to Christian theology has long been recognized.[16] Of course, it does not follow that Christian theology must accept the modern paradigm that re-defines the goal of Christian life in terms of this world rather than the next, still less that it should endorse Heidegger's version of it. On the contrary, it has many reasons, historic and systematic, for adopting a certain critical distance both from the larger modern view and from Heidegger's particular formulation of it. I have sub-titled this work 'A Critical Theological Essay' and I shall at many points register the kinds of objections that a Christian response to Heidegger must make if it is to be true to its sources and its hope. Nevertheless, it is a basic premise of everything that follows that whilst there is much that is distinctive to Heidegger, his central claims are not just the more or less arbitrary views of an individual philosopher but articulate something central to the modern conception of being human. And insofar as his work is indeed distinctive, it is so largely by the persistent rigour with which he thinks through the human condition in the perspective of its thrownness towards death. Whatever criticisms this work contains – and there are not a few – they therefore presuppose a perhaps more fundamental appreciation

---

[14] P. Tillich, *The New Being* (New York: Scribner, 1955), p. 171.

[15] On the analogies between Hegel's and Heidegger's views of death, see Chapter 2 below.

[16] See, e.g., J. Macquarrie, 'Death and Its Existential Significance' in J. Macquarrie (ed.), *Studies in Christian Existentialism* (Montreal: McGill University Press, 1965), pp. 45–57.

both of the intention and of the way in which Heidegger develops his thoughts on death. Heidegger may not have been right (whatever being right might mean in this context), but he takes us to the point at which the truly serious questions arise and his case must be answered.

What form might such an 'answer' take? We have already seen how Schleiermacher sought to re-envision Christian teaching on immortality in such a way as to give greater emphasis to the infinite quality of life in this world than to speculations on human beings' post-mortem states. A more recent version of such a revisionist approach is D.Z. Phillips's *Death and Immortality*, where he argued that belief in post-mortem survival is not integral to Christian belief in immortality, since 'For the believer, his death, like his life, is to be in God. For him, this is the life eternal which death cannot touch; the immortality which finally places the soul beyond the reach of the snares and temptations of this mortal life'.[17] More radically still, Don Cupitt states that it is a basic principle of a genuinely contemporary faith that 'one should not believe in life after death but should instead strive to attain the goal of spiritual life in history'.[18] Yet, even apart from any theological difficulties to which such revisionary approaches are exposed, they seem scarcely to respond to what, for want of a better term, we might call the 'ontological shock' that Heidegger sees in human thrownness towards death. If death is indeed all that Heidegger says it is, then it is question begging to assume that we have options on living in the world in such a way as not to be touched by death (Phillips) or that there is any 'goal' at all to 'spiritual life in history' (Cupitt). Similarly, John Hick's speculative approach to the kind of existence after death that might (a) be compatible with a scientific worldview and (b) reflect the wisdom of a multi-religious perspective seems simply to bypass the scandal of the entire annihilation of self and world that Heidegger is prepared to contemplate. Moreover, it treats death and human beings' post-life fate as if these were the sort of objective entities that Heidegger's existential approach rules to be inappropriate in relation to the unique character of human Dasein.[19]

A very different possibility would be simply to refuse the terms of the modern paradigm. For Karl Barth, for example, the resurrection of the dead remained a defining affirmation of Christian faith, although he consistently refused to engage in speculating on just what this meant regarding post-mortem states and emphasized instead the sovereign Lordship of God in both life and death.[20] Indeed, such reticence is characteristic of most more recent theological approaches to the question. Even

---

[17] D.Z. Phillips, *Death and Immortality* (London: Macmillan, 1970), p. 60.

[18] D. Cupitt, *Taking Leave of God* (London: SCM Press, 1980), p. 10.

[19] See J. Hick, *Death and Eternal Life* (London: Collins, 1976). In this regard it is illuminating that Hick, for his part, treats Heidegger's analysis as simply a 'psychological analysis', thereby missing the defining role of Heidegger's own guiding question as to the meaning of being. See Hick, *Death*, pp. 97–101.

[20] See K. Barth, *The Resurrection of the Dead*, trans. H.J. Stanning (London: Hodder and Stoughton, 1933).

when Cupitt's preferred option of disavowing any version of 'survival' is rejected, the issue is less whether death does in fact mark the cessation of any temporally extended self-conscious existence than whether, faced with death, we still have the possibility of embracing hope as a basic human attitude. And if hope remains possible, what might that mean in the face of death? Going one step further, we might add that if hope is indeed a basic desideratum of any Christian view of death, another no less essential element of such a view is gratitude. And what could gratitude mean for a creature such as the human being that lives only on condition of having to die?

It is striking that recent philosophical discussions of death seem to show little need to engage with Christian views.[21] This may not just be because of a general secular disinterest in theology but because the Christian approach has itself been fragmented, uncertain, and often simply evasive, and even if it continues to use the older language of immortality, resurrection, and eternity it is often in the this-worldly sense of the revisionary theologies we have been considering. This, however, gives the philosophers little enough to go on. A similar crisis is apparent in the changing culture of funerary rites. Even in a Christian funeral service it is now more frequent to hear a eulogy of the dead than preaching concerning the last things. 'The Lord's my shepherd' has yielded to 'I did it my way' and liturgical rigour has similarly yielded to personal choices. As in the Westminster Abbey service for Diana, Princess of Wales, the result may be far removed from what would have been a standard Church funeral service 50 years ago. In many respects this is welcome. Any priest who has conducted fully traditional funeral services for congregations unschooled either in the traditional liturgies or in the Church's doctrine of death will have been painfully aware of the epistemic and emotional gap between what is said and what the bereaved are experiencing. Such liturgy is so far from addressing grief and arousing hope as all the more to abandon the mourners to themselves. But as long as such practical responses are not supported by a steady and consistent thinking through of the underlying issues they remain exposed to short-term cultural shifts and, often, to symbolic and linguistic incoherence.

In this situation it would seem best for the theologian to be cautious in offering too many or too loud pronouncements ex cathedra. It is for this reason that this present essay seeks to meet philosophy on its own ground and to explore what possibilities for a genuinely hopeful response to death might be opened up from within modern philosophy's most consistent portrayal of human existence as thrown towards an ineluctable death from which there is neither appeal nor deliverance. Therefore the critical response to Heidegger that follows will by no means attempt to 'refute' Heidegger but, instead, to think with Heidegger in such a way as to show as accurately as possible the point at which Heideggerian existentialism and Christian faith – even, if I may put it like this, Christian existential faith – will part company and, at the same time, also attempt to explore how Heidegger's

---

[21]   See, e.g., J. Malpas and R.C. Solomon, *Death and Philosophy* (London: Routledge, 1988) in which the Christian tradition is represented by Aquinas, Kierkegaard, and Jesus Christ, who respectively get one, two, and three mentions.

way of thinking may help Christian faith in preparing its own thinking response to human mortality. For, taken as a whole, Heidegger's approach to death is not merely 'negative' and if the present essay is 'critical' it is also and at the same time constructive, thinking with Heidegger and, with Heidegger, working its way towards the hope and gratitude with which a Christian response to death must begin.

Some, perhaps many, theological colleagues will see this essay as conceding much too much ground to a philosophy that is, from the outset, anti-theological. Even in its own terms, they are likely to say, it scarcely reaches the point at which a properly theological response to Heidegger or to the question of death can and must begin: with the self-revelation of God in Jesus Christ. However, whilst this kind of robust talk goes down well with fellow theologians, I have long been convinced that theology will only hold its place in the contemporary academy to the extent that it is able to demonstrate that its particular textual and intellectual resources can prove fruitful for the ongoing work of colleagues in other faculties, especially in other humanistic faculties. Loudly proclaiming theology's queenly dominion over the other sciences is simply a waste of time if it is unable to produce work that constructively helps fellow workers in the academy in their own thinking, teaching, and research. Today's theologian is neither above nor below the philosopher (or historian or literary critic) but engaged in an essentially shared discourse – and, for that matter, an essentially shared struggle for survival in a political context that is rapidly abandoning the fig leaf of a declared faith in the value of a humanistic education as such.[22]

The general aims of this essay should by now be clear. It should also be clear that, as an avowedly Christian and theological study it is not primarily intended as a contribution to the ever-growing philosophical literature on Heidegger. Heidegger is taken as a companion on a path of enquiry and not as an object of study in his own right. In any case, philosophers will often – mostly – come to his work with very different questions from the one that is at issue here. Nevertheless, at least some philosophers are attentive to the question of death in Heidegger's thought and philosophers too can only interpret Heidegger on the basis of reading his texts with a view to what those texts are actually 'saying' or 'about'. Alongside the task of reading Heidegger in such a way as to illuminate the question of death it will therefore be appropriate to comment briefly on the most relevant philosophical literature, over and above the references that will be made in passing in the text.

Since its treatment of death rapidly became one of the most commented-on features of *Being and Time*, it is inevitable that nearly all introductory works on Heidegger make some mention of it.[23] At the same time, and as some commentators

---

[22]   Of course, it should also be said that, for a religious believer, expulsion from the academy would by no means be the worst of fates. However, to the extent that theology seeks to maintain its place at this particular table, it needs to accept the proper rigour and humility of all genuinely scholarly work.

[23]   As, e.g., S. Mulhall, *Routledge Philosophy Guidebook to Heidegger and* Being and Time (London: Routledge, 1996), pp. 114–20.

acknowledge, there has been relatively little sustained attention to death in the larger scholarly literature, at least not in relation to its apparent importance in *Being and Time*. A good general expository survey of the theme is found in James M. Demske's *Sein, Mensch und Tod. Der Todesproblem bei Martin Heidegger* (Being, Man and Death. The Problem of Death in Martin Heidegger).[24] Although published in 1963 and therefore not able to deal with some of the relevant works that have been published since then, this still provides a good account of how the theme of death persists beyond *Being and Time* into Heidegger's later philosophy. It remains the best survey work on the subject.

A very different kind of work is Paul Edwards's notorious *Heidegger on Death: A Critical Evaluation*. Although this present essay shares the term 'critical' with Edwards's work, it soon becomes clear that, in his case, it also carries the connotation of 'hostile', as can already be guessed from the dedication to Bertrand Russell as the 'enemy of humbug and mystification'. 'Humbug and mystification' just about sums up Edwards's entire view of Heidegger's approach. As he himself puts it, 'The few good ideas that are found in Heidegger's works are shrouded in the obscure and barbarous jargon of his writings'.[25] Unfortunately, whilst a philosopher must expect his work to be subject to ruthless scrutiny, Edwards's approach is so negative as to obscure even the 'few good' criticisms he makes in passing.[26] Generally, whether with regard to philosophy or literature, it is never going to be possible to understand a work unless we are prepared to engage in some kind of suspension of disbelief sufficient to allow us to enter the world of the text. Wilfully to misinterpret whatever the text says is the technique of the interrogator, not the thinker. Thus, to take one example, Edwards treats Heidegger's discussion of the essential solitude of death as implying that 'a Heideggerian should not send for his family' if taken to hospital after an accident likely to cause his death.[27] This has so little to do with what Heidegger is saying as to make it virtually irrefutable, not to mention laughable! As a pencilled marginal note on page 29 of the copy of Edwards's work in Oxford's Bodleian Library puts it, 'Why should we expect a philosopher to be meaningful if we wilfully and consciously use their work in ways they explicitly advised us not to?' Whilst deprecating writing in library copies of books, it is hard not to disagree with the anonymous commentator. Good reading requires a minimum of hermeneutical generosity that is simply absent from Edwards's work.

More recent work on the question amongst Anglo-American philosophers often reflects Taylor Carman's assertion that, in Heidegger, death 'does not mean

---

[24]   J.M. Demske, *Sein, Mensch und Tod. Der Todesproblem bei Martin Heidegger* (Freiburg and Munich: Karl Alber, 1963).

[25]   P. Edwards, *Heidegger on Death: A Critical Evaluation* (La Salle: The Hegeler Institute, 1979), p. 3.

[26]   I shall, in Chapter 2, flag one point on which I am in agreement with him.

[27]   Edwards, *Heidegger*, p. 9. For discussion of how to understand this question in a way that is truer to the text see Chapter 1 below, p. 23n12.

quite what is commonly meant by the word'.[28] When Heidegger talks about being towards death he is not talking about pondering our future biological demise but about the kind of self-understanding attainable by Dasein when it authentically relates to the possibility of its own death and does so by way of a certain modification of its relation to its world. For Carman himself, this seems primarily to involve recognition of the fact that we are always losing certain life possibilities and that even when we act in such a way as to realize one possibility we thereby close down others that are by that very same act lost irretrievably.[29] Perhaps not dissimilarly, William D. Blattner writes that, for Heidegger, death 'is the name for a certain condition in which Dasein can find itself, viz., the condition of not being able to be anyone. This condition besets Dasein when it finds itself suffering anxiety, which is a global indifference to all the possibilities that present themselves to Dasein'.[30] In an unfinished and posthumously published work Carol White separates the central thrust of Heidegger's approach to death from its association with an excessively subjective absorption in the prospect of my death in order to throw a bridge across from *Being and Time* to the 'history of being' themes of the later Heidegger. 'Death' is not primarily my biological decease but the collapse or unavailability of the background assumptions that make it possible for us to have a world at all. What is at issue in Dasein, she says, 'is the community and more expansively, the culture'.[31] Death is thus the death of sustaining and implicit cultural foundations, such as became apparent in the transition from paganism to Christianity or from the Middle Ages to the modern world. 'Old possibilities are left behind in this transformation, and new ones take their place in the "there" of being'. [32] Yet (she suggests) there is something more going on here than the simple replacement of one culture by another. For what such moments of transition reveal is also that no new construction is going to be able to gather up the totality of everything that is of concern to Dasein and bring it to the light. There will always be a 'realm of being that proves impenetrable to our understanding' and this realm is death.[33] In these terms death is 'the shadow' that bears testimony to 'the concealed emitting of light' – an illusion of the interdependence of concealment and revelation in Heidegger's fully developed theory of truth.[34] An authentic comportment towards

---

[28] T. Carman, *Heidegger's Analytic: Interpretation, Discourse and Authenticity in Being and Time* (Cambridge: Cambridge University Press, 2009), p. 276.

[29] Ibid., p. 281.

[30] W.D. Blattner, 'The Concept of Death in *Being and Time'* in H.L. Dreyfus and M. Wrathall (eds.), *Heidegger Re-Examined* (New York: Routledge, 2002), pp. 325–6.

[31] C.J. White, *Time and Death: Heidegger's Analysis of Finitude* (Aldershot: Ashgate, 2005), p. 35.

[32] Ibid., p. 21.

[33] Ibid., p. 21.

[34] Ibid., p. 74. For further discussion of this interdependence of concealment and revelation, darkness and light see my *Routledge Philosophy Guidebook to the Later Heidegger* (London: Routledge, 2000), pp. 100–101, 154.

death, then, is 'not just having the courage to face your own death' but, aware of the inevitable limitations of any human construction of cultural or individual life (that is, aware of the essential finitude of human self-understanding), 'having the courage to risk something on your own that goes against the conventional wisdom of the age'.[35] With these thoughts White suggests translating Heidegger's key term *Vorlaufen* (translated as 'anticipation' by Robinson and Macquarrie) as 'forerunning', since 'Authentic Dasein is indeed a forerunner or harbinger of a new understanding of being'.[36]

There is much in such revisionary interpretations that I would not resist. However – and as Carman also points out – if Heidegger doesn't quite mean 'death' when he speaks about the existential–ontological conception of death 'neither is his existential conception of death wholly alien to our ordinary understanding'.[37] More generally, Heidegger's ontological analyses are systematically developed through a radical interpretation of what calls the existentiell or ontic experience and understanding of existence, i.e., life as we know it in an 'average everyday' kind of way or through the scholarly study of a particular aspect of life. In this case, that means that whatever 'work' the concept of death is doing in relation to Heidegger's ontological enquiry into the meaning of being is being done in and through an interpretation of how Dasein relates to death in something like the ordinary sense of the word. If 'death' simply becomes a cipher for the inherent unfinishedness of life, a mood of anxious incapacity to relate fully to life, cultural relativity, or the limitations of knowledge, then it seems to be rhetorically over-dramatic. Whilst all of these may indeed come into view in and as a result of an authentic attitude towards death, the fact that it is death that provides the vantage point from which they can be seen for what and as they are adds something more, namely, that such truths about human existence are only available to me on the condition that I accept my own annihilation in death as a thinking, feeling, self-conscious individual. To use a biblical analogy, those who are to be forerunners in White's sense must be prepared not just to leave behind the Egypt of their old understanding of being for the sake of some new promised land; they must also be prepared to leave the Egypt of the past and to venture the journey into the wilderness without a prospect of any future promised land, accepting to the full the possibility that the desert is all that they will ever know. Only such total self-renunciation can prepare the possibility of a new beginning 'beyond the wasteland', a possibility we can for now know only in the mode of poetry. An authentic Heideggerian forerunner, therefore, will – to borrow a phrase of Kierkegaard's – become a 'sacrificed one', even if the 'sacrifice' concerned is not a publicly authorized sacrifice such as Agamemnon's sacrifice of Iphigenia or the self-sacrifice of a soldier in battle but a sacrifice 'for nothing'. Whatever venture of thought such a one undertakes will be undertaken in the unflinching recognition

---

[35]   White, *Time and Death*, pp. 82–3.

[36]   Ibid., p. 89.

[37]   Carman, *Analytic*, p. 276.

that they may simply be throwing away the one life they have and that there is no second chance. 'Death', then, may not 'quite' mean 'what is commonly meant by the word', but if we are to take Heidegger in his own terms it must mean more and not less than 'what is commonly meant'. That is to say, 'death' must comprise *death* and will, as we shall hear Heidegger himself acknowledge, be no more than a 'fantastical exaction' if it cannot be related to the concrete existentiell realities of human life as it is lived – including death as it is feared, faced, and undergone.

A further issue that I do not intend to address here, although it is a legitimate if painful issue in its own right, is that of how Heidegger's conception of human authenticity being pre-eminently attainable through a clear-sighted and freely chosen relation to death as our ownmost possibility relates to what Edith Wyschogrod has called 'man-made mass death'.[38] This further involves Heidegger's much-discussed relation to National Socialism (he himself joined the Nazi party in 1933) and raises the spectre that the kind of obsession with death that some see in *Being and Time* prepared the way for the 'death dance' of National Socialism's terrible 12-year Reich. Such a link is suggested by the German title of Rüdiger Safranski's biography of Heidegger: *A Master from Germany*, an allusion to Paul Celan's poem 'Fugue of Death', which is in turn a poetic exploration of the experience of death in the extermination camps that he himself lived through and that speaks emphatically of death as 'a Master from Germany' in lines 28, 32, 34, and 38. The issue is further compounded by Heidegger's own inability to give any clear post-war accounting of the responsibility he felt for the crimes committed by the Reich and, in several enigmatic statements, seems to suggest (a) that the death camps were morally (or, at any rate, ontologically) on the same level as industrialized agriculture and (b) that the Jews and other who died in the camps did not 'die' in the radical authentic sense of the term but merely 'perished'. However, these comments are, as I have said, enigmatic and could be read in a way that, far from trivializing the crimes of the Holocaust, sees them in the horizon of the broader modern phenomenon of a military–industrial complex that continues to threaten the diminishment of human life.[39] In these terms, Heidegger's comments could be seen as analogous to those of a left-wing commentator such as Adorno.[40]

---

[38]   See E. Wyschogrod, *Spirit in Ashes: Hegel, Heidegger, and Man-Made Mass Death* (New Haven: Yale University Press, 1985).

[39]   For discussion see my *The Later Heidegger*, pp. 28–30. For a more negative appraisal see J.D. Caputo, *Demythologizing Heidegger* (Bloomington: Indiana University Press, 1993), pp. 131–47. A further dimension of the sensitivity and complexity of the issue is signalled by Melissa Raphael's observation that many male Jewish commentaries on the Holocaust have reserved accounts of 'authentic' dying for male victims, whilst figuring women's deaths as precisely 'perishing', i.e., as dying like animals. See M. Raphael, *The Female Face of God in Auschwitz: A Jewish Feminist Theology of the Holocaust* (London: Routledge, 2003), pp. 21–7.

[40]   This is Safranski's argument, for example. See R. Safranski, *Martin Heidegger: Between Good and Evil* (Cambridge: Harvard University Press, 1998), p. 414.

However, fully to explore what is going on in these remarks would require an extension of this essay in a direction that is not proper to it, since, as I have said, it is in the first instance an essay about death that uses Heidegger, especially the Heidegger of *Being and Time*, as a way of thinking about the question of death in a Christian and theological perspective. As such it does not therefore need to offer a total account of every death-related question that arises in connection with Heidegger. All I shall say here is that even a harsh view of how Heidegger's philosophy fed into the ideology of Nazism need not conclude that his philosophy did not contain other possibilities, pointing towards other paths. Without prejudice to the issue of Heidegger's Nazism, then, it is to the identification, exploration, and – through critical discussion – further development of these possibilities that this essay is dedicated. In these terms it is neither about justifying Heidegger nor refuting him but learning with him, from him, and, only so, beyond him.

Chapter 1

Running towards Death

Introduction

Many of Heidegger's early readers interpreted his philosophy, especially as articulated in *Being and Time*, as a philosophy of death. As such it could be read (and perhaps dismissed) as a philosophical reaction to the trauma of mass death in the First World War.[1] Culminating, it seemed, in the claim that authentic existence was to be found exclusively in a resolute anticipation of death and that human being – Dasein – was most profoundly a being towards death, *Being and Time* was certainly open to such readings. But whether they really or adequately reflect all that is going on in that work or even the most essential tendency of its thought is another matter. Indeed, as we have seen, it is open to question whether, when Heidegger writes of 'death' in that work, he actually or primarily means death in the everyday sense of the biological cessation of life. If it is a general rule in philosophy that one should always be prepared to take a second look at what seems most obvious, this is nowhere more true than with regard to Heidegger's treatment of death.

This last comment calls for a general clarification regarding the aim of this essay, namely (and to repeat what was said in the Introduction), that it is not intended simply as a commentary on what Heidegger had to say about death and, as such, a contribution to the ever-expanding field of Heidegger studies. Although I shall seek to attend as closely as possible to what Heidegger is actually saying, the chief aim will be to address the question of death itself, whilst taking Heidegger as my main interlocutor, since (in my view) it is Heidegger who has offered the most intellectually consistent and rigorous account of death in modern philosophy. Reading Heidegger on death, then, requires us to get and to keep 'the thing itself' in view in good phenomenological manner. We are reading Heidegger here in order better to understand the meaning of death and not just as a formal philosophical exercise or a study in the history of human thinking about death. As this study develops, it will become clear that I regard Heidegger's view of

---

[1] Let us just remind ourselves of the terrible reality of that trauma. Germany lost in the order of two million military personnel, with a further half-a-million direct or indirect civilian deaths; Austro-Hungary lost over one million military personnel and suffered over 400,000 direct or indirect civilian deaths. Figures for those wounded are generally double, whilst these countries, like the rest of the world, also suffered the further trauma of a flu epidemic that, globally, killed a still undetermined number between 50 million and well over a hundred million.

death as essentially flawed, but I understand it to be flawed precisely in terms of his own idea of truth as unconcealment or disclosure. That is to say, I regard it as failing to bring into view all that needs to be seen if we are to have an adequate understanding of death. A constant refrain of *Being and Time* is the claim that one or other approach to a question fails because it does not 'penetrate' the matter at issue to a sufficient depth and my contention here is that the same judgement can be applied to Heidegger's own treatment of the question of death. But – and again in keeping with his own understanding of truth – this is not to say that Heidegger is simply 'wrong' or incorrect. On the contrary, if Heidegger does not see and consequently does not say all that belongs to the matter at issue, he sees sufficiently clearly and deeply to bring us to the point at which some of the key issues concerning death start to emerge. Few, if any, of the great thinkers of the past can lead us so convincingly to what is most decisive in this matter, not merely despite but perhaps also because of those points at which we cannot follow him. In this regard it is, as so often, obligatory to acknowledge that we can only see what we see because we are able to stand on giants' shoulders.

But if we get to the point of seeing further than Heidegger, this is not just a matter of incremental growth. It is not as if Heidegger was the inventor of some new technology that we are now attempting to apply or adapt. Heidegger's own approach to death stresses that how we understand death will depend on the attitude we take towards it, so that what we say about death is in complex and intimate ways interrelated with how we feel, think, and talk about ourselves, about how we *are*. This means that Heidegger's own approach is inevitably connected with his own self-understanding, and one strand of my argument in this essay will be that his interpretation of death is strongly influenced in both positive and negative ways by his own ambivalent relation to the religious traditions on which he draws heavily but which he also systematically resists. As will become clear, this is much more complicated than a straightforward confrontation between a Heideggerian view that declares death to be the simple and final annihilation of self-conscious subjectivity and a religious view that promises some kind of post-mortem future. Heidegger is not 'wrong' from a religious point of view because he denies an afterlife[2] (in fact, he claims, somewhat implausibly, that his analysis is without prejudice to such a question[3]) but rather because of how he portrays the defining characteristics of human Dasein in the here and now. Since what this means is the matter of this essay as a whole, I shall not now pursue this comment further and my point here is simply to make clear, from the beginning, that this is a reading that is both deeply and gratefully indebted to Heidegger and that, to a

---

[2]   This is the objection made by Edith Stein. Her criticism of Heidegger is found in an appendix to the work *Endliches und Ewiges Sein. Gesamtausgabe*, vols 11/12 (Freiburg: Herder, 2006), pp. 445–99 (not included in the English translation).

[3]   This is one of the few points on which I agree with Paul Edwards, namely, that the main thrust of Heidegger's presentation makes any discourse about life 'after' death not only otiose but existentially pernicious.

considerable extent, is reading *with* Heidegger but that, finally, breaks away from Heidegger to offer an alternative reading of the human condition, a reading that is both Christian and existential.

But before we go any further in considering the rights and wrongs and strengths and weaknesses of Heidegger's account of death, it is perhaps necessary to have some idea as to what that account actually says. In the following chapters I shall take up a sequence of specific themes from the discussion of death in *Being and Time* and some later works, but I shall begin now by giving a preliminary summary of the relevant chapters of *Being and Time* itself. Inevitably, even the most pedestrian exposition will already involve significant interpretative moves, especially when what is to be presented is a philosophical argument of some subtlety and complexity. I certainly do not pretend that the précis that follows is entirely neutral. I am in particular aware that my decision to include the chapter on conscience and guilt in my exposition of the discussion of death will be resisted by some Heidegger scholars.[4] Nevertheless, and even if my account might seem to invite the misreading that *Being and Time* simply is a 'philosophy of death', I shall attempt to set out Heidegger's basic argument in as straightforward a way as I can. That we shall then need to qualify this account on a number of important points does not negate the value of establishing a maximally clear if also pedestrian base from which to begin. Indeed, such a procedure reflects something of Heidegger's own 'method' in *Being and Time* and other writings, as, having set out a certain view of the matter at issue, he repeatedly stops to question the account he has given thus far, to identify its inadequacies, and then to move on to a new level of questioning that, sometimes, effectively undermines all that has gone before. With that procedure in mind, let us then attempt in as straightforward a way as possible to address the question as to how death finds its way into the argument of *Being and Time*.

Introducing Death

Heidegger introduces the theme of death in the opening section, ¶45, of Division II of *Being and Time*. But to understand why he does so we have first to see where his argument has at this point got to.

Being and Time begins with Heidegger stating the need to re-open the classical metaphysical question of being and to do so in a philosophical context in which even the meaning of the question has been forgotten and obscured. If we are to start again, he says, we can do so only at the point at which being is most directly and uncontroversially present to us, namely, in our selves, in our own capacity to raise the question as to the kind of beings that we are, the being that makes us the beings that we experience ourselves as being: the being that is 'there' – Dasein.

---

[4]   I shall give reasons for why I think this is not only permissible but even necessary at the appropriate point.

Against what he sees as the characteristically post-Cartesian move of beginning with the knowing subject and then attempting to account for how such a subject can genuinely come to 'know' the world out there in reality, Heidegger offers a radical alternative based on his view of Dasein as being in the world. On this view, it is simply a myth to think that we begin with the consciousness of ourselves as knowing subjects. In fact, we never have any experience of ourselves that is not bound up with our experience of the world. Experiencing ourselves as eating, hammering, talking, observing beings, our sense of who we ourselves are is and can only be developed through a constant and uninterrupted traffic with our world – and, equally, we never have any experience of the world as a pure, detached ensemble of objects independent of our practical and noetic interest in it. Being-in-the-world is in this sense a structural given that precedes both subjectivity and objectivity, and it is only through interpreting this being-in-the-world that we can get to find out who we ourselves are and the kind of being that is proper to us (noting that, in Heidegger's German, the word for 'proper', *eigen*, is essentially related to the word customarily translated 'authentic', *eigentlich*).

On this basis, Division I of *Being and Time* sets out what Heidegger calls the 'Preparatory Fundamental Analysis of Dasein'. Here too he makes another important and original, though less conspicuously advertised, move. Previous philosophers have tended more or less explicitly to take one particular way of being human as definitive for what is truly human as such. For Plato it is the philosopher who is the exemplary human being, for the Christian philosophy of the Middle Ages it is the saint, for Nietzsche the artist. By way of contrast, Heidegger resolves to limit himself to what can be known from the analysis of what he calls 'average everydayness', in other words, human beings as we find them ('we', as we find ourselves) existing in their everyday lives without any particular claim or capacity for extraordinary insight into the truth of their condition. In this situation human self-understanding is typically formed by the way in which we identify ourselves with how we are involved in the world, as engineers, husbands, cleaners, or soldiers. Our self-image is a reflex of our world in us.

The development of this self-image or self-understanding primarily occurs in and as language (or 'discourse', *Rede*), that is, as the way in which we speak about ourselves with one another. For the most part we do so without reflecting fully on all that is potentially conveyed by what we say and much conversation is simply a matter of passing on views, opinions, and phrases that we have picked up from others, which Heidegger calls 'idle talk' (*Gerede*). The issue here is not that we mostly talk about day-to-day trivia. Rather, it is about *how* we talk and, in this perspective, political or philosophical debate can be (and perhaps mostly is) just as much a matter of 'idle talk' as neighbourhood gossip.[5] Truth, in Heidegger's view, is not just a matter of saying what is correct but occurs when we are able to bring the matter at issue out of a state of forgetfulness or concealment and come to see it

---

5   Many of Heidegger's lecture series contain a steady stream of disparaging asides suggesting that this also applies to much contemporary philosophy.

for what and as it is. Already in the Introduction he makes clear how it is discourse (*logos*) that is the primary means of revealing the world and bringing what is being talked about into view. This is always a matter, as he puts it, 'penetrating' more or less deeply into what is under discussion, and the problem with *Gerede* is therefore precisely that it speaks in such a way as to inhibit a more penetrating or a more encompassing view of what is being discussed to be developed. And perhaps it is not hard for us to see that even philosophers talking together about death may do so in such a way as to obscure rather than illuminate the true human meaning of the subject. All too often and at all levels of discourse our talking together is guided by 'curiosity' (a term Heidegger takes from Augustine) rather than really wanting to know and it is therefore unsurprising if it ends in 'ambiguity' rather than clarification.

We are, as Heidegger puts it, 'thrown' into our world and, so to speak, wake up to ourselves in a situation that is far from perspicuous. We never exist without a certain awareness that Heidegger characterizes in terms of state-of-mind, understanding, and language that precede a developed self-consciousness. Macquarrie and Robinson's 'state-of-mind' is a rendering of Heidegger's term *Befindlichkeit*, a word containing a root element recognizably cognate with the English 'find'. This suggests not that our mental states are what we ourselves have planned or chosen in advance but that we are always 'finding' ourselves to be in some way or other. If asked how we are, we are rarely without an instant response: 'good', 'alright', 'so-so', 'a bit down', etc. This is just how we find ourselves being – we can work on it, try to cheer up, or, as the case may be, quieten down, but we can't not start out from some given mood or state-of-mind that we did not in the first instance plan or invent. Moreover, as my example suggests, we can normally spontaneously articulate our mood in language, as 'good', 'alright', etc. and, to complete Heidegger's triad of terms, what we say expresses and conveys a certain understanding of how we are: when I say 'good' or 'alright' I do so on the assumption that I am saying something meaningful that will be understood by the person to whom I am talking. Yet, Heidegger says, carrying on in this way only ever gets us so far. We never get to say all we could say about how we are but are always falling short of an adequate self-understanding. The situation of Dasein in its average everyday way of being in the world is therefore one of 'fallenness', which, Heidegger insists, should not carry the moral or religious connotations of the Christian idea of the Fall.

But if we are always falling short of an adequate self-understanding, how do we ever get to know that we are doing so, i.e., that we are in error? Lacking other evidence, aren't the prisoners in Plato's cave-parable justifiably convinced that their shadow-world is the only reality there is? What's going to make anyone think that there's more to life than their average everyday experience of it? How are we ever going to become aware of what Heidegger calls our 'more primordial' possibilities?

Heidegger's answer to this question is focussed on two further terms. The first of these is anxiety (*Angst*), a term he takes from Kierkegaard but also

characteristically transforms in the process. Like Kierkegaard, he distinguishes
anxiety from fear. Fear is fear of something particular, the wild beasts in the forest
or failure in an upcoming examination or competition. In the case of anxiety,
however, 'That in the face of which one has anxiety is Being-in-the-world as such'
(186/230). Anxiety has no specific object but is an all-encompassing sense that
in my being-in-the-world I am not who I am, that I am constantly falling short
of knowing and being who I am, that I am missing myself in my life. Anxiety 'is
nothing and nowhere' (187/231), and yet this 'nothing' unsettles us in the whole
compass of our dealings with the world and with others. It makes us feel that we
are not at home in our world or in ourselves. In this way it is anxiety that reveals
our fallenness – and yet, precisely for this reason, it is anxiety that makes us flee the
sense of 'uncanniness' (*Unheimlichkeit* – literally the state of not being at home)
that it arouses and seek to absorb ourselves all the more in our average everyday
preoccupations as if they were all there was. For the most part, Heidegger says,
'we have no existentiell understanding' (190/234) of anxiety and assiduously but
more or less unconsciously avert our gaze from what anxiety discloses. But the
busier we are in assuring ourselves that 'everything's alright' the more apparent it
becomes that perhaps it isn't and perhaps there's something missing.

Before we can understand what this 'something missing' might be, we need to
take account of another key Heideggerian term, 'care'. The importance of this term
can be gauged by the statement in the opening paragraph of Division II, summing
up the outcome of Division I, that 'The totality of Being-in-the-world as a structural
whole has revealed itself as care' (231/274). With regard to our question of death,
care, as we shall see, is also the hinge on which Heidegger moves from the analysis
of being in the world offered in Division I to the 'existential Interpretation' that
centres on the account of Dasein's being as being towards death.

In its inception the idea of care is elegantly simple. We have already seen how,
for Heidegger, our way of being is distinctive by virtue of the fact that we are the
beings for whom our being can itself become an issue. But this means that we
are able to step beyond our immediate state of just being and, as it were, look at
ourselves from beyond ourselves and think of ourselves in the light of how we
might be or could become. How we are now involves us considering what we want
to do next and how we might become in the future – shall I go for that new job,
get married, or seek early retirement? As Heidegger says, 'Dasein is already *ahead*
of itself in its Being. Dasein is always "beyond itself", not as a way of behaving
towards other entities which it is not, but as Being towards the potentiality-for-
Being which it is itself' (191–2/236). Implicitly this already broaches the goal
of Heidegger's enquiry that time establishes the sole horizon within which the
question of the meaning of being can be addressed. To be ahead of oneself is to
understand one's present way of being in the light of one's future possibilities,
and if care – being ahead of ourselves – is structurally basic to Dasein then we are
ineluctably temporal beings.

But does care address the sense of something missing that is manifested in
anxiety? Is knowing ourselves as future-directed temporal beings all we need to

know about ourselves? Is it enough genuinely to assuage our anxiety? It is such questions that drive Heidegger's transition from the simple analysis of being-in-the-world to the attempt to interpret what it actually means for us, in our existence, to be this way. So, he ends Division I with a string of questions to himself:

> If in care we have arrived at Dasein's primordial state of Being, then this must also be the basis for conceptualizing that understanding of Being which lies in care; that is to say, it must be possible to define the meaning of Being. But *is* the phenomenon of care one in which the most primordial existential–ontological state of Dasein is disclosed? And has the structural manifoldness which lies in this phenomenon, presented us with the most primordial totality of factical Dasein's Being? Has our investigation up to this point ever brought Dasein into view *as a whole*? (230/273)

By virtue of care, I am always seeing myself in the light of my future possibilities, as getting that new job, as being married, as retiring – but can I ever really anticipate the whole of my life? How, being in the midst of life, might I ever get to see how it might look as a whole? If the meaning of my life is the meaning of my whole life, won't it always necessarily escape me? As Kierkegaard famously put it, life is lived forwards but understood backwards – therefore, since we're not yet at the point at which we can look backwards on all we've lived through, suffered, and done, a full self-understanding is surely always going to escape us. So, in ¶46, in the first full chapter of Division II (¶45 being a transitional and introductory chapter), Heidegger addresses the question that will lead him directly to the question of death, namely, 'the seeming impossibility of getting Dasein's Being-a-whole into our grasp ontologically and determining its character'.

Facing Death

And so we come to Division II, entitled 'Dasein and Temporality'. Heidegger's analysis of the structure of care has revealed that Dasein is ineluctably temporal, since care involves it in always being ahead of itself and understanding itself in the light of its projected future possibilities. But this is not enough for what Heidegger calls a 'primordial' interpretation (his term *Ursprung* suggests that this is an interpretation that grasps Dasein in its very origins and not a matter of simply tracking it along its current trajectory or seeing it simply as it is or happens to be right now). And, he says, 'it [his enquiry] also requires an explicit assurance that the *whole* of the entity which it has taken as its theme has been brought into its fore-having' (232/75). Without this it is impossible to be assured of the *unity* of the phenomenon – Dasein – being investigated. The problem, as Heidegger puts it, is that 'as long as Dasein exists, it must in each case ... *not yet* be something' (233/276). To understand Dasein as a whole, then, it would seem to be necessary to see it in the light of its end, the point at which it has or will have completed its passage from birth to death. But 'The "end" of Being-in-the-world is death' (234/277) – which immediately confronts us with the classical dilemma that, in the moment in which Dasein gains its wholeness, i.e., reaches its end, 'this gain becomes the utter loss of its Being-in the-world. In such a case, it can never again be experienced *as an entity*' (235/280). As he explains a few pages later, 'When Dasein reaches its wholeness in death it simultaneously loses the Being of its "there"' (237/281). Although he does not explicitly allude to it, the thought is essentially that of the Epicurean adage that, as regards death, 'so long as I am, it is not; when it is, I am not'.

Is there any way through this conundrum? An important question, which Heidegger raises at the outset but does not immediately emphasize, is that of the relationship between what he calls 'biological' death and 'existential–ontological' death (237/280). Since it is specifically the latter that concerns him, this raises the question as to whether or how the entire discussion relates to what, in an average everyday kind of way, we human beings mostly mean by the word 'death' – a question to which, as we have seen, contemporary philosophical discussion is especially alert.[6]

The point hinges on Heidegger's understanding of the inter-relationship between the ontic and the ontological and between the existentiell and the existential, an inter-relationship that is crucial to the whole structure and method of *Being and Time*. We recall that his aim in *Being and Time* is the elucidation of the meaning of being, that is, bringing to view the kind of being that is disclosed in Dasein's own (unique) capacity to question itself as to its manner of existing. In pursuit of this aim he began, as we have seen, with a phenomenological analysis of Dasein as we find it in its average everydayness, where we find it engaged in a multiplicity of what he would call existentiell tasks – working, shopping, career building, cultural activities, and moral, political, and religious decision making. This is the material to be interrogated, but the aim is not just to produce a compendium of such existentiell practices: it is to press through to and disclose the underlying structures that make them possible. These are the structures he calls the 'existentialia', corresponding (in a certain sense) to the categories of traditional philosophy. 'Care' was found to be the most basic of these existentialia and we can see it manifesting in any of the activities listed above. Similarly in the case of death, what is at issue is not just having to die and what that means in relation to a multiplicity of, e.g., familial, medical, religious, and cultural practices, but what it means for the meaning of the kind of beings that we are. This is – or, if we could find it, would be – the 'existential–ontological' meaning of death. But – and this is crucial – the 'levels' of the existentiell and the existential are never, in reality, separable.[7] Unlike ancient models of ascetic ascent in which the soul progressed towards its true being by sloughing off the encumbrances of the flesh, Dasein does not and cannot leave its average everyday life behind as it progresses in insight into

---

[6]   See Introduction, pp. 8–10 above.

[7]   And in this regard the notion of 'levels' is itself already potentially misleading.

its ontological structures. Even if it comes to the point of achieving an authentic and unsurpassable realization regarding the truth of its being, it is not absolved from housekeeping, career building, cultural life, etc. It remains a part of average everyday humanity. Authentic existence is not a separation from but a modification of average everydayness.[8] All of this means that it is hard to draw a hard and fast line between the existentiell and the existential: the existentiell is necessary for the existential and the existential does not exist apart from the existentiell. In fact, the closest Heidegger seems to come to offering any criteria for defining the difference is that knowledge of the existential has the quality of being more 'penetrating' than knowledge focussed merely on the existentiell. It is in this sense that although Kierkegaard is praised for 'having seized upon the problem of existence as an existentiell problem, and thought it through in a penetrating fashion' (235/494), he did not 'penetrate' through to a genuinely existential–ontological insight – which is just what Heidegger himself is now attempting in *Being and Time*.[9]

One aspect of this situation is that, in his discussion of death, Heidegger repeatedly emphasizes the distinction between an approach that aims at a fundamental ontology and the various approaches of the manifold ontic sciences. These can, of course, throw considerable light on death as a biological occurrence or a cultural phenomenon or on its psychological impact on human beings. What they cannot do, however, is to show the meaning of death for the whole of our existence, if only because their entire manner of proceeding is defined by the demands of specialization. But, again, the distinction is not always easy to draw, and whilst Heidegger insists that his approach is neither biological nor medical, neither psychological nor theological, he also has to take account of these discourses in order to distinguish his own undertaking from them. This distinction is the burden of ¶49 of *Being and Time*. Here, Heidegger notes that 'Death, in the widest sense, is a phenomenon of life' (246/290) and, in this regard, is the legitimate object of, e.g., statistical analysis. However, in order to secure the distinctiveness of his own approach, Heidegger differentiates 'perishing' (*Verenden*), 'dying' (*Sterben*), and 'demise' (*Ableben*). These are, respectively, mere biological 'perishing' (like the biblical 'beasts of the field'); 'dying', understood as an exclusively ontological category; and a specifically human kind of dying that qua conscious is different from that of the animal although it lacks fundamental ontological insight into what its death really means.

The distinctiveness of an ontological approach not only sets it apart from sociological or anthropological surveys of human attitudes towards death or studies of how we psychologically experience death (247/291–2), it also separates

---

[8]   This will be especially dealt with in Division II, Chapter IV, 'Temporality and Everydayness'.

[9]   See the discussion in my article 'Existence, Anxiety and the Moment of Vision: Fundamental Ontology and Existentiell Faith Revisited' in A.P. Smith and D. Whistler (eds), *After the Postsecular and the Postmodern: New Essays in Continental Philosophy of Religion* (Newcastle-upon-Tyne: Cambridge Scholars Publishing, 2010), pp. 128–49.

it from 'any ontical decision whether "after death" still another being is possible, either higher or lower, or whether Dasein "lives on" or even "outlasts" itself and is "immortal"' (247–8/292). Such questions are not ruled out in principle, even though Heidegger insists on the this-worldly limitations of his own enquiry. Possibly, he hints, one might legitimately ask 'what *may be after death*' (248/292), but this could only happen after death has been conceived 'in its full ontological essence (248/292), and he therefore refrains from even considering it at this point. Whether this agnosticism is more than rhetorical, however, is questionable. In the light of the existential–ontological understanding of Dasein's being towards death that Heidegger in fact arrives at, it is hard to imagine any way of affirming some kind of post-mortem existence that would not undermine the entire structure involved in such a being towards death.[10]

Similarly, Heidegger declares that he is simply not going to address the kinds of questions that would be of interest to a 'metaphysics of death'. Such questions might include why there is such a thing as death at all, how it came into the world, and whether it is to be regarded 'as an evil and affliction in the aggregate of entities' (248/292). No less than biology, etc., such a metaphysics – which sounds rather like what Christian theology might attempt – is looking for an 'explanation' of death or seeking to offer edification in the face of death, but this is not Heidegger's concern. And he is no more interested in justifying the goodness of life or of God: his aim is not a 'theodicy or theology of death' (248/292). His aim is, simply, to ask about the meaning of Dasein's being and, in particular, to do so with regard to getting the *whole* of that being into view and in such a way as to ensure that the interpretation is properly 'primordial'.

This returns us once more to the question as to how such a view of the whole might be possible if, as seems to be the case, the end point from which alone it might be attained is also the moment in which Dasein ceases to exist. Where I am, it is not – where it is, I am not! But perhaps this is mere verbal sleight of hand. Although we will never be in a position from which to survey our own individual lives retrospectively 'as a whole', we do have plentiful experience of historical and contemporary human beings having lived their lives through to the end. Can we then use what we know of others' deaths as a basis for the interpretation we are seeking?

Heidegger's answer to this question is a clear negative, although the way in which he explains why such knowledge cannot help an ontological interpretation of death is not entirely clearly set out. The key issue seems to be this: although we continue to relate to the dead in a variety of ways, none of these relationships allows us to grasp what we might call an 'inside' view of what *their* dying means. In death, Dasein does not cease to be in any possible way: it becomes something else, whether it is the corpse on the anatomist's slab or 'the departed one' who is the object of funerary rites and family mourning. Although the deceased is no longer *there* (*Da*), we are – or believe ourselves to be – somehow with him: 'the

---

[10]   As previously noted, this is one point on which I do agree with Paul Edwards.

deceased has abandoned our "*world*" and left it behind. But *in terms of that world* those who remain can still *be with him*' (238/282). But in this way, what 'the end' means to the one whose life has ended is all the more occluded. The corpse on the anatomist's slab 'is "more" than a *lifeless* material thing. In it we encounter something *unalive*, which has lost its life' (238/282). Nevertheless, this doesn't help us at all with regard to 'the ontological meaning of the dying of the person who dies, as a possibility of Being which belongs to his being' (239/283). We can be alongside them, but we can neither see their death as they see it nor experience it as they experience it.

This raises the question of representability or substitutability. In everyday life you can go to the shop for me, a colleague can chair a committee in my place, professors who have research assistants can get them to write their footnotes for them – Sydney Carton can even go to the scaffold for Charles Darnay[11] – but no one can take my having to die from me: even if, in the last case, Charles Darnay will live happily ever after with Lucie he too will, one day, have to die. '[I]f "ending", as dying, is constitutive of Dasein's totality, then the Being of this wholeness itself must be conceived as an existential phenomenon of a Dasein which is in each case one's own' (240/284). Death qua end is utterly and unqualifiedly singular and in death we are each of us utterly and unqualifiedly solitary.[12]

But this further prompts Heidegger to underline the radicality of what he means by 'end'. We have seen that as long as Dasein has not yet reached its end and cannot be grasped as a whole in a first-person perspective, 'this "not-yet" "belongs" to Dasein as long as it is' (242/286). But how are we to understand this 'not-yet' itself? Not, says Heidegger, by analogy with the outstanding balance of a debt, nor with the aspect of the moon concealed by the earth's shadow. In the former case it is a matter of the quantitative completion of a sum that has already been defined (i.e., we know what it is that needs to be paid off), while in the latter it is merely a limitation of our perceptual capacities that makes it impossible for us to see what is actually already there but invisible (ignoring, as Heidegger himself remarks, the further question as to the moon's dark side!). A further important

---

[11]   See Charles Dickens, *A Tale of Two Cities*.

[12]   In a particularly egregious example of how not to read Heidegger, Edwards takes this to mean that Heidegger believes that we are each of us psychologically alone at the moment of death. However, if we take seriously Heidegger's own distinction between the existential–ontological approach and that of existentiell life or the deliverances of the ontic or regional sciences, we can see that this misses the point entirely. That point, I take it, is that even if I die a good death, surrounded by those who love me most and having time to say farewell to those I have cherished on earth, the fact of having to die and of thus losing all my possibilities of continuing to relate to others and to my world as a whole reveals the essential solitude of my existence. Thus it is not as if having lived an averagely sociable life I then have to abandon society and go alone to death but rather that death reveals how, even when I am most sociable, I am also essentially solitary, i.e., because of having to die I am just as solitary as I sit here writing this as I will be on the day of my death. See Edwards, *Heidegger*, pp. 9ff.

point is that in neither of these cases is the object in question essentially defined by its temporality. The debt is, let us say, £200, and even if the passage of time adds a further interest payment of £35 to this sum, such interest is calculable in advance on the basis of the original amount owed. Similarly, the waxing and waning of the moon is not, in reality, intrinsic to the nature of the moon itself: it does not change simply because, at a given moment of time, we can only see it as new, as crescent, as a quarter, etc.

Can we find a closer analogy, then – an entity for which change was integral to its very being? As Heidegger poses the question, do we know of entities 'to whose kind of Being becoming belongs' (243/287)? It seems we do. Think of a fruiting plant. The fruit is what it is and only becomes 'fruit' – what it is – through the temporal process of ripening. This suggests a certain analogy to Dasein, as Heidegger acknowledges, but, he adds, 'this does not signify that ripeness as an "end" and death as an "end" coincide with regard to their ontological structure as ends' (244/288). With regard to the fruit, it is, as it were, 'fulfilled' in becoming ripe, completing its life cycle and fulfilling its *telos*. In the case of Dasein, however, death is so far from being a fulfilment as to mean the loss of its specific possibilities. Heidegger does not at this point explicitly say, although he may be thought to imply, that even if there were, from time to time and here or there, individuals who had lived in such a way as to be able to say at the moment of death that they had fulfilled all they had to do in their lives, such fulfilment is purely random, i.e., dependent on contingent circumstance, and does not belong to their end as such. Take the case of Marshal Pétain. Had he died in 1939, he might have been regarded as having lived a fulfilled life and an outstanding example of military and national virtue and, already in his 80s, as having lived out his natural span of life. Because he did not die and went on to head the collaborationist Vichy government, he ended his days in prison as a convicted war criminal. Conversely, we can imagine other cases where a person seems to be moving towards all that they have worked for in life only to be robbed of it by death – their own or, perhaps, that of the beloved with whom they had hoped to share it. As Heidegger writes,

> With its death, Dasein has indeed 'fulfilled' its course. But in doing so, has it necessarily exhausted its specific possibilities? Rather, are not these precisely what gets taken away from Dasein? Even 'unfulfilled' Dasein ends. On the other hand, so little is it the case that Dasein comes to ripeness with its end, that Dasein may well have passed its ripeness before the end. For the most part, Dasein ends in unfulfilment, or else by having disintegrated and been used up. (244/288)

Death qua end is neither fulfilment nor, as Heidegger goes on to say, is it just stopping, getting finished, or disappearing. Instead 'The "ending" which we have in view when we speak of death, does not signify Dasein's Being-at-an-end, but a Being-towards-the-end of this entity. Death is a way to be, which Dasein takes over as soon as it is. "As soon as a man comes to life, he is at once old enough to die"' (245/289).

This clarification enables Heidegger to make his next move. If the 'not-yet' of care 'has the character of something *towards which* Dasein *comports itself*' (250/293), then death cannot be treated as an object ready-at-hand but '*is something that stands before us – something impending*' (250/294). Of course, death is not the only thing we experience as 'impending'. As Heidegger says, 'a storm, the remodelling of the house, or the arrival of a friend' (250/294) may all be experienced as impending. But what is at issue in such cases is more or less accidental and is determined by the practically infinite variety of existentiell life. Death, by way of contrast, 'is a possibility of Being which Dasein has to take over in every case' (250/294). And then, Heidegger adds, 'With death, Dasein stands before itself in its ownmost potentiality-for-Being. This is a possibility in which the issue is nothing less than Dasein's Being-in-the-world' (250/294). What such a total view of death might mean has been well described by the modern Russian spiritual writer Sophrony Sakharov, who, although writing with a very different intention from Heidegger's, articulates just this point: my death is not so much a matter of my falling out of a world that, nevertheless, carries on but the end of the entire world in which I have lived and moved and had my being. He writes,

> My inevitable death was not just mine, someone of no account, 'one of these little ones'. No. In me, with me, all that had formed part of my consciousness would die: people close to me, their sufferings and love, the whole historical progress, the universe in general, the sun, the stars, endless space; even the Creator of the world Himself – He, too, would die in me .... The fact that with his death the whole world, even God, dies is possible only if he himself, of himself, is in a certain sense the centre of all creation.[13]

In light of the preceding discussion, this means that death – having to die – brings to a head the question as to whether we are, in fact, capable of grasping our lives as a whole and, consequently, whether we are capable of interpreting the kind of being that belongs to our life *as a whole*. Having to die confronts us with the possibility that our lives may be without meaning or – which amounts to the same thing – that whatever meaning our lives may have is a meaning that will always escape us and that we will never be able to grasp. It always slips through our hands – literally at the very last moment. Death, then, 'is the possibility of the absolute impossibility of Dasein. Thus death reveals itself as that possibility which is one's ownmost, which is non-relational, and unsurpassable' (250–51/294).

---

[13] A. Sophrony (Sakharov), *We Shall See Him as He Is* (Tolleshunt Knights: Stavropegic Monastery of St John the Baptist, 2004), p. 12. Heidegger would not endorse the religious beliefs articulated by Sakharov, nor perhaps the notion of the individual human person as 'the centre of all creation', but he would affirm that, in death, even God – as God is for me – also in a sense dies. Death is the total annihilation of the entirety of the structure of meaning that is, for me, the world.

Heidegger has earlier described human *Existenz* as having the character of thrownness, and this too plays an important part in relation to the meaning of death. Death is not a possibility we choose for ourselves: it is a possibility into or towards which we are thrown – whether we are conscious of it or not. Previously, in connection with care, we noted that Heidegger had drawn attention to the special role of anxiety in human Dasein. Contrasting anxiety with fear, he argued that whereas fear is always fear of this or that (including fear of dying, e.g., of cancer or in battle), anxiety is a state in which we feel insecure about our lives as a whole. As Heidegger puts it, it engenders a sense of *Unheimlichkeit*, which, as I have already noted, Macquarrie and Robinson translate as 'uncanniness' but which could be more literally rendered as 'the sense of not-being-at-home', as in 'not-being-at-home' in our own lives or not being at ease with who we are. It is the sense that 'I am not what I am' (as Shakespeare's Iago put it, although with a somewhat different meaning).

Now, having introduced the theme of death, we are in a position to see a further – and defining – feature of anxiety. For it now starts to appear that what lies behind my not-being-able-to-be-at-home in the world is the sense that my life might run out on me before I am able to fulfil my possibilities, i.e., before I am really able to be all that I have it in me to be.[14] In this sense,

> Anxiety in the face of death must not be confused with fear in the face of one's demise. This anxiety is not an accidental or random mood of 'weakness' in some individual; but, as a basic state-of-mind of Dasein, it amounts to the disclosedness of the fact that Dasein exists as thrown Being towards its end. (251/295)

In this sense, being willing to let anxiety come to the surface is a positive step, since the fact that our being is a being-towards-the-end is something we are habitually inclined to avoid thinking about – thereby also inhibiting such possibilities as we have for grasping the meaning of our being as a whole. Dasein, as we have seen, typically exists in the mode of falling, of not realizing all its possibilities, and, in this case and especially, not realizing the meaning of the possibility of its own impossibility. Nevertheless, if being towards death does belong 'primordially and essentially to Dasein's being, then', Heidegger says, 'it must also be exhibitable in everydayness, even if in the first instance in a way which is inauthentic' (252/296). So, once more, Heidegger returns to what is both his point of departure and a constant point of reference, that is, to average everydayness and, in this case, to how death is revealed in the context of average everydayness.

As has been indicated, an especially salient feature of average everydayness is what Heidegger calls *Gerede* ('idle talk'), that is, discourse that is so far from revealing what is at issue as actively to block off access to it. In such discourse we

---

[14] Or, conversely, I might so overshoot my possibilities as to live on in what I subjectively experience as a 'useless' old age, no matter how often my friends and family reassure me as to the value of my being here.

speak neither from our own personal centre nor in the light of a clear understanding of the matter that we are claiming to have insight into. Instead we pass on what others – '*das Man*', translated variously as 'they' or 'one' – have said (and, remember, this is as likely to be true of academic discourse as of office tittle-tattle). The subject matter of such discourse is not necessarily concealed in a direct sense. It may be something that is a matter of public knowledge, something that is talked about by everyone, but talked about in such a way as to prevent it from being seen for what and as it is. And this, Heidegger says, is mostly how it is with regard to death. Few people are totally oblivious of their mortality, but when we do speak of death it is mostly in terms of 'a case of death', of 'someone or other is dying'. We do also acknowledge that 'one of these days one will die too, in the end; but right now it has nothing to do with us' (253/297). The outcome of all this is succinctly described by Heidegger in terms that can surely be corroborated by most people who have spent time with the dying and the bereaved:

> This evasive concealment in the face of death dominates everydayness so stubbornly that, in being with one another, the 'neighbours' often still keep talking the 'dying person' into the belief that he will escape death and soon return to the tranquillized everydayness of the word of his concern. Such 'solicitude' is meant to 'console' him. (253/297)[15]

A further consequence of such tranquillization is that it inhibits the consciousness of anxiety. But whereas 'they' will inevitably interpret anxiety as morbid or obsessive, the courage to face up to and accept and even identify with one's anxiety is, as we have seen, a condition for raising the question as to the meaning of our being as a whole – and therefore also a condition for bringing that question into connection with what we have now learned is our ownmost, non-relational, and not-to-be-surpassed possibility of death.[16]

It should be clear that what 'they' say about death is not necessarily incorrect. The problem is that even when what they say is true, it is said in such a way as

---

[15] Heidegger illustrates this scenario with reference to Tolstoy's novella *The Death of Ivan Ilych*, a reference to which we shall return in Chapter 3.

[16] It is plausible to see Heidegger's comments here as playing a role in gradually changing cultural attitudes towards death and engendering the contemporary tendency towards the more 'open' attitude towards death that is characteristic of much palliative care practice. See, for example, the references to 'existentialist' perspectives in H.M. Chochinov, 'Dying, Dignity and New Horizons in Palliative End-of-Life Care'. *CA: A Cancer Journal for Clinicians*, American Cancer Society (October 2009): 82–103. This is doubtless a subject that merits a more extensive discussion, which might include how Heidegger's comments on such 'idle talk' could be linked via his later critique of technology to some negative aspects of the medicalization of death. See, e.g., references to Heidegger in J. Bishop, *The Anticipatory Corpse: Medicine, Power, and the Care of the Dying* (Notre Dame: University of Notre Dame Press, 2011). However, real and even pressing as they are, such practical extensions and applications of Heidegger's view are not the matter of this essay.

not to enable the kind of truth at issue to be seen for what or as it really is. Thus with regard to the certainty of death, 'they' know that death is certain and that, as an empirical fact, all human beings will, one day, certainly die. In fact, most of us are taught explicitly through literature, religious texts, and services, or biology classes that we will one day die. But real conviction, Heidegger says, depends on 'let[ting] the evidence of the thing itself which has been uncovered (the true thing itself) be the sole determinant for its Being towards that thing in such a way as to understand it' (256/300). But it is just this kind of conviction or certainty – 'Being-certain' (258/302) – that is eroded in the average everyday way of talking about death. Death is spoken of as something that will happen sometime later and this 'cover[s] up what is peculiar in death's certainty – *that it is possible at any moment.* Along with the certainty of death goes the *indefiniteness* of its "when"' (258/302). Heidegger had doubtless read Kierkegaard's upbuilding discourse 'At a Graveside' in which a similar thought is expressed by an allusion to Jesus' parable of the rich man who fills his barns with provisions for the future only to be told 'this night your life will be demanded of you' (Luke 12.20).[17]

We cannot avoid or opt out of being towards death. As existing we are thrown towards it. Indeed, since Heidegger's German *Sein*, usually translated 'being', is in fact the infinitive 'to be', we could summarize his position even more succinctly as 'To be is to be towards death'.[18] But, even if this is how it is with us, we mostly relate to it in the way typical of '*das Man*', as an inauthentic being towards death (259/303). Yet Heidegger immediately adds that 'inauthenticity is based on the possibility of authenticity. Inauthenticity characterizes a kind of Being into which Dasein can divert itself and has for the most part always diverted itself; but Dasein does not necessarily and constantly *have to* [emphasis added] divert itself into this kind of being' (259/303). This suggests that Dasein can choose to relate otherwise to death than in the manner of inauthenticity – but what would such an authentic relation to death be?

Heidegger does not at this point say, although he will later acknowledge it to be the case, that the account of an authentic being towards death that follows in ¶53 is of the nature of what Kierkegaard might have called a 'thought-experiment'. That is to say, whilst we all probably have experience of people comforting the dying by telling them to cheer up and that it'll all be alright soon, we don't necessarily have much if any experience of how people are when they relate authentically to death. Indeed, for reasons that we have seen, we could only really know such an authentic relationship to death from a first-person perspective. Seeing how someone else relates authentically to death could never (on Heidegger's terms) ground our own possibility for doing likewise. For now, then, Heidegger is assuming that his

---

[17]   I shall discuss the *difference* between Heidegger and Kierkegaard on this point in Chapters 3 and 4 below.

[18]   Heidegger gives an extended discussion of the meaning of *Sein* as an infinitive form in his *Einführung in die Metaphysik* (Tübingen: Niemeyer, 1998), pp. 42–55 (GA40, pp. 60–75).

readers may not know what it would be for them as the individual subjects that they are to have such an authentic relation to death. And yet, he suggests, they are in a position to do so by virtue of the mirror image of such a relationship given in the inauthentic mode of average everydayness.

In the first instance – and like every other existential state – being towards death has the character of 'being-towards-a-possibility' (261/305). But whereas most of our other life possibilities are of such a kind as to invite us to try to actualize them, death cannot be actualized while remaining an existential possibility – when it is, we are not! But whilst death is not at our disposal in the same way as training for an athletics competition or building a career (so that actualizing it cannot be made into a life project in the same way as these and other possibilities), we still have the option (which we have in relation to any other possibility) of 'expecting' it (262/306). But 'expectation' too seems not quite right, since it is a kind of waiting in which, as Heidegger puts it, 'the possible is drawn into the actual, arising out of the actual and returning to it' (262/306) – and this is not the case with the possibility of death: our dying will not return us to the actuality of life! What is needed therefore is an attitude that brings death qua possibility to consciousness and keeps it there. This is what Heidegger calls 'anticipation', his German term *Vorlaufen* conveying the sense of actively running towards what is anticipated and not merely waiting for it. Keeping a sense of death as a possibility that is never actual is necessary, Heidegger says, because, for us (and for reasons which we have seen), death never can become actual. Death is *'the possibility of the impossibility of any existence at all'* (262/307).

'Anticipation' is thus more than one attitude amongst others: it is the way in which we authentically exist in relation to the ultimate possibility of our existence, a possibility that is both our ownmost and, so to speak, our uttermost – uttermost to the point of impossibility. 'Death, as possibility, gives Dasein nothing to be "actualized", nothing which Dasein, as actual, could itself *be*' (262/307). Yet, at the same time, 'Death is Dasein's ownmost possibility. Being towards this possibility discloses to Dasein its ownmost potentiality-for-Being, in which its very Being is the issue' (263/307) – and does so precisely by 'wrenching' Dasein away from the attitudes embedded in the 'idle talk' of the 'they'.

Again Heidegger re-iterates the three attributes of being towards death that he has previously flagged up without extensive discussion: that this distinctive possibility is Dasein's ownmost, that it is non-relational, and that it is unsurpassable. As our ownmost possibility it is entirely non-relational because it 'individualizes Dasein down to itself. This individualizing is the way in which the "there" [*Da*] is disclosed for existence' (263/308) (which, as we have seen, is a comment not just on the psychological process of dying but on the character of human existence as a whole and, as such, the contrary of the evasive tranquillization of idle talk). It is unsurpassable because, in the face of death, there are no possibilities held, as it were, in reserve. 'Anticipation [running-towards] discloses to existence that its uttermost possibility lies in giving itself up, and thus it shatters all one's tenaciousness to whatever existence one has reached' (264/308). In contrast to the inauthentic attitude of '*das Man*', anticipation is and remains certain, because it does not see death simply as a fact that will one day come to pass but because, in and through its own action of actively 'running towards' death, 'Dasein *makes* this possibility *possible* for itself as its ownmost potentiality-for-being' (264/309). This, then – more than just taking on board the fact that, by virtue of our thrownness, we have to die – is a matter of understanding our having to die as intrinsic to our capacity to choose our lives *as a whole* and as our own project. It is not just a question of submitting to our fate but, as Nietzsche put it, 'to turn "It was" into "I willed it thus"'.[19]

But there is a tension here. Anticipation is indeed an essentially free act and, as such, involves an act of will. Yet, at the same time, this act of will is possible only as or in the light of a certain 'disclosure'. We have seen how Heidegger understood truth in terms of bringing the matter at issue out of a state of concealment or forgetfulness so that it could be seen for what and how it is, and here too the idea of truth is in play. Why? Because Dasein's being convinced of the need for it to embrace death as its ownmost possibility cannot be just a matter of some arbitrary whim but is only possible, according to Heidegger, if it reflects or rests upon a disclosure of how things really are, i.e., if and only if Dasein can be brought to see that this is indeed the 'truth' of its being. Whereas Nietzsche's 'I willed it thus' can be interpreted as the expression of a kind of willing that is heedless of how the world really is – a sovereign, creative will, as it were – Dasein's action in making this possibility possible is therefore in one respect a response to how things actually are. As Heidegger's final summing-up of his argument thus far makes clear, what is involved is both an action on Dasein's part – it must choose to run freely towards its death – and a revelation or disclosure of how it is in its very being:

> Anticipation reveals to Dasein its lostness in the they-self, and brings it face to face with the possibility of being itself, primarily unsupported by concernful solicitude, but of being itself, rather, in an impassioned *freedom towards death* – a freedom which has been released from the Illusions of the 'they' and which is factical, certain of itself, and anxious. (266/311)

I suggested that, in the first instance, this sketch of an authentic existential–ontological being towards death has the character of a thought experiment. Now, having completed the experiment, Heidegger himself seems to step back and ask, is it true – that is, is it an attitude that any actually existing human being could take up? Is it (as Heidegger puts it in a phrase perhaps deliberately evocative of Kierkegaard's critique of Hegelianism) 'a fantastical exaction' (266/311)? Is there any evidence from what we know of Dasein that it is capable of such a seemingly

---

[19]   F. Nietzsche, *Also Sprach Zarathustra. Werke* II (Frankfurt am Main: Ullstein, 1972), p. 669. This characterization of being towards death in terms of will is central to Heidegger's complex relation to German Idealism. See Chapter 2 below.

heroic – we might even say super-human – unflinchingness? As Heidegger himself puts it, '… we must investigate whether to *any* extent and in any way Dasein *gives testimony*, from its ownmost potentiality-for-being, as to a possible *authenticity* of its existence, so that it not only makes known that in an existentiell manner such authenticity is possible, but *demands* this of itself' (267/311). Only if this is the case can what has been projected as an ontological possibility be regarded as meaningful for human beings living their average everyday lives in an existentiell manner. Heidegger's further reflections on this question lead him, in the following chapter, to an account of conscience and guilt. But how does this address the worry about the whole thing being a 'fantastical exaction'?

Guilty of Death

The starting point of Heidegger's analysis of Dasein is, as we have seen, Dasein as we encounter it in its average everyday way of existing, caught up in the life of 'das Man', the 'they' or 'one', and understanding itself in the mode of *Gerede* or 'idle talk'. How, then could we come to be otherwise? How could even the possibility of another way of relating to our own being come about? And how might such another way direct us towards the possibility of authentically running towards death?

Given the course of the discussion thus far, we might expect Heidegger to offer examples of those who have gone towards death with clear unflinching knowledge of the annihilation that awaits them. Yet Chapter II of Division II, in which he turns to the question of the existentiell attestation of an authentic potentiality for being one's self, scarcely mentions death at all but turns instead to the question of conscience. In Chapter 4 I shall return to further aspects of how we might see this discussion as central to the treatment of death, but, for now, limit myself to pointing out that (a) it is introduced as offering existentiell testimony to the possibility of authentic being towards death and (b) this connection is expressly affirmed in the résumé of the chapter offered at the start of ¶61. So far from being a new topic or even the mere continuation of the discussion of death, this chapter is its conclusion and completion – and precisely in the sense of consummation.

Heidegger characteristically begins with Dasein lost in the 'they-self' of average everydayness. In this situation its self-understanding is determined by what it hears of itself from others. Yet in listening to others 'it fails to hear its own Self' (271/315). If it is to exist more authentically, then, it must be called away from such distracted hearing and, Heidegger says, 'That which, by calling in this manner, gives us to understand, is the conscience,' which, he adds, is 'a mode of discourse. Discourse articulates intelligibility' (271/316). Here again, the principle that Dasein's self-relation always involves *Befindlichkeit*, understanding, and *logos* or discourse is unavoidably central. The call of conscience is not just a vague, moody stirring or sense of unease, or, if is that, it is also always a distinct way of understanding who we are in our lives articulated in speech. But what is being talked about in such speech? Dasein itself, answers Heidegger. And to whom is the call of conscience directed? Again, it is to Dasein itself. The call of conscience thus calls Dasein back to itself.[20]

But if this seems relatively straightforward, Heidegger's next move is rather more unusual. To the question as to what conscience might say to Dasein, his answer is 'Taken strictly, nothing. The call asserts nothing, gives no information about world-events, has nothing to tell .... Conscience discourses solely and constantly in the mode of keeping silent' (273/318). Heidegger further explicates this in terms of Dasein's situation as having been thrown into existence. By way of preparation for this, he makes a further clarification: although conscience calls me to myself, it is in a certain sense not 'I' that calls. Rather, as he puts it, '"It" calls, against our expectations and even against our will .... The call comes from me and yet from beyond me' (275/320). This strange situation is, however, explicable if we note that Dasein's thrownness means that 'It exists as an entity which has to be as it is and can be' (276/321). In other words, its existence is not simply a project it has freely created for itself; instead, its existence – its truth, so to speak – is something it can only acquire through decisions and actions it finds itself called upon to make or perform. This situation, Heidegger suggests, arouses anxiety and is experienced as 'uncanny' (again, Heidegger's term *unheimlich* also expresses the sense of not being at home in the world or in ourselves, as if – to evoke a motif that is both Neoplatonic and Christian – its true home were elsewhere[21]). Of course, Heidegger himself does not understand this 'elsewhere' as 'another life' or 'another world' beyond this life and this world but as a kind of not-yet revealed from within our current experience of this-worldly existence. Only, as a matter of fact, it is mostly not revealed, precisely because it is so unsettling and disturbing. Faced with our thrownness we mostly don't face it, but instead 'Dasein flees to the relief which comes with the supposed freedom of the they-self' (276/322). In this way it avoids the anxiety in which it would be confronted with the disclosure of its essential nothingness. On the other hand, 'Uncanniness reveals itself authentically in the basic state-of-mind (*Befindlichkeit*) of anxiety' (276/321). Thus, Heidegger says

> The caller is Dasein in its uncanniness: primordial, thrown Being-in-the-world as the 'not-at-home' – the bare 'that-it-is' in the 'nothing' of the world. The caller is unfamiliar to the everyday they-self; it is something like an *alien* voice. What could be more alien to the 'they', lost in the manifold 'world' of its concern, than the Self which has been individualized down to itself in uncanniness and been thrown into the 'nothing'? (277/321–2)

Now Heidegger does not expressly identify this 'nothing' with the annihilation of the self in death, but surely, at this point, he doesn't need to. Even if there

---

[20]   For further discussion of the role of 'call' in Heidegger, see the section 'Who Shall I Say Is Calling' in Chapter 6 below.

[21]   Again, see Chapter 6 below, especially the concluding section 'Eternal Life?'

is no direct identification, the preceding meditation on death seems to make abundantly clear that it is precisely as thrown towards death, that is, thrown towards its entire annihilation and the final impossibility of its going on existing, that Dasein essentially lacks substantial being and is, instead, to be defined by 'nothing'. And, as his previous discussion also showed, the mood of anxiety in which the homelessness of Dasein's being is disclosed is especially associated with death – an association we shall later have occasion to discuss further.[22] And, again, Heidegger affirms that the way in which conscience calls us to anxious awareness of our thrownness and ontological homelessness is, precisely, by 'keeping silent' (277/322). Is this, then, the silence of the grave?

Passing over further features of the account of conscience, we move on to note its association with guilt. As we might by now expect, guilt, for Heidegger, does not mean being guilty in the sense of having perpetrated some specific transgression nor (as might be suggested by the German term *Schuld* also and indeed primarily meaning 'debt') being indebted in a financial or personal sense. On the contrary, law breaking and indebtedness are possible forms of human life only because, at a more profound level, our being is such that we are responsible for our actions and, indeed, for being the way that we are. Thus, the 'guilt' of which conscience makes us aware is, most fundamentally, '*a primordial Being-guilty*' (284/329). But this primordial 'being-guilty' is not simply another way of saying 'responsible' since, as Heidegger suggests, 'guilt' always implies a 'not' or, as he glosses it, '*Being-the-basis-of-a-nullity*' (283/329). And what is this 'nullity'? Ultimately it is we ourselves – Dasein itself – as thrown. In other words, existing as being responsible for being the beings that we are by virtue of our thrownness, i.e., beings that we did not choose to be before coming into existence but now find ourselves having to be, means existing as beings who are not defined by any pre-existent essence but have to, as it were, become who we are (but are not-yet) through our free choices. 'The nullity we have in mind,' writes Heidegger, belongs to Dasein's being-free for its existentiell possibilities' (285/331). Yet, I suggest, the freedom (i.e., the lack of ontological pre-determination) that Heidegger has in mind is not a freedom that exists or can exist outside what, in the previous chapter, he had described as a fundamental freedom for death since it is only this freedom in which we grasp our existence in its thrownness and as a whole and it is only this freedom that reveals my possibilities in all their finitude and 'mineness'. In any case, as freedom it is essentially the readiness to act and to be according to what is disclosed in conscience – whatever that may be and however 'uncanny'. This is what Heidegger calls 'wanting to have a conscience' (288/334), but 'Wanting-to-have-a-conscience becomes a readiness for anxiety' (296/342) – which, as has several times been noted, is precisely the mood in which we become aware of our thrownness as a thrownness towards annihilation in death. And, once more, Heidegger recurs to his theme of conscience as discoursing in the mode of keeping

---

[22] Again, see Chapter 6 for further discussion of the connection between the themes of death and home.

silent, which he now restates as *reticence* and which he contrasts with 'the loud idle talk which goes with the common sense of the "they"' (296/432).

Again, as in the projection of an authentic existential–ontological being towards death, we can see here a combination of active and passive elements. Dasein is thrown towards its annihilation, and its freedom is possible only on the (null) ground of this thrownness. Yet it must also want to have a conscience and want to live in the light of the uncanny and anxiety-inducing truth of what conscience silently discloses. As Heidegger puts it, 'This distinctive and authentic disclosedness, which is attested in Dasein itself by its conscience – this reticent self-projection upon one's ownmost Being-guilty, in which one is ready for anxiety – we call "resoluteness"' (296–7/343). As Macquarrie and Robinson note in their footnote, the term translated 'resoluteness', *Entschloßenheit*, is etymologically akin to the term for 'disclosedness', *Erschloßenheit*, suggesting that against at least some versions of existentialist freedom, resoluteness is not merely an arbitrary act of self-assertion on the part of a supposedly sovereign subjectivity but, on the contrary, is also an appropriate and fitting response to what is revealed to it in conscience. This, then, is 'that truth of Dasein which is most primordial because it is authentic' (297/343), i.e., 'proper' to the kind of being that it is.

Now it is certainly possible to see this as some general feature of Dasein, but, again, we should not lose sight of the role of death in this entire discussion – even when the word 'death' itself is not immediately present (after all, if we have once inscribed ourselves into the ranks of the reticent we cannot be expected to talk loudly about what most concerns us every few sentences). As so often, Heidegger shows himself aware of the issue and opens the following chapter by asking,

> What can death and the 'concrete Situation' of taking action have in common? In attempting to bring resoluteness and anticipation [which, remember, is the way in which an authentic being-towards-death is revealed to us] forcibly together, are we not seduced into an intolerable and quite unphenomenological construction for which we can no longer claim that it has the character of an ontological projection, based upon the phenomena? (302/349)

Yet, whilst thus acknowledging the potential scandal of his procedure, Heidegger nevertheless insists that resoluteness and anticipation really do belong together. Rhetorically he asks, 'What if it is only in the *anticipation* of death that all the factical "*anticipatoriness*" of resolving would be authentically understood – in other words, that it would be caught up with in an existentiell way?' (302/350). A positive answer to this question frees the proposal from the charge of being an arbitrary construction and becomes instead 'a way of Interpreting whereby Dasein is liberated for its uttermost possibility of existence' (303/350). And, finally, when Dasein does thus come 'face-to-face' with its 'individualized potentiality-for-being' in 'sober anxiety' it will at the same time experience 'an unshakable joy in this possibility' – although Heidegger immediately admits that to say more about this 'would transgress the limits which we have drawn for the present Interpretation by aiming towards fundamental ontology' (310/358).

Conclusion

The sheer pace of Heidegger's argument is at times overwhelming, but if we are capable of resisting its forward surge *and even if we are broadly sympathetic to key elements in it*, we may soon find much to question. Does being towards death really have the exclusive role vis-à-vis an authentic understanding of human Dasein that Heidegger claims for it? And just how persuasive is his account of the relationship between conscience, guilt, and being towards death? Is the ontological possibility of an authentic being towards death in fact and in any sense realizable at the level of existentiell life? We shall return to such questions in Chapters 3 and 4. First, however, we move to consider an important aspect of the philosophical background to *Being and Time* that is often overlooked in the secondary literature, namely, its relation to German Idealism. Doing so will help to clarify some of the central issues raised by Heidegger's proposal concerning the possibility of relating through death in the manner of anticipation or running-towards. Especially it will help us to see how the 'freedom' enacted in running towards death can be related to the situation of existing as thrown into a world and into possibilities not of our own making and, in connection with this, how running towards death is both an act of freedom and the revelation of how and who we really are. In the light of this discussion, we shall then start to see how a theological response to the nexus of issues brought to light by German Idealism might offer a significant alternative to that of Heidegger.

Chapter 2

Death and I

We have now seen in outline how Heidegger introduces and proposes his idea that the way – the only way – in which Dasein can gain an authentic relation to its own way of being is by 'running towards death', understanding this as an existential–ontological project and not some 'merely' psychological rebooting. Heidegger himself anticipates this being seen as a 'fantastical exaction' unless it can be shown to be a concrete possibility for Dasein at the level of its existentiell life and his account of conscience, guilt, and 'anticipatory resoluteness' is his attempt to give just such 'existentiell attestation' to the possibility of an authentic existential–ontological running towards death. I have indicated that I do not regard this as unproblematic. But before developing a critical response to Heidegger's position, I want to step back and consider an important aspect of the philosophical context of his argument. Apart from this being a way of helping us to see what is going on in *Being and Time* itself, it will also help us be more precise as to just where a Christian account of death might agree and where it might disagree with Heidegger's argument. The first half of this chapter, then, will, like the last, be of a largely expository character before, in the second half, I start to develop a more critical discussion.

In 1928 Heidegger's friend and colleague Rudolf Bultmann was asked to write an article on Heidegger for the prestigious encyclopaedia *Religion in Geschichte und Gegenwart* (Religion in History and Today). Having drafted his article, Bultmann then sent it to Heidegger, who made a number of amendments and clarifications. Here is an extract:

> His work … repeats the problems of ancient ontology in order to radicalize them and outlines universal ontology which in addition includes the region of history. The fundament of this problematic is developed by starting from the 'subject' properly understood as 'human Dasein', such that, with the radicalizing of this approach the true motives of German idealism come into their own. Augustine, Luther, and Kierkegaard were influential [Heidegger's own preferred wording was 'philosophically essential'] for H. in the development of the [H.: a more radical] understanding of Dasein ….[1]

Bultmann's article also lists other sources and contexts, such as Husserlian phenomenology, Aristotle, scholasticism, Dilthey and neo-Kantianism, that were

---

[1]   T. Kisiel and T. Sheehan (eds), *Becoming Heidegger* (Evanston: Northwestern University Press, 2007), p. 331.

also important for Heidegger – a formidable testimony to the wealth of sources active in the genesis of *Being and Time*. In this chapter and the next, however, I shall give particular weight to Heidegger's 'theological' sources – Augustine and, chiefly, Luther and Kierkegaard – and to German Idealism. The presence of Kierkegaard is, of course, well known, and if Shestov's view that *Being and Time* was an attempt to smuggle Kierkegaardian ideas into philosophy under the guise of phenomenology is extreme,[2] some kind of kinship is broadly acknowledged and is likely to be flagged in even the most cursory introductions to Heidegger. The role of German Idealism is less obvious, yet – perhaps counter-intuitively – Kant and Hegel are amongst the most extensively referenced authors in *Being and Time* itself. Nor was this any sudden new interest on Heidegger's part. On the contrary, there is evidence of its having been present from the very start of his philosophical journey.

Heidegger's *Habilitationschrift* (the post-doctoral qualification for teaching in a German university) was dedicated to Duns Scotus's doctrine of the categories. The work was submitted and examined in 1915 and published in 1916. The published version contains a short but important supplement in which Heidegger sketches an answer to what we might call the 'So what?' question, i.e., why the problem of the categories is philosophically important. In presenting an English translation of this supplement, Theodor Kisiel and Thomas Sheehan comment that 'Although Heidegger's immediate interlocutors are neo-Kantian contemporaries, the position that he takes from them is especially informed by the Idealist–Romantic reception of transcendental Idealism that plays out between Kant and Hegel'.[3] Heidegger's own comments show that he is especially concerned, as he puts it, with 'consciously working the problem of judgment into the subject–object relationship, and, second, bringing the category into relation with the judgment'.[4] However, as he goes on to say, 'we cannot view logic and its problems in their true light at all if we do not interpret them *from* a translogical perspective'.[5] In other words, as he immediately adds, this means grounding logic in 'a metaphysical and teleological interpretation of consciousness' that will do justice to consciousness as 'a living deed [*lebendige Tat*] that is itself meaningful and actualizes meaning'.[6] With reference to the Romantic thinker Friedrich Schlegel, he sees this as calling for a deeper investigation of 'the concept of living spirit and its "eternal affirmations"' and this 'living spirit' is also to be grasped as 'essentially historical

---

[2]   For a provocative discussion of the role of Heidegger in Shestov's study of Kierkegaard see B. Guérin, 'Chestov – Kierkegaard: faux ami, étrange fraternité' in R. Fotiade and F. Schwab (eds), *Léon Chestov – Vladimir Jankélévitch. Du tragique à l'ineffable* (Saarbrücken: Editions Universitaires Européennes, 2011), pp. 113–32.

[3]   Kisiel and Sheehan, *Becoming Heidegger*, p. 75.

[4]   Ibid., p. 80.

[5]   Ibid., p. 82.

[6]   Ibid.

in the broadest sense of the term'.[7] The philosophical task, therefore, is to show how the categories we use to structure our knowledge of the world are grounded in the history of Spirit, which, he also says, 'provides [philosophically] a continually increasing means for a living conception of the absolute spirit of God'.[8]

The work to which these remarks are a supplement is, of course, dedicated to a medieval philosopher. In his introduction to the thesis Heidegger had flagged the distinctive character of medieval thought as especially suited to such a deepening of philosophical concerns. If, as he there asserts, philosophy is more than a merely technical or theoretical undertaking and necessarily involves the living personality, the medieval attitude of 'absolute devotional and affective immersion in the received stuff of knowledge' provides a helpful means of effecting such deepening.[9] The medieval individual loses himself in the 'matter at issue', 'the material' and 'the universal'. The medieval thinker is not a 'subject' in the modern sense and has no clear sense of method nor of the 'what' or the 'that' of knowledge, but is concerned with the 'how'.[10] In the case of Duns Scotus, this proximity to life is evidenced in his distinctive category of *haecceitas* ('thusness' or 'suchness').[11] In this regard the 'mysticism' of the Middle Ages also receives a positive evaluation, and, despite having by then moved away from scholasticism (to the point at which he can speak of it as a 'pseudo-philosophy'[12]), Heidegger subsequently takes medieval mysticism as the theme for a phenomenological investigation of the basic constitution of human being as such.[13]

This project is never completed, but whatever the more precise reasons for his not having pursued it further, not only the supplement but also the conclusion of the thesis on Duns Scotus already indicates that it is especially in relation to German Idealism that the decisive philosophical questions are most likely to get properly formulated. This is the clear implication of the extraordinary concluding sentence:

> The philosophy of the living spirit, of deedful [*tatvoll*] love, of revering intimacy with God, whose most general aims we can only allude to, especially a theory of categories that is guided by its basic tendencies, faces the major task of a fundamental confrontation with that system of a historical worldview that commands the greatest wealth of experience and concept formation, as abundant

---

[7]   Ibid., pp. 82–3.

[8]   Ibid., p. 83.

[9]   M. Heidegger, *Frühe Schriften. Gesamtausgabe*, vol. 1 (Frankfurt am Main: Klostermann, 1978), p. 198.

[10]   Ibid., pp. 198–201.

[11]   Ibid., p. 203.

[12]   M. Heidegger, *Phänomenologie des religiösen Lebens. Gesamtausgabe*, vol. 60 (Frankfurt am Main: Klostermann, 1995), p. 313.

[13]   See 'Die philosophischen Grundlagen der mittelalterlichen Mystik' in *Phänomenologie des religiösen Lebens*, pp. 303–37.

as it is profound, a system that took up into itself all of the fundamental motives previously operative in philosophical problems – that is, a confrontation with Hegel.[14]

In fact, it would be 10 years – and after the publication of *Being and Time* itself – before Heidegger turned directly to German Idealism in a series of lectures on Kant (winter semester 1927–28;[15] on Fichte, Schelling, and Hegel (summer semester 1929); Hegel (winter semester 1931–32); and Schelling (summer semester 1936, also 1941). Yet the fact that these lectures post-date *Being and Time* by no means invalidates them from being used to highlight a philosophical debate or *Auseinandersetzung* that had been underway since the time of the Duns Scotus thesis, even if it had also been running underground for much of that period. On the contrary, as I hope to show, they can help see more precisely just what is at issue in that work itself and, in particular, with regard to the question of death. At the same time, this debate cannot itself be entirely separated from Heidegger's reading of Kierkegaard and the latter's own critique of German Idealism, and, as we shall see, Heidegger's own critical appropriation of German Idealism repeats in some measure what we already find in the Danish thinker.

But just how might the argument of *Being and Time* be a way of revealing the 'true motives' of German Idealism and helping them come into their own? And how, if it also reflects Kierkegaard's earlier critical response to that same philosophical movement, does it do so? It is to address such questions that I turn now to the 1929 lectures on German Idealism and, in particular, the interpretation of Fichte, whom Heidegger regards as setting the agenda for subsequent representatives of the movement.

The True Motives of German Idealism

We have been seeing the importance of freedom in *Being and Time*, and the lectures on German Idealism, which start with some general reflections on the nature of philosophy, underline that importance. Philosophy, Heidegger suggests, is not an attempt to deal with a string of discrete questions nor even to provide 'useful' knowledge, but, if it is to be genuinely philosophical, must address the question as to what is *greatest* in human being. In relation to this he says that 'Only when we bring freedom to the point at which it can bring us to ourselves does it make any sense to get involved with philosophy'.[16] It is typical of contemporary philosophy to start with the question of the human, with anthropology in the broadest sense

---

[14]   Kisiel and Sheehan, *Becoming Heidegger*, p. 86 (*Frühe Schriften*, pp. 352–3).

[15]   These lectures evolved into the book *Kant and the Problem of Metaphysics*.

[16]   M. Heidegger, *Der Deutsche Idealismus (Fichte, Schelling, Hegel) und die philosophische Grundlage der Gegenwart. Gesamtausgabe*, vol. 28 (Frankfurt am Main: Klostermann, 1997), p. 7. Further references are given in the text as DI.

of the term – a tendency he sees in, e.g., Max Scheler. But philosophy cannot stop there because the study of humanity, like the study of the history of philosophy (another contemporary trend), cannot avoid claims about the nature of reality, being, and truth and is therefore driven ineluctably towards metaphysics, namely, to Heidegger's own questions as to the essence of being as such and as a whole. These were indeed questions that came to the fore in German Idealism itself, although subsequent philosophy is, in this regard, decadent (Heidegger holds).

How might one go about reversing this situation? By going back to Aristotle? To some extent this might seem to have been Heidegger's own tactic through the 1920s, when he lectured repeatedly on different aspects of Aristotle's philosophy.[17] However, he now asserts that Aristotle won't do because 'he did not at all pose the problem regarding the inner possibility, that is, regarding the essence, of first philosophy' (DI, 34). This problem is implicit in ancient, i.e. Platonic and Aristotelian, metaphysics, indeed. It is its 'hidden basic problem' (DI, 35), but it is not thematized there as such. After the eclipse of ancient philosophy, it is only with Kant that the possibility of a genuinely new beginning is made. Why? Because Kant understands reason as essentially finite. 'The question is about finitude, about what it is, about the essence of human finitude, which is the basis on which alone being human is possible' (DI, 38). Yet Kant himself doesn't succeed in making the bridge from the study of the human to the grounding of the human in metaphysics, that is, a 'metaphysics of Dasein' (DI, 41). Kant sees the connection between temporality and finitude but doesn't work it through. As for German Idealism itself, it entirely misconceives the problem and, despite (or perhaps because of) its 'monstrous efforts to focus on the "I" and the subject' (DI, 46), causes finitude to once more vanish from sight. The study of German Idealism, then, is for Heidegger the study of an error. Yet, at the same time, he affirms its impulse to think through the 'I' and the subject as the path to a new grounding of metaphysics. The study then becomes fruitful if he can identify the point at which German Idealism veers away from the path along which its guiding question could have taken it. The basic error, I suggest, becomes apparent in the treatment of Fichte, which constitutes the larger part of the lecture series. This treatment has the form of an exposition of Fichte's *Science of Knowledge*, but although – like so many of Heidegger's lecture series – it is in large part expository, it also provides him with the occasion both for critical comment and for his own counter-proposals.

Noting that the German Idealists regarded themselves as Kantian and considered being only insofar as it is knowable, finite being, i.e., what can become an object for a knowing subject, he sees their central concern as being to eliminate the unknowability of the thing-in-itself and to ground the thing in absolute subjectivity. In pursuance of this aim, they saw philosophy itself as a kind of science and, like all sciences, as resting upon a certain founding principle, a *Grundsatz* or basic

---

[17]   For an overview of these lectures see T. Kisiel, *The Genesis of Heidegger's Being and Time* (Berkeley: University of California Press, 1993), esp. pp. 221–308.

proposition that is not derived from any other science and that is utterly certain. This is what Fichte's science of knowledge seeks to identify and explicate.

As concerning knowledge, such a science is directed towards the organ of knowledge: thought. But thought does not exist apart from an 'I' that thinks. The ground of knowledge is therefore the thinking 'I' but, since thinking does not occur except as an activity, this 'I' is 'the "I" that acts' in what Fichte calls an 'act-action' (*Tat-handlung*[18]). But this 'I' is not that of any particular human individual but '"I" qua "I" as such, the I-ness of any "I"' (DI, 53). In a manner not unlike Heidegger's own application of phenomenological method and the 'formal indication',[19] Fichte proceeds to 'construct' his system of knowledge on the basis of this I-qua-I not, as Heidegger puts it, by 'de-monstrating' but simply by 'monstrating', i.e., indicating or showing its own internal structure (DI, 54). Again, not unlike Heidegger's own procedure in *Being and Time* this is said to be both a 'projection' (*ein Entwerfen*) and a distinctive way of letting the matter be seen (*ein Sehen-lassen eigener Art*) (DI, 54).

What, then, comes to view when we let the matter be seen in this way?

In expounding Fichte's answer, Heidegger explains how the founding principle of knowledge has three interconnected forms, namely, the principle of identity, the principle of contradiction, and the principle of sufficient reason.[20] In order to identify what is of most relevance to the question we are pursuing here (that is, the question of how 'running towards death' might be seen as illuminating the basic motives of German Idealism), I shall merely sketch Heidegger's exposition and move fairly rapidly towards the point at which he offers his own decisive criticism of Fichte's position.

The first principle, that of identity, is summed up in the classic Fichtean formulation of the logical copula A is A. Here, Heidegger says, the emphasis is on the 'is' and in such a way that what is highlighted is how the predicate is related to its subject – A *is* A ('the grass *is* green', etc.). But – and already this is a sign of how the Idealists veered away from the possibility of genuinely uncovering the

---

[18]   Cf. Heidegger's commendation in the supplement to the *Habilitationsschrift* of Hegel's view of consciousness as *lebendige Tat* or 'living act'.

[19]   'Formal indication' refers to a recurrent feature of Heidegger's approach in the 1920s. See references in Kisiel, *Genesis*.

[20]   In both Fichte and Heidegger an important thread in the whole discussion is the role of the verb *setzen* and the noun *Satz* that is hard to sustain in English. *Setzen* is often, in this context, translated as 'posit' (cf. the Latin *ponere*); the *Satz* is what is then posited in the act of positing. *Satz*, however, may be variously translated 'sentence', 'proposition', or 'principle'. The German thus testifies to an immediate connection between 'positing' and, e.g., 'principle' that is lost in English. A further key term is *Grund*, translatable both as 'ground' (or 'basis') and 'reason' and, again, both Heidegger and Fichte seem to invoke the metaphorical force of the former also in discussing 'reason'. The third principle of knowledge, the principle of sufficient reason, is thus, in German, *der Satz vom Grunde*, i.e., the positing of the ground.

ontological question – this is understood by Fichte in such a way as to absorb the being of whatever is being considered into the judgement that it 'is' whatever it is, which serves to occlude the relation between judgement and ontology. What Fichte seizes on is that this principle (*Satz*) is something that the thinking subject who thinks it posits (*setzt*). What is generatively active in this principle, then, is not the variable content of the subject and predicate but the act of the 'I' in which the 'is' that binds them is posited. In this perspective, A is A can be reformulated more precisely and more fundamentally as I = I. What this means is that the act of thinking is an act in which the I always and continually posits itself and 'I am' is the highest *Tatsache*, a word regularly translated as 'fact' but which might be better rendered here as 'act–fact'. A *Tatsache* in this sense is not a merely occurring 'fact' (what just happens to be the case) but a fact that it grounded in an act (*Tat*). This act is a pure activity of the I as act–fact and it is the basic action (*Tathandlung*) in which the I is (self-)established in the absoluteness of its I-ness as the absolute subject (although, as Heidegger notes, it is open to question whether what is being talked about here is God or the empirical subject – an issue that was important in Kierkegaard's criticism of post-Fichtean irony).

This, for Fichte, (de-)monstrates that the self-relating I is the proper[21] and primary grounding essence and first principle of all human knowing. Yet, at the same time, and precisely by constituting itself as a knowing subject in this way, the I projects or represents what it knows as a Not-I. Once more, the metaphoric force of the relevant German term *Vor-stellen*, 'placing in front of', plays a significant role in interpreting the matter at issue, in this case 'representation'. Thus, 'We apprehend and understand the essence of the Not-I only as regards [a manifestation of] the positing–representing I' (DI, 77). That is to say, the Not-I, what I affirm to be the case out there in the world (e.g., 'the grass is green'), is basically grounded in and constructed by and to that extent *is* the product of the I. This then provides the basis for the second principle of knowledge, the principle of contradiction.

We are now presented with a twofold structure of consciousness, the I and the Not-I, in which the I is not only capable of knowing what is not itself but also knows this to be its own representation or what it itself represents to itself in the act of thinking. In a move that is important with regard to the question of finitude as that emerges in *Being and Time*, Fichte argues that the relationship of the I and Not-I will always be a relationship of mutual limitation and negation. But this is only ever partial and never total – the I is not annihilated by the Not-I or the Not-I dissolved by the I, but the I knows itself as limited by the Not-I in some particular respect or aspect. Otherwise the contradiction would be all encompassing and consciousness would annihilate itself. This, however, means that we are now presented with a model in which a manifold of divisible or quantitative relationships is displayed: the I never knows the Not-I simply as 'Not-I' but as this particular something, e.g., as this green grass or distant mountain range. In this way, the pure activity of the

---

[21]   The word translated 'proper' here is *eigentlich*, which, in the context of *Being and Time*, is generally translated as 'authentic'.

I as such spontaneously renders the objects that constitute its known world finite. Only in this way is the I whole.

Yet, Heidegger suggests, Fichte is only bringing to consciousness what is already there to be found in it. He is not creating a subject and its world ex nihilo but trying to account for the certitude we actually have of existing as subjects in a world. In this way he implicitly prioritizes the need for certitude over the question of truth (Heidegger says). But can the finite I – you or I in our everyday lives – ever really give ourselves such certitude? Isn't Fichte's procedure less of a deduction and more of an expression for what Heidegger calls a *Machtanspruch*, a mere claim that it must be so?

With these critical suggestions, Heidegger moves to the third principle of knowing, the principle of sufficient reason. With this we move beyond the simple fact of representation to a more complex model of positive and negative relationship, *synthesis* and *diairesis*. That the Not-I is only knowable as a particular something means that it is knowable as what it is only in the form of a judgement ('This is a tree' or 'This tree is an oak') and any statement in which such a judgement comes to expression must be such as to have a ground or reason.

By following the path from the self-evidence of 'A is A' to the necessity of concrete judgements concerning particulars, Fichte now believes himself to have shown how synthetic propositions are a priori possible and therewith to have solved the basic problem of metaphysics as bequeathed by Kant. However, Heidegger says, he has overlooked what for Heidegger himself is the decisive question: that of the possibility of knowing being. But how might that question have been addressed in terms of Fichte's starting point? Heidegger suggests that whilst Fichte rightly traces synthetic judgements back to the founding activity of the I, he does not reflect that this I itself is groundless. The only judgement that the I can make concerning itself is that it is – 'I am' – leaving the place of the predicate infinitely open. But this means that my 'I am', my being, can never be understood in the light of any entity or complex of entities predicated of me since it itself precedes all possible predicates. The way in which my 'I am' is knowable must therefore be quite different from the way in which I know objects in the world. As Heidegger says, 'My being is never a being that is present-at-hand, but something that is given to me as my own task. The being of the I is an ought-to-be, thus and thus, or, regarding what it concerns, thus or thus' (DI, 107). The I cannot know itself as a 'what' but only as regards 'how' it is to be. To say 'Human beings are free' looks like a synthetic judgement, but this is an illusion since we know of no class of 'free beings' (as opposed, say, to 'beings that reproduce sexually'). 'Freedom' is not an element of the world but can be known only in relation to the I that 'is' free. Freedom 'is' only in and through my self-liberation. But where Fichte sees the human being as absolute subject, and whilst Heidegger too depicts the I as standing before an open field of infinite possibilities, the latter sees the finite I as *existing* only by virtue of the concrete ways in which it relates itself – finitely – to these possibilities.

By overlooking the question of being, Fichte – preparing the way also for Hegel – understands the I precisely in the line of Descartes's thinking substance and consequently conceives of the I essentially and solely as the thinking – rather than the existing – I. And (as we might say the title of Fichte's work on which Heidegger is commenting already indicates) what is at issue for Fichte is precisely not being but knowledge and he therefore he overlooks the question of finitude as it confronts existing human Dasein, 'the most intimate and secret question of Dasein itself' (DI, 133). Of course, Fichte is not ignorant of finitude, but he locates it in the representing activity of the knowing subject and in such a way that the Not-I is, as we have seen, only real for us in representation. Thus his position is essentially idealistic.

Now, as Heidegger acknowledges, all of the foregoing relates only to one part of Fichte's system, namely, the theoretical part. Fichte himself sees that he must go further and account for how the I is affected by and not simply productive of what is external to it, and he attempts to do this in his practical philosophy. Yet here too he ends only by offering a further *Machtanspruch* and cannot surrender his basic conviction that even the affects that the self experiences in the mode of passivity are traceable to the causative activity of absolute subjectivity. As Heidegger puts it, suffering (in the technical sense of the passions) is only a lesser quantum of activity (DI, 157). In exploring the reciprocity of the I and its world, Fichte invokes an analogy of the threefold relation of night, day, and dusk, but to Heidegger's mind this suggests that the difference between self and other is, for Fichte, finally and solely a quantitative difference, just as night, day, and dusk gradually shade off into or emerge out of each other. What Fichte does not give an adequate account of is what Heidegger calls the *Anstoß* or, we might say, push back offered by the world to the world-creating I, and one of the reasons why he does not do so is that (like Kant) he overlooks the role of temporality (DI, 169). In other words, what obliges human Dasein to recognize that it is not the sovereign creator of its world but is also responsive to it is that it exists in time and that it cannot of itself determine the coming and going of its own temporality. Heidegger affirms Fichte's guiding insight that the self is to be conceived as active, i.e., as a centre of freedom, but where he parts ways with his predecessor and with the other Idealists who followed him is that this activity never exists except as confronted by the demands of having to be in time. And, as we have seen in *Being and Time*, the determining instance of our passivity in relation to time is the manner in which we are, beyond any possibility of choice, thrown towards our entire annihilation in death. Human finitude is not something posited by the infinite creative activity of the 'I' but is disclosed to us in the ineluctability of our thrownness towards death.

The lectures on Fichte set out the basic shape of Heidegger's response to German Idealism as a whole. As regards this course, the following lectures on Schelling and Hegel show how they amplified the Fichtean paradigm. Schelling's early nature philosophy (the only part of his work discussed here) depicts nature itself as grounded in the productive imagination (DI, 191[22]), whilst Hegel sees both intelligence and nature as comprising the subjective and objective polarities that are mutually mediated in the synthesis created by absolute Spirit – a paradoxical idea that, nevertheless, is rooted in an act of imagination, i.e., productive reason (DI, 200–208). But this productive act of reason is not subject to time. Instead, it is conceived of by Hegel as an 'absolute present', equivalent to the nunc stans of medieval philosophy (DI, 211). Yet, characteristically, this does not lead Heidegger simply to dismiss the Idealists. Their error belongs to the history of philosophy, and if they cannot offer us the right 'answers', they nevertheless lead us to the decisive questions and, indeed, point us back to where the issue must be decided: to Dasein itself and the manner of its actual ontological constitution (DI, 231–2).

The lectures on Hegel's *Phenomenology* repeat many of the themes from the earlier series on German Idealism. 'Hegel and German Idealism as a whole can grasp the totality of beings in their being from out of I-hood as infinity', Heidegger says,[23] and again this leads to the occlusion of the temporal character of the I. Hegel construes being 'egologically' as the essence of time, where Heidegger sees time as the essence of Being: 'it is not the concept which is "the power of time," but it is time which is the power of the concept'.[24] Where Hegel sees being in the light of its being posited by absolute Spirit, Heidegger sees it as 'the horizon of ecstatic time'.[25] But this is not a simple opposition. Again, Hegel is not simply 'wrong' but sums up and recapitulates the guiding assumptions of the philosophical tradition as a whole, which Heidegger characterizes as 'onto-theological' and 'onto-ego-theo-logical'.[26]

To some extent the 1936 lectures on Schelling's treatise on human freedom do strike new ground, since Heidegger sees Schelling as making explicit the limits of German Idealism, whilst not actually breaking with its guiding assumptions. Here the emphasis is especially on will and the Schellingian interpretation of Fichte's abstract I as a centre of active and creative volition, grounding itself in the unfathomable abyss of its own freedom and capable of both good and evil, the latter being understood in terms of the capacity of the individual will to break loose from

---

[22]   However, Heidegger also notes how Schelling considers the possibility that the I is only one outworking of nature itself, a possibility he regards as 'suspect' (*bedenklich*) (DI, 192–3).

[23]   M. Heidegger, *Hegel's Phenomenology of Spirit*, trans. P. Emad and K. Maly (Bloomington: Indiana University Press, 1994), p. 78 (GA32, p. 111).

[24]   Heidegger, *Hegel's Phenomenology*, p. 100 (GA32, p. 144).

[25]   Ibid., p. 100 (GA32, p. 145).

[26]   Ibid., pp. 97ff., 145 (GA32, pp. 141ff., 209). The lectures on Schelling will also invoke the idea of onto-theology that, through the post-war paper on 'The Onto-theological Constitution of Metaphysics' would come to play such a large part of late-twentieth- and early-twenty-first-century philosophy of religion. Strikingly, this paper too is set up as a response to Hegel, underlining the continuing importance of the debate with German Idealism to Heidegger's thought.

the universal order of things and establish itself as an original centre of existence, perhaps what Kierkegaard would call 'the despair of defiance'. As Heidegger cites Schelling, "'Ultimately, there is no being other than willing. Willing is primordial being." That is to say: original being (*Seyn*) is willing'.[27] Although this points beyond the Idealist conception of human freedom as grounded in intelligence, in the abstract I, Schelling is unable to think together the exigencies of wilful existence and the coherence of beings as a whole. The critical implications of thinking of human freedom solely in terms of will (as well as the connection between Schelling's and Nietzsche's idea of the will to power) are brought out in further lectures from 1941, where such 'wilfulness' is seen as a defining trait of human beings' (or at least of Germans') self-conception. Here – in what might be his most explicit negative comment about Nazism – Heidegger comments,

> The metaphysics of the unconditional will to power has been expressed in three short statements that were cited in a leading article in the June issue of the weekly *The Reich*. Here we saw cited as the briefest epitome [of this position] the remarks of a Berlin taxi-driver (not as a joke but quite seriously, agreeing with him, and as offering insight into how things are). The remark is: 'Adolf knows it, God guesses (*ahnt*) it, and what's it got to do with you'. This expresses the unconditional consummation of Western metaphysics. These three statements are the genuine Berlin interpretation of Nietzsche's *Thus Spoke Zarathustra*; they outweigh everything in the entire Nietzsche-literature.[28]

That would seem to sum up, albeit in non-philosophical language, Heidegger's view that, despite re-directing philosophy to the human subject as the point of entry to any future metaphysics, German Idealism's conception of this subject in terms of pure subjectivity (or egoity, or wilfulness, or self-assertion) effaces the co-presence of passive as well as active elements in the constitution of the self and thereby obscures also the essential temporality of human Dasein. If *Being and Time* seeks to elucidate the true motives of German Idealism in such a way as to allow them to 'come into their own', it would seem that it does so by (a) bringing to the fore and re-affirming the freedom of the self with regard to its possibilities but (b) critically re-describing these possibilities in terms of thrownness, epitomized in Dasein's thrownness towards death, and (c) therewith bringing to the fore the fundamentally temporal character of Dasein. Nevertheless – and this is perhaps what, though briefly said, is most striking – even as thrown towards death, Dasein qua capable of freely and resolutely running towards this impossible possibility can, as it were, reclaim and take on its thrownness, making itself guilty of being the nullity that it is. Precisely by taking account of what Fichte and the other

---

[27] M. Heidegger, *Schelling: Vom Wesen der menschlichen Freiheit. Gesamtausgabe*, vol. 42 (Frankfurt am Main: Klostermann, 1988), p. 164.

[28] M. Heidegger, *Die Metaphysik des deutschen Idealismus. Gesamtausgabe*, vol. 49 (Frankfurt am Main: Klostermann, 1991), p. 122.

German Idealists did not take account of, Heidegger is thus able to restate – and, he would claim, do so as a statement of truth and not merely as expressive of the need for certitude – that even the thrown self can be the agent of its own world of meaning. Again, we may say, it is a kind of self-redemption in the mould of Nietzsche's resolve to turn 'It was' into 'I willed it thus'.[29] This is certainly a subtler picture than that offered by the anonymous Berlin taxi-driver – but perhaps Heidegger's comment on that anecdote may be taken as an exercise in implicit self-criticism 12 years on from *Being and Time* and at a point at which he had come to see the Nazi experiment as one more manifestation of technological will to power. For is it not at least possible that, in his account of Dasein's possibility of resolutely running towards death, Heidegger finally betrays his own insistence on the thrown character of existence and on the relationless, unsurpassable, and *impossible* character of the possibility of death?

Mortality and Createdness

In order to develop these critical questions further, I turn now to another aspect of Heidegger's early 'programme'. As we read in Bultmann's article, Heidegger

---

[29] Another angle on this relationship (Heidegger and German Idealism) is provided by Alexandre Kojève's influential Paris lectures on Hegel and, in particular, by the 1933–34 lectures on Hegel's philosophy of death. Starting with the passage from the *Introduction to the Phenomenology of Spirit* in which Hegel asserts that he intends to re-think truth as not only substance but also subject, Kojève interprets this as requiring an account of truth that incorporates the totality of historically attested discourse concerning truth, which, as such, further involves the negation of a merely 'natural' relation to an immanent order of things defined in terms of what they substantially and timelessly 'are'. But where Judaeo-Christian traditions ground human beings' capacity to exist as world-transcending Spirit in their religious postulate of another world, Hegel reconceived this transcendence in terms of temporality and finitude. Thus, 'according to Hegel, the revelation of Being by means of discourse is only possible if the being that effects this revelation by speaking it forth is finite or mortal ... a natural being limited in its existence by time and space'. And 'Hegel's Absolute Knowledge (or Wisdom) and the complete acceptance of death, understood as complete and definitive annihilation' are one and the same'. A. Kojève, *Introduction à la lecture de Hegel* (Paris: Gallimard, 1947), pp. 539, 540. It should immediately be added that this interpretation is itself carried out under the auspices of Kojève's reading of Heidegger, reading Hegel through Heideggerian lenses, as it were. However, to the extent that Kojève's reading is persuasive, this reinforces Heidegger's own view that what he is doing in *Being and Time* is, *inter alia*, uncovering the true motives of German Idealism, namely, the attempt to understand human knowing as grounded in and manifesting the interplay of historicity, language, finitude, and death. On the role of Heidegger in Kojève's thought see Kojève, *Introduction à la lecture de Hegel*, p. 575 (n. 1); idem., 'Note inédite sur Hegel et Heidegger', *Rue Descartes*, no. 7 (1993): 37; see also S. Geroulanos, *An Atheism That Is Not Humanist Emerges in French Thought* (Stanford, CA: Stanford University Press, 2010), pp. 130–72.

regarded Augustine, Luther, and Kierkegaard as 'philosophically essential' for the development of the 'more radical understanding of Dasein' that he was seeking.[30] I shall return in Chapter 4 to further aspects of his relation to these theological sources, but wish now to focus (a) on how Heidegger reprises aspects of Kierkegaard's own criticism of German Idealism and of the difference between the former's methodologically a-theistic and the latter's theologically inflected criticism; and (b) the differences in their way of dealing with the inconceivability of death. Both these concern the nature of human thrownness and of how such thrownness nevertheless also allows us to experience ourselves as free.[31]

Kierkegaard was, from the beginning of his intellectual career, engaged with the questions posed to religion by German Idealism. His thesis *On the Concept of Irony* addresses Fichte, briefly but incisively, as preparing the way for what he sees as Early Romanticism's nihilistic celebration of the spontaneous creative freedom the individual self or I. In what could be read as an effective summing-up of the more extensive exposition offered by Heidegger's 1929 lectures, he sees Fichte as having placed the *an sich* (or in-itself) of Being 'within thought' since, on Fichte's account of knowledge, 'the producing *I* is the same as the produced *I*'.[32] 'By so doing,' Kierkegaard continues, '[Fichte] infinitely liberated thought'. But

---

[30] Kisiel and Sheehan, *Becoming Heidegger*, p. 331.

[31] Of course, a theological response to Heidegger's argument as I have presented it here could choose to go in a more fundamental theological direction at this point by looking at how the German Idealist portrayal of the self as a kind of pure activity, an act–fact, relates to the scholastic view of God as *actus purus*, the pure act in which all possibilities are always already actualized and who may therefore also be spoken of as Being–Itself, *ipsum esse*, He Who Is. There are elements of Heidegger's discussion that suggest he might have envisaged Dasein itself as playing the part of the *actus purus* and therefore being the ultimate ground of its own being. This might seem to be implicit in the opening definitions of *Being and Time* ¶9, as when Heidegger states that 'The essence of Dasein lies in its existence' (42/67) and 'All the being-as-it-is which this entity possesses is primarily being (*Alles so-sein dieses Seienden ist primär Sein*)' (42/67). This seems exactly to mirror the scholastic claim that God is the unique being whose being is simply to-be and, as such, is also pure act. However, Heidegger also differentiates the German *Wesen* and *Existenz* from the Latin *essentia* and *existential* in such a way as to make clear that the relationship between essence and existence in Dasein is quite differently understood from how it is in the case of the scholastics' God. As we have now seen, existent Dasein exists only as thrown, as having freely to take over possibilities – including the impossible possibility of death – into which it has been thrown. And we have now also heard Heidegger's criticisms of the Idealist version of understanding human Dasein as any kind of absolute subject. Yet – and this is precisely the question that the following discussion may be read as indirectly addressing – we may still ask whether his account of our capacity freely to run towards this impossible possibility allows him a kind of backdoor to re-asserting a kind of sovereignty on the part of the human being that mirrors the sovereignty of a God who is 'pure act'.

[32] S. Kierkegaard, *Af en endu Levendes Papirer/Om Begrebet Ironi. Søren Kierkegaards Skrifter*, vol. 1 (Gad: Copenhagen, 1997), p. 309; *The Concept of Irony*, trans. H.V. Hong and E.H. Hong (Princeton: Princeton University Press, 1989), p. 273.

the outcome is a purely idealistic infinity: 'When Fichte infinitized the *I* in this way, he advanced an idealism beside which any actuality turned pale, an acosmism in which his idealism became actuality even though it was Docetism'.[33] The universe of which the Fichtean subject was creator and centre was a purely abstract universe. However successful this might be as an account of the principles of knowledge, it is disastrous when the I is identified with the I of the individual subject (you or I or he or she), which is precisely how (according to Kierkegaard) the Romantics developed Fichte's ideas, living as if each individual was the creator of his own world. But, he argues, such wilful neglect of the claims of external reality leads inevitably to arbitrariness and nihilism. To echo Heidegger, we may say that Kierkegaard sees Fichte's transcendental project as a 'fantastic exaction' when taken as a basis on which to live out one's life on the level or in the mode of the existentiell.[34]

On the Concept of Irony itself seeks to show how this nihilism manifests itself in the literary and theoretical work of Friedrich Schlegel and other early Romantic figures and does so in a fairly straightforward scholarly way – the work was, after all, offered as a thesis for the degree of Master of Philosophy. But when Kierkegaard takes up his pen without the constraints of academic formality, he restates his argument in looser and more imaginative terms. In *Either/Or*, his first major publication after the thesis, he presents the kind of nihilism he sees resulting from Romantic, i.e., post-Fichtean, irony by means of a series of papers supposedly written by a nameless advocate of this ironic view of life, supplemented by two extensive letters to this same person from an older friend, a legal Assessor whose first name we learn is Vilhelm. It is especially in the second of these letters that we have a further more or less direct criticism of the Fichtean view of the self that anticipates Heidegger's account of Dasein as a 'thrown project', that is, a centre of freedom tasked with taking over the factical content of a life it has not created for itself. For the Assessor, the issue centres on what we mean by choice, which, as he explains (and despite his own designation of the position he is representing as 'ethical'), is not the choice between good and evil but something more basic – a choice that makes choice itself possible (just as, for Heidegger, it is existential–ontological guilt that first makes it possible to be 'guilty' in the more familiar moral or forensic senses of the word). It is, as he puts it, a matter of 'choosing to choose'[35] and also, as such, an affirmation of the basic freedom of the self: it is a matter of, so to speak, activating, enacting, and owning the freedom to choose and, in choosing, choosing ourselves as free.

---

[33]   Ibid.

[34]   For further discussion see my *Kierkegaard and the Theology of the Nineteenth Century* (Cambridge: Cambridge University Press, 2012), pp. 82–92; also L. Hühn and P. Schwab, 'Kierkegaard and German Idealism' in J.A. Lippitt and G. Pattison (eds), *The Oxford Handbook of Kierkegaard* (Oxford: Oxford University Press, 2013), pp. 54–85.

[35]   S. Kierkegaard, *Enten-Eller 2. Søren Kierkegaards Skrifter*, vol. 3 (Copenhagen: Gad, 1997), p. 165; *Either/Or, Part II*, trans. H.V. Hong and E.H. Hong (Princeton: Princeton University Press, 1987), p. 169.

But what is it, then, that I choose, is it this or that? No, for I choose absolutely, and the absolute element in my choice is precisely that I am not choosing this or that. I am choosing the absolute, and what is the absolute? It is myself in my eternal validity. I can never choose anything external to my self absolutely, for then I am choosing something external, then I am choosing something finite, and therefore do not choose it absolutely.[36]

Now this might sound as if the Assessor too, like the Romantics whom Kierkegaard criticized in *On the Concept of Irony*, is subscribing to some sort of Fichtean programme of absolute self-assertion, envisaging the self as the sole, absolute creative power in existence. In choosing myself absolutely, I unconditionally accept that I am who I am and as I am and there is no parallel universe into which I can escape. I am infinitely responsible for the self that I am, and there is no one else who is or can be responsible for it in the same way. However, the Assessor also places great emphasis on the difference between self-creation and self-choice. Choice is not ex nihilo or contextless.[37] Precisely as an act of self-choice and not an act of self-creation, the self we become through this choice is also a received self. Self-choice is always *situated* and, the Assessor says – again anticipating Heidegger – is situated by virtue of its inherent temporality: in choosing ourselves as who we are we acquire a history, as he puts it; that is, we accept ourselves as the people we have become through the experiences that have brought us to this point. He also calls this 'repentance', but although this seems to foreground the idea of accepting ourselves *despite* everything there might have been in our lives that fell short of how we would like to have been, notions of moral wrongdoing or sin are not – or, at least, not at this point – salient in the Assessor's account. What 'repentance' reveals is precisely that 'no man is an island', since those who repent repent themselves 'back into the self, into the family, the race, until he finds himself in God'.[38] And, as he goes on to say, 'His self is, so to speak, outside him, and it has to be acquired, and repentance is his love for it, because he chooses it absolutely from the hand of the eternal God'.[39] In theological terms, the act of choice by which I become who I am is the act in which I learn to understand myself as created by God – or, in the language of Schleiermacher (the one early Romantic thinker who offered a far-reaching critique of the view of the self as absolute subjectivity), I learn to understand myself as infinitely and absolutely dependent on God.[40]

---

[36] Kierkegaard, *Enten-Eller 2*, p. 199; Hong and Hong, *Either/Or II*, p. 214.

[37] On, e.g., Alasdair MacIntyre's misreading of Kierkegaard (and the Assessor) on this point, see J. Davenport and A. Rudd (eds), *Kierkegaard after MacIntyre: Essays on Freedom, Narrative, and Virtue* (Chicago: Open Court, 2001).

[38] Kierkegaard, *Enten-Eller 2*, p. 201; Hong and Hong, *Either/Or II*, p. 216.

[39] Kierkegaard, *Enten-Eller 2*, p. 208; Hong and Hong, *Either/Or II*, p. 217.

[40] On Kierkegaard's relation to Schleiermacher, see Pattison, *Kierkegaard and the Theology of the Nineteenth Century*, Chapter 1.

Here, as with Heidegger, the absolute activity of the subject is limited by a passivity over which it has no control. However, I suggest that, in fact, the Schleiermacherian–Kierkegaardian view of the self as infinitely and absolutely dependent even in the moment of its constitution as a self through an act of free self-choice offers a passivity more profound than the passivity of our thrownness towards death. For we have seen that, despite the ineluctability of death, Dasein is, according to Heidegger, capable of rousing itself resolutely to a freedom towards death and running towards death in such a way as to make death its 'project' – not as in seeking suicide or a hero's or martyr's death but as a contingency that it can take back without remainder into its self-understanding. However, and although there is a considerable formal analogy between this and Kierkegaard's account of the dependence of the self on God, the fact that God is understood as transcendent to the whole world of human relationships (including a human being's self-relationship) and not, like death, a mere contingency means that, in this case (i.e., of the creaturely relation to God), freedom can never retrieve itself entirely but, as Kierkegaard would put it elsewhere, will always remain open to and dependent on 'the power that posits it'.[41] That the human being is created by God inscribes a passivity in the self that is more basic, more radically non-convertible into an act of freedom, and therefore more basically transcendent than that of thrownness towards death.

As is also the case in Heidegger, this understanding is reinforced by a view of the thoroughgoing temporality of human existence and the consequent impossibility of the human subject ever reaching a state of complete actuality. On the contrary, as an extended discussion in *Concluding Unscientific Postscript* makes clear, human 'actuality' is always a blending of actuality and possibility, always in motion, and we have no possibility of a view *sub specie æternitatis*. Now although Kierkegaard's target here is Hegelian claims about speculative knowledge of God rather than the Heideggerian understanding of *Existenz*, it seems nevertheless that Kierkegaard's account also places an obstacle in the way of any understanding of existence that might run on ahead of itself so as to grasp itself *as a whole*. A holistic view on human existence is possible only for God. As long as we are in time, we see only in part, in a glass darkly. But Kierkegaard is certainly not far from Heidegger when he concludes that this also requires us to surrender the attempt to define human being in terms of a 'what' or essence but to focus instead on the 'how' of existence.[42] And for Kierkegaard too this is eminently focussed in the how of our relation to death.

It has been claimed that one of the 'sources' for Heidegger's own discussion of death is Kierkegaard's discourse 'At a Graveside' from the *Upbuilding Discourses*

---

[41]   S. Kierkegaard, *Sygdommen til Døden. Søren Kierkegaards Skrifter*, vol. 11 (Copenhagen: Gad, 2006), p. 130; *The Sickness unto Death*, trans. H.V. Hong and E.H. Hong (Princeton: Princeton University Press, 1980), p. 13.

[42]   See *Concluding Unscientific Postscript*, vol. 1, trans. H.V. Hong and E.H. Hong (Princeton: Princeton University Press, 1992), Part II, Section 2, Chapter 3.

on Imagined Occasions of 1846. It is certainly a text Heidegger is likely to have been familiar with, since it was published in German translation in the spring 1915 edition of *Der Brenner*, a radical Austrian cultural journal that he read, and, in this case, would have been especially memorable by virtue of its dedication to the memory of Georg Trakl and the inclusion of Trakl's *Last Poems* (amongst them *Heimkehr*, to which Heidegger would many years later devote an important interpretative essay). The relevance of this particular discourse to Heidegger's position has been argued by Michael Theunissen, who claims that Heidegger's position is both close to and yet less radical than that of the Danish Christian writer. What does Theunissen mean by this? Let me begin to answer that question by looking briefly at some of the key points of the discourse itself.

Very much like Heidegger, Kierkegaard (writing in his own name and not under a pseudonym) insists that the only way to talk appropriately about death is to do so in such a way as to keep one's own death in view: the person who wants to think seriously about death must do so 'under four eyes', to use Kierkegaard's vivid Danish expression. The Epicurean ruse – or jest, as Kierkegaard refers to it – that says, 'Where death is I am not, where I am death is not' merely imagines death as something external, as a characteristic of 'the race', but not as my own. 'If one merely thinks death but not oneself in death' then one is jesting, no matter how gruesomely one depicts the horrors of death.[43] 'To think of oneself as dead is seriousness; to be witness to another's death is whimsy'[44] – even if it is oneself one represents as 'another'. Thus far, thus Heideggerian, we might say. 'Seriousness' remains a defining theme of the discourse, and if we are to think or say anything significant about death, it has to be in the mode of 'seriousness'. This applies to death's 'decisiveness', its 'indeterminateness' (i.e., that it is indifferent with regard to all earthly differences), and its 'inexplicability'. We shall return to further aspects of this discourse in Chapter 4, but for now I shall focus particularly on this last point of 'inexplicability'.

Of course, Kierkegaard concedes, people have explained it in many ways, as 'a transition, a transformation, a suffering, a battle, the final battle, a punishment, the wages of sin' and each of these, he adds, imply a whole view of life.[45] But these do not 'explain' *death* so much as the enquirer's own life, and the question is not whether they are correct – which cannot be answered, if death is inexplicable – but whether they are able to have retroactive power in relation to how the individual is living. Death and our attitude to death is, in the end, a test of how we are living. This, Kierkegaard concedes, doesn't tell us all that much about death itself, but this is part of the point and, as he characteristically adds, this ignorance can remind

---

[43] S. Kierkegaard, *Tre Taler ved tænkte Leiligheder. Søren Kierkegaards Skrifter*, vol. 5 (Copenhagen: Gad, 1998), p. 444; *Three Discourses on Imagined Occasions*, trans. H.V. Hong and E.H. Hong (Princeton: Princeton University Press, 1993), p. 73.

[44] Kierkegaard, *Tre Taler*, p. 445; *Three Discourses*, p. 73.

[45] Kierkegaard, *Tre Taler*, p. 466; *Three Discourses*, p. 99.

us that 'knowing much is not an unconditional good'.[46] Death and whatever knowledge we may have of death cannot be incorporated into life, so that the condition of being towards death cannot define the character of human life as a whole. 'That death is inexplicable is not a request to solve riddles, an invitation to be witty, but is death's serious warning to the living: I need no explanation; but remember that in this decisive moment all is over and that this can happen at any moment; this, look you, is worth thinking about'.[47] The blank wall of death, beyond which consciousness simply cannot penetrate, throws the individual back into life and designates life as his proper field of concern. And this life, as (in Kierkegaard's view) created by and infinitely and absolutely dependent on God, is itself marked by a passivity (perhaps akin to Lévinas's 'passivity before passivity') that cannot be exhaustively re-enacted in consciousness.

According to Theunissen, all of this means that 'the discourse scarcely gives expression to the content of what Heidegger refers to as anticipation ("running-towards")', which, I suggest, is precisely connected with Kierkegaard's reserve over against the possibility of the existing human individual ever being able to view himself as a whole.[48] Moreover, by defining Dasein itself through its relation to death, Heidegger ends (according to Theunissen) by dissolving death into life. Such a position, Theunissen argues, 'cannot be articulated without contradiction' and 'there is a contradiction in its fundamental claim,' namely in the idea of an 'end', 'which can be understood both as process and as result'.[49] In other words, resolute anticipation claims to give to Dasein just that conclusive view of its own life that, according to Kierkegaard's *Postscript*, is made impossible by the temporal structure of human life. Of course, Kierkegaard is there polemically directing his remarks against a speculative view that sees human life *sub specie aeternitatis* and that abstracts from time and motion. Yet, at one point (and that a crucial one), Heidegger has laid himself open to the same objection. In Kierkegaardian terms, the disclosure that is offered to anticipation and that provides it with the basis for its resolute self-commitment is essentially abstract and concerns only possibility, not actuality.[50] That is to say, it is an event solely in pure thought, not in the unfinalizable tension between thought and existence that is characteristic of the existential thinker. None of us actually existing human beings who really do have

---

[46]   Kierkegaard, *Tre Taler*, p. 468; *Three Discourses*, p. 101.

[47]   Kierkegaard, *Tre Taler*, p. 468; *Three Discourses*, p. 101.

[48]   M. Theunissen, 'The Upbuilding in the Thought of Death: Traditional Elements, Innovative Ideas, and Unexhausted Possibilities', trans. G. Pattison, in R. Perkins (ed.), *International Kierkegaard Commentary*: *Prefaces and Writing Sampler* and *Three Discourses on Imagined Occasions*, vols 9 and 10 combined (Macon: Mercer University Press, 2006), p. 338.

[49]   Theunissen, 'The Upbuilding in the Thought of Death', p. 339.

[50]   S. Kierkegaard, *Afsluttende uvidenskabelige Efterskrift. Søren Kierkegaards Skrifter*, vol. 7 (Copenhagen: Gad, 2002), p. 286; Hong and Hong, *Concluding Unscientific Postscript*, p. 314.

to die can anticipate our deaths other than in thought. But this is really something quite different from running towards death itself. It is striking that at the close of ¶62, dealing with 'Anticipatory Resoluteness as the Way in which Dasein's potentiality-for-being-a-whole has Existentiell Authenticity', and introducing his evocation of the 'unshakable joy' that resoluteness bestows, Heidegger himself asserts that 'Neither does anticipatory resoluteness stem from "idealistic" exactions soaring above existence and its possibilities' (358/ 310), as if 'anticipating' just such a bucketful of Kierkegaardian cold water.

Yet it might be objected that Kierkegaard's position, as I have presented it here, relies on an appeal to God and to the possibility of divine transcendence that is essentially alien to a secular age. As Theunissen puts it, it seems to 'bring into play convictions that, by the standards of a purely human concept of death, it should not be able to take into account'.[51] However, he argues that even the secular reader should not 'argue away' the reference to God nor see it as a 'mere dogmatic residue'.[52] What is at issue is not, in the first instance, a set of metaphysical propositions but a matter of existential comportment and self-understanding. Theunissen's claim, then, is that whereas Heidegger's position ultimately leads us into a closed circuit in which the individual thinking the death that is exclusively his own achieves authenticity on the basis of a kind of negative solipsism, Kierkegaard's view leaves the self essentially open both to the other and to a future that is not simply the projection of its own possibilities. In fact, faced with death's assertion that 'all is over', the serious person will characteristically make the counter-assertion, 'All is not over', and where death says, 'Maybe today' the serious person will say, 'It may be today or it may not, but I say "This very day"', i.e., this very day is the day in which I must be doing the good work that I am today being called upon to do.[53]

Again, we shall look at further aspects of what this means in Chapter 4, but by way of anticipation we may say that even if the secular reader will hesitate before the name of God (and religious readers too might do well to hesitate before invoking this name too casually), Kierkegaard might not object if, while the issue of faith in God remains undecided at the bar of reason, we speak of 'the good' (as in 'the good that I must be doing today') and 'hope' (as in 'the hope that I will have time to do it'). And both 'the good' and 'hope' also signify that life is not self-invented but a task, a challenge, or an opportunity that we have not made up for ourselves but have received and that a fundamental passivity therefore precedes the very possibility of our activity and does so in such a way that it can never itself be transformed into act. To the extent that Heidegger repeats the German Idealist aspiration that substance might become subject and subject become the ground of substance he risks not only being charged with '"idealistic" exactions soaring above existence and its possibilities' but also foreclosing on an

---

[51]   Theunissen, 'The Upbuilding in the Thought of Death', p. 345.

[52]   Ibid.

[53]   Kierkegaard, *Tre Taler*, p. 454; *Three Discourses*, p. 85.

open discourse and practice concerning both *the good* and *hope*. The possibility of such a more open discourse and practice, however, is not exclusive to those who are able to embrace a religious faith in a future beyond this life in which all contradictions and injustices are made good. It is also, I suggest, a possibility for purely secular readers of Heidegger who, fascinated as they may be by the call to run authentically towards death, are able to find an alternative path to authenticity in the present claims of life.[54]

Running from Death

Heidegger has described Dasein's average everyday 'flight from death' as largely unconscious and carried out in such a way that death is not even consciously thought about. But if death becomes imminent, and if we do then start thinking about it – what then? Does it follow that 'running towards' is the sole authentic attitude? A striking counter-example to Heidegger's activist and heroic metaphorics is provided by the opening pages of Franz Rosenzweig's *The Star of Redemption*, a text nearly contemporary with *Being and Time*, similarly gesturing back towards Kierkegaard and not lacking a certain kinship with Heidegger's thought.[55]

If the First World War and its aftermath may be seen as contributing to, as it were, the cultural 'mood' of *Being and Time*, this is even clearer in the case of Rosenzweig, who served in the frontline and famously began writing *The Star* on postcards in the trenches. But – or precisely for this reason – his account of 'man's' comportment in the face of death is very far from invoking any kind of 'running towards':

> All cognition of the All originates in death, in the fear of death. Let man creep like a worm into the folds of the naked earth before the fast-approaching volleys of a blind death from which there is no appeal; let him sense there, forcibly, inexorably, what he otherwise never senses: that his I would be but an It if it died; let him therefore cry his very I out with every cry that is still in his throat against Him from whom there is no appeal, from whom such unthinkable annihilation threatens – for all this dire necessity philosophy has only its vacuous smile.[56]

---

[54] For further discussion of some of these points, see Chapter 4 below and comments on Lévinas, Bloch, and Lear.

[55] On the relationship between Rosenzweig and Heidegger, see P.E. Gordon, *Rosenzweig and Heidegger: Between Judaism and German Philosophy* (Berkeley: University of California Press, 2003). Rosenzweig himself seems to have believed that his idea of a 'new thinking' had some kinship with Heidegger's project.

[56] F. Rosenzweig, *The Star of Redemption*, trans. W.H. Hallo (Notre Dame: Notre Dame University Press, 1985), p. 3.

Of course, 'philosophy' here is very definitely not the kind of philosophy that Heidegger will develop in *Being and Time*, but, as Rosenzweig goes on to say, it is the kind of philosophy that 'with index finger outstretched directs the creature, whose limbs are quivering with terror for its this-worldly existence, to a Beyond of which it doesn't care to know anything at all. For man does not really want to escape any kind of fetters; he wants to remain, he wants to – live.' And, as he adds, 'Man is not to throw off the fear of the earthly; he is to remain in the fear of death – but he is to remain. He is to remain. He shall do none other than what he already wills: to remain'.[57]

This sounds like a very different confrontation with death from that figured in the Heideggerian 'running towards death' and talk of Dasein finding its being 'in an impassioned freedom towards death'. Indeed, Rosenzweig evinces no desire heroically to run towards death: he just wants to remain, to stay alive! And even if we might say that Heidegger nevertheless, like Rosenzweig, resists the impulse to direct the trembling soul away from this world towards some other world where death counts for nothing, Rosenzweig's further comments on the connection between philosophy, cognition of the All, and nothingness are at least thought provoking in relation to the argument of *Being and Time*:

> By denying the somber presupposition of all life, that is by not allowing death to count as Aught but turning it into Nought, philosophy creates for itself an apparent freedom from presuppositions. For now the premise of all cognition of the All is – nothing. Before the one and universal cognition of the All the only thing that still counts is the one and universal Nought. Philosophy plugs up its ears before the cry of terrorized humanity. We want no philosophy which joins death's retinue and deceives and diverts us about its enduring sovereignty by the one-and-all music of its dance. We want no deception at all. If death is something, then henceforth no philosophy is to divert our glance from it by the assertion that philosophy presupposes Nothing.[58]

The 'philosophy' Rosenzweig is speaking about here is precisely that of Hegel, and he seems fairly clearly to be alluding precisely to the trope of philosophy beginning with nothing, which was such a salient theme of Kierkegaard's attack on speculation in *Concluding Unscientific Postscript*. For Rosenzweig as for Kierkegaard, such 'beginning with nothing' is the hallmark of a self-forgetful kind of philosophizing that abstracts from the concrete reality of the human condition and especially from the very concrete and ever-present possibility of death. But the Hegelian way of 'beginning' philosophy with nothing, i.e., by abstracting from all presuppositions, seems very different from Heidegger's way of beginning with Dasein in its concrete thrownness towards annihilation. Nevertheless, how Rosenzweig links together the All, nothingness, and deafness to 'the cry of

---

[57]   Ibid., p. 4.

[58]   Ibid., p. 5.

terrorized humanity' seems also to suggest a possible analogy between Hegel and
what we see going on in Heidegger's text – an analogy that is all the more pertinent
if we are able to take seriously the kind of Heideggerian reading of Hegel found in
Kojève in which Heidegger and Hegel are seen as essentially convergent.[59]

Remember that the issue of death is raised by Heidegger with specific reference
to the problem of Dasein's being-a-whole or of Dasein getting its being as a whole
into view. The ahead-of-itself structure of care means that Dasein is, in a sense,
always looking back on itself from a projected future – I understand my getting
up from the chair by reference to the act of answering the door that I have not yet
accomplished. But whilst I can do this fairly successfully in relation to a sequence
of proximate futures (such as answering the door or organizing a conference), it
seems impossible for me to complete the circle with regard to my life as a whole.
Yet Heidegger's proposal that we are capable of a readiness to run anxiously and
resolutely towards death and conscientiously to take upon ourselves the debt of
this nothingness, to accept ourselves as the 'five-foot nothing' that we are and
thus disclose the truth of our being as a whole, seems to promise just that.[60] In
relation to this 'impassioned freedom towards death' (266/311) Heidegger
speaks of an 'unshakable joy' (310/358). But in the perspective of a Rosenzweig
or a Kierkegaard this seems to mean that death has become a nothing that the
self-assertion of resolute self-choice has transformed into the beginning of the
understanding of Being and, more precisely, of being as a whole. And they might
also see in Heidegger's 'unshakable joy' a repetition of the Hegelian obscuring
of 'the cry of terrorized humanity'. Of course, Heidegger is not Hegel, and the
understanding at which Heidegger's interpretation of human Dasein aims is not
Hegel's absolute knowledge. It is not, in any conventional sense, cognitive. Nor
is it a simple assertion of will, as in Heidegger's own interpretation of Schelling's
'will to will'. Yet here too, by a mysterious philosophical alchemy, the ultimate
passivity of having to die has been transformed into the ultimate activity of a
supremely heroic *but also perhaps self-deceiving* gesture. But the problem is not
primarily in the 'heroism' as such but, more simply, in the unrelenting desire to
understand Dasein 'as a whole' (Rosenzweig's 'cognition of the All'). Even if this
is not to be interpreted as if it were a matter of Hegelian totality, such a relation
to the whole indicates a possibility that, in a religious view of life, is always pre-
empted by the creaturely status of the human being whose life is always surpassed
in every direction by the life of the God who is its source. In this regard Sartre
seems to have been right that, on its own terms, Heidegger's project is set up to
fail. If the task is to take over and, as it were, overtake a possibility that cannot
be overtaken (a more literal rendering of Heidegger's statement that the relation
to death is 'unsurpaasable'), then, on a purely immanent understanding, human
existence must surely be irredeemably self-contradictory. Authenticity will always
elude us, since 'the whole' of our existence is destabilized at its deepest roots

---

[59]   See note 5 above.

[60]   On Abraham à Sancta Clara's expression 'five-foot nothing', see Chapter 6 below.

by the possibility of a death that could come at any moment or that might not arrive at the moment when we feel ourselves ready for it, leaving us suspended in meaningless existence.

Of course, the religious response that sees existence in the context of a divine creation cannot simply be read off the surface phenomena of human life in this world. Whether the view of life in which such a response is grounded is true or in what way it might be true are questions that go beyond the scope of this essay. Certainly, if Kierkegaard was right, it is not a view one can make one's own without much fear and trembling. Indeed, this must be so if the abyss of God is greater than the abyss of death, as a theistic view must claim. God is not a means of avoiding death and silence but is found only on their far side.[61] So far from softening the Heideggerian interpretation and offering a consolatory tranquillization, such a religious view all the more underlines the impossibility of a final appropriation of everything that is given us in, with, and under existence. In this regard, such a view is arguably the more realistic, leaving Heidegger exposed to his own suspicion that securing an authentic or proper relation to Being by resolutely running towards death is, in the end, a fantastic exaction.

---

[61] As is emphasized in S. Craigo-Snell's account of Karl Rahner's treatment of these topics in her *Silence, Love, and Death: Saying "Yes" to God in the Theology of Karl Rahner* (Milwaukee, WI: Marquette University Press, 2008).

Chapter 3

At the Scaffold

We have seen that Heidegger acknowledged the need for his existential–ontological interpretation of death to receive testimony at the level of the existentiell so as not to be accused of being a merely 'fantastical exaction'. We have also seen how he himself approached this existentiell attestation of Dasein's capacity for authentic resoluteness in terms of the phenomena of conscience and guilt. Yet although our readiness to take upon ourselves the guilt of existing as thrown towards death is seen as the guarantee of such an existentiell capacity, as the expression 'anticipatory resoluteness' illustrates, the chapter on conscience and guilt seems almost assiduously to avoid a direct reference to death itself.[1] How, then, in the light of Heidegger's account of resoluteness, might we actually envisage such a confrontation with death on the part of a normal human being, an 'I' in the average everyday 'empirical' sense – you or I or he or she?

Heidegger himself provides a clue as to where we might look for an answer to this question in a reference he makes by way of illustrating the way in which, typically, we unconsciously evade having to face the reality of death. In the discussion of being towards death and everydayness in ¶51, he makes one of his few explicit references to novelistic literature, namely to Tolstoy's novella *The Death of Ivan Ilych*. We have several times touched on how the category of *logos*, or discourse, is central to Heidegger's conception of phenomenology, such that it is precisely in and by means of discourse that Dasein finds and articulates how it understands itself and its world. Across the course of his career, Heidegger is attentive to manifold forms of discourse, from the 'word of Parmenides' to meditations on the poetic word of Hölderlin.[2] But the kind of discourse that finds expression in the modern novel seems on the whole conspicuous by its absence from the many words that accompanied Heidegger on his paths of thinking. It was not entirely absent (note the early [1910] article on the Danish Catholic poet and novelist Johannes Jörgensen[3]) but, relative to the attention given to the words of philosophers and poets, extremely rare.

---

[1] However, for further discussion of its relevance to the question of death, see Chapter 4 below.

[2] On the role of the 'poetic word' in Heidegger's understanding of death, see Chapter 6 below.

[3] See M. Heidegger, *Reden und andere Zeugnisse eines Lebensweges. Gesamtausgabe*, vol. 16 (Frankfurt am Main: Klostermann, 2000), pp. 3–6. Heidegger entitles this short commentary on Jörgensen's *Lebenslüge und Lebenswahrheit* 'Per Mortam ad Vitam' (From death to life). However, this is not itself a novel.

For a thinker living in the wake of the extraordinary expansion of the world of the novel in the nineteenth century and contemporary with writers whose work is in some respects contiguous with this own – Jünger, Mann, and Kafka, to name but three – this is, at the very least, worth noting. Yet it would seem that the novel would offer a resource for the analysis of contemporary Dasein analogous to that of the religious thinkers whose words, although remaining on the level of the ontic or existentiell, nevertheless, offer material for a more fundamental phenomenological reading.[4] This thought is strengthened by Heidegger's own comments in the foreword to the 1972 edition of his early writings, where he speaks of the intellectual background to those works: 'What was contributed by the stimuli of the years between 1900 and 1914 cannot be sufficiently stated, but merely indicated by a small, selective enumeration: the second, more than twofold expanded edition of Nietzsche's *Will to Power*, the translations of the works of Kierkegaard and Dostoevsky, the awakening interest for Hegel and Schelling, Rilke's poetic writing and Trakl's poetry, Dilthey's *Collected Works*'.[5] Heidegger's list is by no means original, as he himself implies, but reflects the intellectual experience of a generation, and many of his contemporaries read Dostoevsky as a resource for theology or philosophy on more or less the same footing as they read Nietzsche or Kierkegaard – Karl Barth, Eduard Thurneysen, Georg Lukács, and Romano Guardini being amongst the more eminent examples.[6] But what is also striking about his 'small, selective enumeration' is that all but one of those listed come to be explicitly discussed in Heidegger's own subsequent work. That one is the novelist, Dostoevsky.

Here, however, it is not Dostoevsky but another Russian novelist, Tolstoy, whom Heidegger takes as providing us with the opportunity to think more closely about what it might mean to run resolutely towards death in the context of an ordinary human life. Tolstoy is, of course, not only often compared with Dostoevsky but equally often contrasted with him; where the latter's novelistic world is described in terms of polyphonic, double-voiced discourse, in which voices blend and

---

[4]   For examples of recent philosophical work (albeit not specifically phenomenological) that takes significant account of novelistic literature, see, e.g., R. Pippin, *Henry James and Modern Moral Life* (Cambridge: Cambridge University Press, 2001); M. Nussbaum, *Love's Knowledge: Essays on Philosophy and Literature* (Oxford: Oxford University Press, 1990); M. Weston, *Philosophy, Literature and the Human Good* (London: Routledge, 2004).

[5]   M. Heidegger, *Frühe Schriften. Gesamtausgabe*, vol. 1 (Frankfurt am Main: Klostermann, 1978), p. 56.

[6]   See, e.g., Barth's comments about the revisions involved in the second edition of his commentary on Romans: K. Barth, *The Letter to the Romans*, trans. E.C. Hoskyns (Oxford: Oxford University Press, 1933), p. 4. Barth himself refers here to the role of Thurneysen in introducing him to the Russian writer. See E. Thurneysen, *Dostoevsky* (London: Epworth Press, 1961). Lukács's unfinished book on Dostoevsky, full of cross-references to Kierkegaard, was posthumously published as G. Lukács, *Dostojewski: Notizen und Entwürfe* (Budapest: Akademia I Kiado, 1985). See also R. Guardini, *Religiöse Gestalten in Dostojewksijs Werk* (Munich: Kösel, 1977 [1st ed. 1933]).

separate without ultimately being harmonized or finalized, Tolstoy seems to be a 'classic' author whose narrator is able to inform the reader as to the true intentions and thoughts of his characters and thus to construct a beautiful and harmonious whole.[7] It would take us far afield to debate the correctness of this view, although, in what follows, we shall in this case see that Dostoevsky can indeed help us to see layers of ambiguity and uncertainty that Tolstoy – and perhaps Heidegger – occludes. If Tolstoy can help us go further into Heidegger's own understanding of an authentic being towards death, Dostoevsky, despite being adduced by Heidegger as influential in his own development, can contribute to further problematizing what such an authentic being towards death might be. First, however, let us turn to Tolstoy's story and the role it plays in Heidegger's argument.

The Death of Ivan Ilych

Being and Time in ¶51 describes how, in the average everydayness of society (*Öffentlichkeit*), death is treated as a third-person occurrence. It is not so much shrouded in silence as spoken of in such a way that it is not encountered as a possibility of my own existence. Talking about death in the manner of *Gerede* establishes a barrier against anxiety in the face of death but, in the mode of 'falling' nevertheless shows, despite itself, that this being towards death is an unavoidable issue for Dasein. Typically, the dying person is spoken of and spoken to as if 'he will escape death and soon return to the tranquilized everydayness of the world of his concern' (253/297). This 'tranquilization' is offered both to the dying person and to those 'who "console" him' (254/298). 'Indeed,' Heidegger adds, 'the dying of Others is seen often enough as a social inconvenience, if not a downright tactlessness, against which the public is to be guarded' (254/298). It is to this comment that Heidegger appends a footnote: 'In his story "The Death of Ivan Ilyitch" Leo Tolstoi has presented the phenomenon of the disruption and breakdown of having "someone die"' (254/298, n. xii). Tolstoy's story, in other words, shows how the *Gerede* that we are accustomed to in relation to death cannot, finally, deal with that which it is purportedly about.

Tolstoy's tale opens with Ivan Ilych's colleagues learning of his death, which '… aroused, as usual, in all who heard of it the complacent feeling that, "it is he who is dead and not I."'[8] Ivan Ilych is a successful lawyer who has lived a life entirely conformed to what might be expected of a successful lawyer. Until he becomes ill. Then, it's not as if he pretends he is not dying, but his dying seems to make no sense. 'The syllogism he had learned from Kiezewetter's Logic: "Caius is a man, men are mortal, therefore Caius is mortal," had always seemed to him

---

[7] See, e.g., G. Steiner, *Tolstoy or Dostoevsky: An Essay in Contrast* (London: Faber and Faber, 1960).

[8] L. Tolstoy, *The Death of Ivan Ilych and Other Stories*, trans. Aylmer Maude (New York: New American Library, 1960), p. 96.

correct as applied to Caius, but certainly not as applied to himself.'[9] Notionally, he now acknowledges its truth, but existentially it seems impossible. He cannot make sense of what this incomprehensible 'It' means:

> And what was worst of all was that *It* drew his attention to itself not in order to make him take some action but only that he should look at *It*, look it straight in the face: look at it and without doing anything, suffer inexpressibly. And to save himself from this condition Ivan Ilyich looked for consolations – new screens – and new screens were found, and for a while seemed to save him, but then they immediately fell to pieces or rather became transparent, as if *It* penetrated them and nothing could veil *It*.[10]

Increasingly aware that he had not, in fact, lived as he ought to have done, it is only at the end of the last three days of his life, days passed in screaming agony, that a moment of compassion for his son takes him outside himself: 'and it was revealed to him that though his life had not been as it should have been, this could still be rectified'.[11] Ivan Ilych is no longer physically capable of communicating this insight to those around him, but the transformation of his inner state that this new orientation towards the world provides is enough.

> 'And death … where is it?'
> He sought his former accustomed fear of death and did not find it. 'Where is it? What death?' There was no fear because there was no death.
> In place of death there was light.
> 'So that's what it is!' he suddenly exclaimed aloud. 'What joy!'
> To him all this happened in a single instant, and the meaning of that instant did not change. For those present his agony continued for another two hours. Something rattled in his throat, his emaciated body twitched, then the gasping and the rattle became less frequent.
> 'It is finished!' said someone near him.
> He heard these words and repeated them in his soul.
> 'Death is finished,' he said to himself. 'It is no more!'
> He drew in a breath, stopped in the midst of a sigh, stretched out, and died.[12]

In these words, Tolstoy seems to dramatize what Heidegger will describe as Dasein's being 'face-to-face with the "nothing" of the possible impossibility of its existence' (266/310). In his last moments, Ivan Ilych exemplifies what it is to tear

---

[9]   Ibid., p. 131.

[10]   Ibid., p. 133.

[11]   Ibid., p. 155. That this sudden movement in Ivan Ilych's relation to his impending death is occasioned by a moment of compassion is significant for considering the relationship between being towards death, conscience, and ethics. See Chapter 4 for further discussion.

[12]   Ibid., pp. 155–6.

free from the 'concernful solicitude' of others, of the 'one dies', and experiences '*an impassioned* freedom towards death – *a freedom which has been released from the Illusions of the "they"* ....' (266/311). Yet *Ivan Ilych* also poses a couple of problems for Heidegger.

We have seen that, compared with Dostoevsky, Tolstoy is often perceived as writing with a kind of objectivity, based upon the assumption of authorial omniscience. In this case, although Tolstoy's tale serves to unsettle the 'average everyday' view of death, it does so in the light of a presumed knowledge on the novelist's part of Ivan Ilych's states of mind that were, in the story, inaccessible even to those who were with him in his death agony. The 'reality' depicted in the story is offered as an objective reality available to third-party scrutiny, for which the differentiation of each individual's interiority is no barrier.[13] But whilst such presumptions may be allowable to omniscient narrators of fiction, are they allowable to philosophers?

Furthermore, even if we allow the novelist correctly to have described his character's interior relation to death, Ivan Ilych is, after all, dying. He does not get up from his deathbed and return to the world. We do not see him *existing* in the complex circumstances and relationships of life with the constant, unchanging knowledge granted to him by his interior moment of vision, face-to-face with the possible impossibility of his non-existence. Such a life, if it was not merely to be offered in the mode of hagiography, and even if its narrator continued to be gifted with the power to read his subject's innermost thoughts, would presumably set a far greater challenge to the novelist. What would it be like to live in the light of such an instant? Could it be done? Could it be made actual?

It is in the light of such questions that we turn now to Dostoevsky.

Dostoevsky in Germany

Dostoevsky, I have suggested, is virtually absent from Heidegger's published writings. The only substantial reference I know of is from the start of the first of

---

[13]   Tolstoy's interest in depicting the inner thoughts of the dying is also illustrated in the perhaps even better-known account of the death of Prince Andrei Bolkonsky in *War and Peace*, vol. 4, Part 1, Chapter 16, which speaks specifically of Prince Andrei's realization of 'awakening' 'in the moment when he died'. Yet Tolstoy's teaching on death also belongs to the general revisionist views considered in the Introduction and according to which 'eternal life' is a way of speaking about participation in true spiritual life in this life. It is 'life' rather than 'my soul' that is eternal, and I am eternal only as or to the extent that I open myself up to participate in the universal stream of spiritual life. It is in keeping with this idea that Tolstoy ends his life of Jesus with the crucifixion and Jesus' words '"It is done! Father, I offer my spirit into your hands." And bowing his head, he surrendered his spirit', i.e., surrendered it to the encompassing stream of life. See L. Tolstoy, *The Gospel in Brief: The Life of Jesus*, trans. D. Condren (New York: Harper, 2011), p. 157.

the 1940 lectures on European nihilism. Here, Heidegger offers a brief comment on the origins of the term nihilism, referring to Jacobi, Turgenev, Jean Paul, and then Dostoevsky. Only in this last case does he offer an extended quotation, from the foreword Dostoevsky wrote for the printed version of the 1880 speech on Pushkin, which may be regarded as a kind of manifesto for Dostoevsky's concept of an authentically Russian literature. Amongst Pushkin's merits, Dostoevsky suggests, is that he was – and I take up Heidegger's quotation –

> the first to see and recognize for what it is a significant, morbid manifestation among our intelligentsia, our rootless society, which seems to hover high above the common people. He recognized it, and enabled us to place graphically before our eyes the typical, negative Russian character: the character who finds no rest and cannot be satisfied with anything permanent, who does not believe in his native soil nor in the strength of his native soil, who fundamentally denies Russia and himself ... who will have nothing to do with his own people, and who sincerely suffers from all this ....[14]

However, this quotation is immediately followed by the comment that 'For Nietzsche, though, the word *nihilism* means something substantially "more."'[15] In other words, Dostoevsky is merely offering a, as it were, local and merely 'ontic' account of what Nietzsche would show to be a fundamental feature of the history of metaphysics. Heidegger does not (and this may or may not surprise us) offer any further justification for this way of dealing with Dostoevsky. He does not, for example, even allude to the far more extended Dostoevskian discussions of nihilism in *The Devils*, *The Idiot*, or *The Brothers Karamazov*, where it is explored in a perspective that is both Russian and European and interpreted as the manifestation of a religious and metaphysical crisis. Although (in *The Devils*, for example), Dostoevsky certainly draws on particular Russian manifestations of nihilism, such as the Nechaev circle, it is clear that Russian nihilism is itself grounded in a rationalizing, utilitarian, and reductionist worldview that is seen as originating in the West and that has many points of contact with what Heidegger himself would portray as 'the age of technology'.[16] In this connection it is worth noting that he seems at one point to have been planning a translation of work by Hegel, probably the history of philosophy.[17] Even though unfulfilled, this plan

---

[14]   M. Heidegger, *Nietzsche*, vol. 4: *Nihilism*, trans. F.A. Capuzzi, ed. D. Farrell Krell (New York: HarperCollins, 1982), pp. 3–4 (GA6.2, p. 24).

[15]   Ibid., p. 4 (GA6.2, p. 24).

[16]   See, e.g., D.O. Thompson, 'Dostoevsky and Science' in W. J. Leatherbarrow (ed.), *The Cambridge Companion to Dostoevskii* (Cambridge: Cambridge University Press, 2002), pp. 191–211. Also J.P. Scanlan, *Dostoevsky the Thinker* (Ithaca: Cornell University Press, 2002).

[17]   See J. Frank, *Dostoevsky: The Years of Ordeal, 1850–1859* (Princeton: Princeton University Press, 1983), pp. 170–71.

indicates something of the philosophical hinterground to the treatment of nihilism in the novels. Indeed, without his portrayal of contemporary and, as it were, local nihilism being grounded in such a larger grasp of the theoretical meaning of nihilism, it is unlikely that it would have had the influence it did on subsequent Russian philosophy, as exemplified in Dostoevsky's contemporary V.S. Soloviev and, in the twentieth century, N.A. Berdyaev.[18]

At this point, we might start to wonder whether Heidegger's strategy vis-à-vis Dostoevsky is not marked by some kind of avoidance (just as, Kierkegaardian readers of Heidegger are likely to feel that although Heidegger acknowledges some points of contact with the Danish Christian writer, there are aspects of the sources that he assiduously avoids[19]). Such a suspicion might be further fuelled by Otto Pöggeler's testimony that for many years Heidegger kept a picture of Dostoevsky in his study, suggesting that the Russian writer had a more than usual significance to the philosopher. Nevertheless, commenting on Heidegger's relation to literature, Kostas Axelos, a co-organizer of Heidegger's 1955 visit to Paris, put the relation to Dostoevsky in essentially negative terms:

> He identifies privileged cases that suit what he wants to say. Hölderlin is one such case. But there is also the matter of his inability to speak about poets and thinkers who are neither German nor Greek. I don't see Heidegger as being able to speak about someone like Dostoevsky. He can only talk of a certain Greece or a certain Germany.[20]

We can refine Axelos's comment somewhat if we note that, as we have heard Heidegger himself imply, he certainly *read* Dostoevsky, but yet he does not *speak of* him. And since, as we shall hear Heidegger himself insist, speaking is inter-dependent with listening and hearing,[21] this would suggest that whatever Dostoevsky he read, he didn't listen to what Dostoevsky was actually saying! Can we go beyond noting this and registering a certain surprise or even disappointment? Can we identify what it was in Dostoevsky (apart from his not having been German

---

[18]   Of course, this is to say much too little about what is a major theme in Dostoevsky's authorship. It would undoubtedly be an interesting task to develop further the comparison between Dostoevsky's and Heidegger's views of nihilism, but this would be to digress too far from the task in hand – although, inevitably, the mortality and finitude of the individual human person is a question that is also central to the whole discussion of nihilism in Dostoevsky.

[19]   The same could also be said of the treatment of Christ in Hölderlin's poetry. See my article 'Heidegger's Hölderlin and Kierkegaard's Christ' in S. Mulhall (ed.), *Martin Heidegger.* International Library of Essays in the History of Social and Political Thought (Aldershot: Ashgate, 2006), esp. p. 403.

[20]   See D. Janicaud, *Heidegger en France. Entretiens*, vol. 2 (Paris: Albin Michel, 2001), p. 30.

[21]   See Chapter 6 below.

or Greek) that might have elicited Heidegger's resistance? Does Dostoevsky have a question for Heidegger that Heidegger would not like to have had asked?

In order to address these questions I shall proceed as follows. Firstly, I shall comment on the general character of the Dostoevsky reception in the German-speaking world in the pre–First World War period. Then, I turn to the recently published letters between Heidegger and his wife Elfride, where we do in fact find a small number of references that go some way to help us reconstruct how Heidegger might have been reading Dostoevsky. Finally, I return to the discussion of being towards death in *Being and Time*, where (I think) we find a scenario that is profoundly Dostoevskian – yet one that Dostoevsky interpreted very differently from Heidegger. This difference in interpretation, I suggest, reading Dostoevsky in the prism of his greatest commentator, Mikhail Bakhtin, throws into relief a more wide-ranging difference between the 'word in the novel' and the respective words of philosophers and poets, thus disrupting one of the basic premises on which some of Heidegger's key contributions rest.

I think it important to proceed in this way, because, as will become apparent, the reception of Dostoevsky by Heidegger's generation was very different from that in Britain and America in the post-war world. If, more recently, the theological (and even the Christian) Dostoevsky has come much more to the fore,[22] the 1950s and 1960s offered a proto-existentialist Dostoevsky, a Dostoevsky read in the light of Shestov, Camus, and Sartre, whose characters were lonely outsiders in a godless universe, anguished by their failure to become the 'supermen' called for by the death of God,[23] whilst the image of Dostoevsky in the German-speaking world in the pre–First World War years was very different again. The Dostoevsky reception of this time has been recounted in William J. Dodd's article, 'Ein Gottträgervolk, ein geistiger Führer'. As the full title of Dodd's article makes clear, what is at issue here is not only Dostoevsky but the whole image of Russia of which, in crucial instants, Dostoevsky became the bearer and/or the creator.[24]

An early wave of Dostoevsky reception saw him in the context of literary naturalism, reading him as a realist writer who described the urban life of capitalist Russia with ruthless honesty, but this was soon superseded by the Dostoevsky of expressionism, a Dostoevsky whose modernity lay not in his urban realism but in his metaphysical and psychological depths, his irrationalism, and his opposition to

---

[22]   See, e.g., D.O. Thompson and G. Pattison (eds.), *Dostoevsky and the Christian Tradition* (Cambridge: Cambridge University Press, 2002); R. Williams, *Dostoevsky. Language, Faith and Fiction* (London: Continuum, 2008).

[23]   As in C. Wilson, *The Outsider* (London: Victor Gollancz, 1956).

[24]   W.J. Dodd, 'Ein Gottträgervolk, ein geistiger Führer – Die Dostojewskij-Rezeption von der Jahrhundertwende bis zu den zwanziger Jahren als Paradigma des deutschen Rußlandbilds' ['A God-bearing people, a spiritual leader – The reception of Dostoevsky from the turn of the century through to the 1920s as a paradigma of the German image of Russia'] in L. Kopelew (ed.), *West-östliche Spiegelungen, Reihe A: Russen und Rußland aus deutscher Sicht*, Bd. 4, *Das zwanzigste Jahrhundert* (Munich: Wilhelm Fink, 2000).

Enlightenment rationalism. In all these respects, Dostoevsky seemed fitted to be the voice of Russia itself. As Dodd comments, '"Dostoevsky" and "Russia" were indeed often separable only with great difficulty"'.[25] This 'Russia' was a Russia whose psychology was shaped by the infinite horizons of its endless steppes and its cultural isolation from the West; it was, in a word, 'mystical Russia'. Paradoxically enough, as Dodd suggests, this 'mystical Russia' became a figure for the German *Zeitgeist* – and Dostoevsky was its prophet. Often, Dostoevsky was contrasted with Tolstoy, and usually to the advantage of the former. In this vein Spengler opposes Tolstoy's Jesus, a mere social moralist, to Dostoevsky's, who looked for a complete transformation of society. Specifically with regard to the years 1910–14, Dodd comments that the reception of Dostoevsky 'was characterized by wonder and awe and from the strange experience … that one was being carried along by what one didn't fully grasp'.[26] This is epitomized by Alexander Döblin's autobiographical remark that, as a schoolboy in this period, he read Goethe and Schiller by day and Dostoevsky by night.

If the English-language reception of Dostoevsky was to be dominated by *Crime and Punishment*, *Notes from Underground*, and *The Brothers Karamazov*, it is indicative of the German-language reception that the first volume of the complete translation published by Piper-Verlag from 1906 onwards was *Demons*, a novel dealing with issues of revolutionary nihilism and nationalism, whilst the second volume was a selection of his *Political Writings* (1907), drawn from the *Diary of a Writer*, a non-fictional periodical in which, amongst other things, Dostoevsky gave extensive expression to his ultra-conservative, ultra-nationalist views, blending Russia's Christian mission with its imperial vocation, often, as in the Pushkin speech, with a strong emphasis on the humiliation of the Russian people as fitting them for a special identification with the kenotic Christ. The volume's editor, Arthur Moeller van den Bruck, spoke of Dostoevsky as prefiguring 'the religious revolution', and his own conception of where this revolution might lead is suggested by the title of his 1922 book *Das Dritte Reich* (The Third Reich), a significant text in the ideological development of Nazism. Another commentator would say, in connection with Dostoevsky, 'that Russia's vocation was, one day, to redeem the religious need of Europe'. At the same time Dostoevsky revealed 'the abyss' that lay beneath the surface of Europe's century of progress.[27] As such, Russia was essentially non-European and the volume of Dostoevsky's political writings was accordingly divided into four parts: Western Europe, Russia itself, the Balkans and the Orient, and Asia. In this perspective Dostoevsky himself could be spoken of as 'the quintessence of the "Asiatic" Russian soul',[28] a comment that

---

[25]   Ibid., p. 853.
[26]   Ibid., p. 856.
[27]   Ibid., p. 861.
[28]   Ibid., p. 860.

could easily be turned in a critical direction, as by Richard M. Meyer, who spoke of Dostoevsky as a 'hysterical half-Asiatic'.[29]

Political events themselves meant that, from 1912 onwards, Russia (and Dostoevsky) came to be seen more as a threat than as a source of mystical redemption, although even after the war Stefan Zweig was only one who could say (in his 1921 introduction to the novels of Dostoevsky) that 'The novel of Dostoevsky is the myth of the new Man and his birth from the womb of the Russian soul'.[30] Similarly, Spengler could say that it would be to Dostoevsky's Christianity that the next thousand years would belong. And still in the post-war period, he could be a decisive intellectual influence on theologians such as Eduard Thurneysen, whose book very much echoes the traits described by Dodd as typical of the pre-war reception.

This impression is further underlined if we turn to the evidence of Heidegger's letters to his wife Elfride. The references are not extensive and are limited to three letters. In the first of these, a letter of 28th August 1918 largely taken up with reporting various facts about life in the barracks, Heidegger asks his wife if she can get hold of a copy of *The Brothers Karamazov*. The second, a letter of 27th October 1918, is far more wide ranging and deserves more extended attention. Describing how the night before he went to bed early to read the last three letters from Elfride that had arrived in a single delivery, he pictures her life with '*der kleine Jörg*' ('little Jörg', i.e., their son) and how, through her, the child will learn 'to feel the sense of being at home and the particularity of each thing, so that his soul is permeated by the parental home, childhood happiness, sunshine and stillness – but also life's clarity and clairvoyant assurance of life and true religiosity'. The letter then goes on to recall the time of their engagement and how he experiences this as a stage of personal formation through its joys, self-giving, and acts of self-entrusting to and self-forgetfulness in the other, in '*Du*'. In this spirit he notes that thinking about her in his quiet moments is like an act of solemn dedication ('*eine Weihe*') for their future reunion. In these moments he realizes 'that every present is only ever the living actuality of what is of value in past and future life – that is to say, truly historic', which in turn leads to insights into forms of thought beyond those known to current ontological and natural sciences. So, he realizes,

> Instead of leading to a pure, empty 'I' the whole problem of the 'I' leads to the fulfilled and primordially living ['I'] and its constituent elements – the fulfilling of values grounded in essential openness to value, pointing back to the essence of personal Spirit that I have apprehended as 'Vocation' – only so do the eternal properties of the Spirit and their absolute confusion become conceivable – it is along these lines that the problems upon which I have hit

---

[29]   Ibid., p. 861.
[30]   Ibid., p. 864.

while out here are moving, the carrying through of the principal of the historical consciousness – ....[31]

This, then, leads him to thoughts about the future of his research and the developments in university life that can be expected in the decade after the end of the war. The 'holy', which, he says, Rudolf Otto has misconceived, will play a central part here. 'As to the problem of the devout life (*'das Problem des Frommseins'*), which you have particularly felt coming out as a principal element from Dostoevsky, another time.'[32]

Now, although it is not clear whether Heidegger had, in fact, received and been reading *The Brothers Karamazov* at this point, the themes of this letter, both in its personal and in its more theoretical aspect, bear comparison with that novel and, especially, key moments in the formation of its 'hero', Alyosha. As readers of the novel will recall, Dostoevsky lays a special emphasis in introducing Alyosha on the boy's childhood memories, a theme that will recur when Alyosha himself, in the closing pages of the book, urges the young boys to whom he has become a kind of informal teacher to live their future lives in the light of the memory of the good actions and friendships that have united them:

> ... although he lost his mother in his fourth year, he remembered her afterwards all his life, her face, her caresses, 'as if she were standing before me.' Such memories can be remembered (everyone knows this) even from an earlier age, even from the age of two, but they only emerge throughout one's life as specks of light, as it were, against the darkness, as a corner torn from a huge picture, which has all faded and disappeared except for that little corner. That is exactly how it was with him: he remembered a quiet summer evening, an open window, the slanting rays of the setting sun (these slanting rays he remembered most of all), an icon in the corner of the room, a lighted oil-lamp in front of it, and before the icon, on her knees, his mother.[33]

As Alyosha's future development will make clear, this is very much a case, to use Heidegger's words, of the child acquiring a formative experience of 'sunshine and stillness – but also life's clarity and clairvoyant assurance of life and true religiosity'.

Like any Dostoevsky character, Alyosha is not to enjoy an uninterrupted fulfilment of such early promises, however. The death of his mother, the brutality

---

[31] G. Heidegger (ed.), *'Mein liebes Seelchen!' Briefe Martin Heideggers an seine Frau Elfride 1915–1970* (Munich: Deutsche-Verlags-Anstalt, 2005), p. 87. We shall return to the notion of the 'I' as 'called' in Chapter 6 below. It also has important connections to the idea of conscience to be discussed in Chapter 4 below.

[32] Heidegger, *'Mein liebes Seelchen'*, p. 88.

[33] F.M. Dostoevsky, *The Brothers Karamazov*, trans. R. Pevear and L. Volokhonsky (London: Vintage, 1992), pp. 18–19.

of his father, and the general chaos of his family life, culminating in the murder of the father at the hands of one of his sons, make the monastery and the devout life at the feet of the blessed Elder Zosima an understandably attractive option. Even here, however, life does not go smoothly. Zosima is envied by a large faction in the monastery, and, on his death, his enemies are gratified when his body begins to rot – an event that dashes the hopes of those who had thought him a saint, worthy of having his body miraculously preserved. Amongst these is Alyosha himself, and it is in the turbulent period after the death of the elder that the youngest Karamazov has what is perhaps the most explicit religious experience in any of Dostoevsky's novels. Sitting by the body of his elder, an overwrought Alyosha falls asleep and, in a dream, sees Zosima as one of the guests at the wedding feast in Cana of Galilee[34] at which Christ himself is present, though unseen. On waking, Alyosha rushes out, 'Filled with rapture, his soul yearned for freedom, space, vastness'.[35] Gazing up at the night sky, 'The silence of the earth seemed to merge with the silence of the heavens, the mystery of the earth touched the mystery of the stars ....' Alyosha throws himself weeping to the ground, kissing the earth, not knowing why, but weeping 'even for the stars that shone on him from the abyss'. The more precise content of 'what happened' is not stated, but

> he felt clearly and almost tangibly something as firm and immovable as the heavenly vault descend into his soul. Some sort of idea, as it were, was coming to reign in his mind – now for the whole of his life and unto ages of ages. He fell to the earth a weak youth and rose up a fighter, steadfast for the rest of his life, and he knew it and felt it suddenly, in that very moment of his ecstasy.[36]

Shortly afterwards, he leaves the monastery and goes out into the world. Is this 'experience', then, expressive of what Heidegger called 'true religiosity', the 'I' becoming open to the eternal properties of spiritual life and its values, and what Elfride feels as 'the devout life' manifested in Dostoevsky's novels? Even if this is not the explicit, unique, or even intended reference, I suggest both that it focusses the 'religious experience' theme as found in Dostoevsky and also that it condenses what other contemporary German readers of Dostoevsky were seeing as his mysticism and his portrayal of 'the new man', of which Alyosha was to be the most developed example.

The third letter in which Heidegger mentions Dostoevsky likewise reflects what we have seen to be a characteristic feature of the German Dostoevsky reception, namely, a focus on his political writings. In a letter from Meßkirch (28th July 1920), Heidegger writes, 'It is rather cool up here .... I am very happy again regarding the homeland, the meadows and fields and gradually I feel what it is to have ground under one's feet – it so precisely fell into place with what is

---

[34]   See John's Gospel, Chapter 2.

[35]   Dostoevsky, *Brothers Karamazov*, p. 362.

[36]   Ibid., pp. 362–3.

in Dostoevsky and I really strongly experience the contrast to people like Afra Geiger and others who simply live in their relationships'. And, later, 'When you have time, do try to read Dostoevsky's Political Writings; you will be very impressed – ....'[37] The motif of 'earth' is, of course, strongly present in Alyosha's 'mystical' experience, but in Dostoevsky's political writings this is further understood in terms of the 'holy ground' of the Russian people, an identity of person and land that gives a rootedness unknown to the cosmopolitan Westerner, a bond that joins the people both to each other and to God. For Dostoevsky, as for Heidegger, it is, of course, one of the salient features of modern science and the technological society that this primordial 'given' relationship is disturbed and even shattered by the reduction of life to a series of calculable relationships. If, on first reading, Alyosha's 'mystical' experience hints at that privileged moment hinted at in *Being and Time*, the moment in which a person acquires authentic resolve to become who they are, the political writings seem to point more towards that confluence of themes of land, nationhood, and personal identity that come more to the fore in Heidegger's lectures of the 1930s.[38]

But if Dostoevsky was so fit for Heideggerian purposes, what reason could there be for the philosopher to refrain from including him in the roll call of existentiell witnesses to existential structures? And how could we even begin to consider a Dostoevskian critique of Heidegger?

I have indicated that the German reception of Dostoevsky, of which Heidegger's own references to the Russian writer are typical, was a very particular reading. In many respects it paradoxically endorsed a certain kind of Slavophilism apparent in Dostoevsky himself, only applying it as a liberative solution to the crisis of German culture.[39] Civilization would be rescued by what was deep, of the abyss, religious, mystical, of the earth, a new event in human history, a third kingdom. Such motifs are found in Dostoevsky's novels and sometimes endorsed by Dostoevsky himself in his non-fictional writings. However, as most Dostoevsky commentators now agree, many of these views are far from naïvely endorsed in the novels themselves. There they are subject to extensive and sometimes decisive critique.

Take Alyosha's religious experience. Not only is Dostoevsky in fact extremely vague as to what this consists in or how it impacts on Alyosha's life, but it is clear that, in his plans for a continuation of the novel, Alyosha would undergo many future permutations. I don't think we need to take at face value the preliminary suggestions thrown out by Dostoevsky that Alyosha would lose his faith and

---

[37] Heidegger, '*Mein liebes Seelchen*', p. 107.

[38] As, for example, in the lectures on Hölderlin's poems 'Germania' and 'The Rhein'. See M. Heidegger, *Hölderlins Hymnen 'Germanien' und 'Der Rhein'. Gesamtausgabe*, vol. 39 (Frankfurt am Main: Klostermann, 1989).

[39] Ironically, perhaps, many of the key tropes of Slavophilism were themselves adapted from German Romanticism and given a Slavic 'twist'. For a good introduction to Slavophilism, see B. Jakim and R. Bird (eds.), *On Spiritual Unity: A Slavophile Reader* (New York: Lindisfarne Books, 1998).

become a terrorist, but it is entirely characteristic of Dostoevsky's treatment of character that it cannot be condensed into a single simple experiential or ideological 'moment'. Another example is Prince Myshkin, the central figure of *The Idiot.* Myshkin too is described as having a kind of mystical experience, only in this case, despite the heavenly visions that the prince seems to have been vouchsafed, Dostoevsky raises the question as to whether the whole thing may not have been merely the effect of epilepsy. In any case, there is a gap between the interior illumination provided by the vision and the working out of that illumination in life, so that Myshkin's religious experience is, in fact, unable to ground any decisive moral or personal transformation for himself or for those poor sinners amongst whom he lives. Religious experience and inner resolve cannot achieve more than ambiguous expression in the world – a situation for which the rotting corpse of Elder Zosima, the most unambiguously and positively 'holy' personage in any of the novels, is an apt symbol.

The same can be said of Dostoevsky's nationalism. In *The Brothers Karamazov*, for example, Ivan's famous roll call of horrors begins by citing such atrocities as those perpetrated by the Muslim Turks on the Christian Slavs of the Balkans – but the list climaxes with atrocities perpetrated by Russians on Russians and Russian parents on Russian children. If Russia has been vouchsafed a special visitation from the Christ, this by no means confers any kind of collective sanctity that is to be had without being earned. Even more pointedly, the idea that Russia is, in some sense, a God-bearing nation is specifically discussed in *The Devils*, where one of the main characters, Shatov, admits to having believed this. But he also says, very clearly, that this too is a form of human hubris and, moreover, that the idea originated with the demonically nihilistic Prince Stavrogin, a kind of Antichrist figure.

All of this, we may say, is testimony to those features of Dostoevsky's novelistic art that Bakhtin would refer to in his 1929 study of *Dostoevsky's Poetics* as Dostoevsky's dialogism, double-voiced discourse, heteroglossia, and polyphony.[40] This is not simply a matter of Dostoevsky setting various ideological viewpoints or life choices against one another (as, for example, he opposes the nihilism of Ivan Karamazov to the holiness of Elder Zosima). Rather, it is Dostoevsky bringing to an extreme expression a basic feature of novelistic discourse as such, as Bakhtin makes clear in the 1934–35 work *Discourse in the Novel* – a work which, bearing in mind Heidegger's emphasis on the category of the 'word' of the philosopher and the poet, we could quite literally translate as *The Word in the Novel.* Discussing a shift in the study of stylistics in the 1920s, Bakhtin notes the gradual emergence of a sustained examination of the stylistics of the novel, as opposed to the stylistics of poetry. Here, he adds, 'these concrete analyses and these attempts at a principled approach [to artistic prose] ... made patently obvious the fact that all the categories of traditional stylistics – in fact the very concept of a *poetic* artistic discourse,

---

[40] See M.M. Bakhtin, *Problems of Dostoevsky's Poetics*, trans. C. Emerson (Minneapolis: University of Minnesota Press, 1984).

which lies at the heart of such categories – were not applicable to novelistic discourse.'[41] He comments, 'The novel as a whole is a phenomenon multiform in style and variform in speech and voice. In it the investigator is confronted with several heterogeneous stylistic unities, often located on different linguistic levels and subject to different stylistic controls.'[42]

We have already seen how, despite portraying an apparently decisive life-changing experience in the life of his 'hero' Alyosha, Dostoevsky nevertheless characteristically left his account sufficiently under-determined to allow for the possibility of significant future change in Alyosha. Even life's decisive moments sometimes turn out to be not so decisive after all. The same might be said of the 'face-to-face' with death.

In this case, of course, Dostoevsky did not need to read anybody else's mind, since he had himself, as literally as is possible, been face-to-face with death when, at the age of 27, he was condemned to death by firing squad, with immediate effect. Although, 20 minutes later, as the first of those condemned with Dostoevsky were tied to the posts, ready for execution, a pardon was read out, commuting the sentence to hard labour, for those 20 minutes Dostoevsky believed that he was facing immediate death. He never described this in a first-person memoir, but in the novel *The Idiot* the eponymous Prince Myshkin tells the story of an acquaintance to whom just this same thing happened. Already, we notice, how this immediately qualifies whatever is said in the story by its association with the curiously ambiguous personality of the prince. As with many of his stories and reflections, there seem to be loose ends and unanswered questions, the story ends abruptly and inconclusively, with the listeners waiting for him to go on and finish – 'You're very fragmentary', one of them remarks.[43] There is to be no triumphant act of resolution à la Tolstoy.

As the prince tells the story, the details of which he has learned by questioning his acquaintance, 'a certain man' whom he had 'encountered' the previous year, the man carefully allotted the time remaining of the last five minutes. 'He said those five minutes seemed like an endless time to him, an enormous wealth. It seemed to him that in those five minutes he would live so many lives that there was no point yet in thinking about his last moment ....'[44] And so, the Prince continues, the manmade arrangements to say goodbye to his friends and decided to reserve just two minutes for thinking about himself and looking around for the last time. When those two minutes come, 'He knew beforehand what he was going to think about: he wanted to picture to himself as quickly and vividly as possible how it could be like this: now he exists and lives, and in three minutes there would be

---

[41] M.M. Bakhtin, *The Dialogic Imagination: Four Essays*, trans. C. Emerson and M. Holquist, ed. M. Holquist (Austin: University of Texas Press, 1981), p. 261.

[42] Ibid., p. 261.

[43] F.M. Dostoevsky, *The Idiot*, trans. R. Pevear and L. Volokhonsky (London: Granta, 2001), p. 61.

[44] Ibid., p. 60.

something, some person or thing – but who?'[45] Seeing the sunlight shining off the gilded dome of a nearby cathedral, 'it seemed to him that those rays were his new nature and in three minutes he would somehow merge with them ....'[46] (His feeling about this and about his ignorance of what is about to come is described as one of 'loathing'; yet even worse, we are told, was the 'constant thought': 'What if I were not to die! What if life were given back to me – what infinity! And it would all be mine! Then I'd turn each minute into a whole age, I'd lose nothing, I'd reckon up every minute separately, I'd let nothing be wasted!'[47] Eventually, this thought so fills him with anger that he starts to wish they'd hurry up and shoot him. At which point the prince stops.

Of course, the very fact that the story is being told lets us know that this 'terrible' thought was, in fact, realized. Unlike Ivan Ilych, but like the putative existential hero who runs towards the possibility of his own impossibility in the power of a moment of vision resolutely affirmed and held fast through the passage of time, he passes from this face-to-face with death back into everyday existence. How will he live? Will his life in fact be transformed by this face-to-face, this new configuration of the self's relation to time and death? The prince is asked,

> ...'what did he do with so much wealth [i.e., of time] afterwards? Did he live "reckoning up" every minute?' 'Oh, no, he told me himself – I asked him about it – he didn't live that way at all and lost many, many minutes.' 'Well, so there's experience for you, so it's impossible to live really "keeping a reckoning." There's always some reason why it's impossible.'[48]

Of course, we do not have to accept this conclusion. After all, these are only characters in a novel exchanging views. But what this exchange of views does highlight is the questionableness of claims to a decisive reorientation towards existence in the light of a face-to-face confrontation with the possible impossibility of my existence. As befits the word of the novelist, the articulation of that possible impossibility occurs in words that are 'variform in speech and voice', that combine 'heterogeneous stylistic unities, often located on different linguistic levels and subject to different stylistic controls'. Even in being uttered the possible impossibility beheld in the moment of decisive vision slides back into the polyphony of many voices, opinions, and points of view. It cannot be held to in existence, other than one possibility amongst others. Nor – and this is Bakhtin's view, at least – is the novelist obliged to offer us anything more. All he need do is open and engage for us a world of multiply conflicting possibilities. If he wants to do more than that, he ceases to be a novelist and dons the mantle of the prophet, as Dostoevsky himself seemed to be prone to doing in his non-fiction.

---

[45]   Ibid., pp. 60–61.
[46]   Ibid., p. 61.
[47]   Ibid.
[48]   Ibid.

Although the autobiographically informed story of the mock execution provides the sharpest possible instance of the face-to-face confrontation with death, it is more generally true that Dostoevsky consistently refrains from giving us the kind of commentary on the dying person's inner stream of consciousness that is found in Tolstoy. Although rather a lot of Dostoevskian characters do die, and sometimes rather dramatically, we typically see their deaths from the outside and they are often described with not a little hint of irony.[49] One exception might be the death of Alyosha's beloved elder, Zosima, who, we are told, 'silently lowered himself from his armchair to the floor and knelt, then bowed down his face to the ground, stretched out his arms, and, as if in joyful ecstasy, kissing the earth and praying (as he himself taught), quietly and joyfully gave up his soul to God'.[50] Yet even in this case, the continuation of the story shows that, as we have heard, many in and beyond the monastery refused to accept that this was a holy death and the subsequent decomposition of the elder's body confirms them in their view that he was no saint. Alyosha's vision of the elder's heavenly transfiguration is just that, a vision, a dream, and Dostoevsky – despite (or perhaps even because of) being committed to a view of immortality that is more 'objective' than Tolstoy's notion of the infinity of life – consistently draws a veil of ignorance over what happens in the final moments of an individual human life. Death – comprising dying, the moment of death, and whatever may be 'beyond' death – is as subject to the polyphonic, variform indeterminacy of the novelistic world as any of this world's other great themes.

Can the philosopher deal with this merely by affirming the secondariness of the novelist's word in comparison, say, with that of the poet? Is the novelist condemned in advance merely to recycle *Gerede*? Does the philosopher's faith in the primordial nature of the poetic word stem from antiquated assumptions about its temporal priority? But should the late arrival of the novel (if late it is[51]) preclude the possibility that, in its own way, the novelistic word brings to the fore a certain primordial quality of language, of the word as such; that what happens to 'the word' in the complex, stratified, multiply fractured, and unfinalized space of novelistic discourse is (at least) 'equi-primordial' with the 'gathering' of being effected in the poetic word? And might it then be the case that, to adapt a Heideggerian formulation, the word, any word, is inevitably and necessarily 'always already' falling, or that 'falling' is what language does (a possibility, incidentally, hinted at by Kierkegaard when, dismissing the myth of the serpent, he suggests that

---

[49] Perhaps the most striking example of this is the death of Stepan Trofimovich Verkhovensky in *The Devils*, where the narrator expressly suggests that it is an open question as to whether his final reconciliation to the Church and his reception of the sacrament was a genuine conversion or merely for aesthetic effect.

[50] Dostoevsky, *Brothers Karamazov*.

[51] Bakhtin, at least, connects its origins with the Socratic dialogues.

it was language itself that first tempted Adam[52])? But if that is so, how might the philosopher persuade us that the self can become consciously (and therefore articulately) unified around a decisive act of self-choice in the face of death (as is argued in *Being and Time*), *or* (if we apply the same question to the later works) that the poet is in a position to inaugurate an anticipatory celebration of the festal unity of gods and mortals? For the implication of the novelistic scenario of *The Idiot* seems to be that any anticipatory act or word, even when it seems most serious and most decisive, is liable to unravel in time or to slip into any one of the innumerable crevices that crisscross the space between actually speaking persons.

Heidegger's account of anticipatory resoluteness in the face of death may offer one possibility for engaging the possible impossibility of my own existence; but it is only one possibility. As such it seems to fall far short of what might be required for grounding a general and reliable moment of vision that might bring our being as a whole into view. Exposed to the hum, the ebb and flow, and incompleteness of the novelistic word, the heroic profile struck by the philosopher becomes blurred, lost in the crowd, a possibility amongst possibilities, providing a key to the whole only to those capable of an act of faith that runs on ahead of any possible evidence.

We might think again of Rosenzweig: 'Man is not to throw off the fear of the earthly; he is to remain in the fear of death – but he is to remain. He is to remain. He shall do none other than what he already wills: to remain'.[53] And, as he adds,

> By denying the somber presupposition of all life, that is by not allowing death to count as Aught but turning it into Nought, philosophy creates for itself an apparent freedom from presuppositions. For now the premise of all cognition of the All is – nothing. Before the one and universal cognition of the All the only thing that still counts is the one and universal Nought. Philosophy plugs up its ears before the cry of terrorized humanity .... We want no philosophy which joins death's retinue and deceives and diverts us about its enduring sovereignty by the one-and-all music of its dance. We want no deception at all. If death is something, then henceforth no philosophy is to divert our glance from it by the assertion that philosophy presupposes Nothing.[54]

Like Rosenzweig, Dostoevsky too is a writer determined not to let us forget 'the cry of terrorized humanity'. But is that all there is? Is there no one to hear this cry? Is there no one to respond? These questions may be taken in a theological sense, clearly, but they also point us to a further possibility: whatever meaning is to be found in our uniquely human consciousness of having to die is not a

---

[52] See S. Kierkegaard, *Begrebet Angest. Søren Kierkegaards Skrifter*, vol. 4 (Copenhagen: Gad, 1997), p. 353; *The Concept of Anxiety*, trans. R. Thomte (Princeton: Princeton University Press, 1980), pp. 47–48.

[53] F. Rosenzweig, *The Star of Redemption*, trans. W.H. Hallo (Notre Dame: Notre Dame University Press, 1985). p. 4.

[54] Ibid., p. 5.

meaning that we can find as solitary individuals thrown towards a solitary death. For to cry, to cry out, to rage against the coming of the night is to direct ourselves to what is *other-than-myself*, whether that other is God or another human being. But this is to say that the relation to death is, in the end, inseparable from the social and ethical constitution of the human being – ethical, that is, in the sense of concerning how we are in our being-with-one-another as mutually responsible and as mutually engaged in articulating, in language, the meaning that our lives might possibly have. We have already seen how Heidegger himself placed the question of conscience at the centre of his response to the challenge posed by our being thrown towards death. But the question we must now address is whether 'conscience' in Heidegger's sense can help us connect the human being's having to die to the world of ethical relationships and ethical responsibility. And this, in turn (and as we shall see), is also connected to how we might interpret death in the horizon of a religious view of life.

Chapter 4
Guilt, Death, and the Ethical

Why 'Conscience' and 'Death'?

We have seen how, at the end of Division II, Chapter 1, Heidegger wondered whether his projection of an authentic existential–ontological freedom for death might, 'from an existentiell point of view', seem to be 'a fantastical exaction' (266/311). We have also seen how Heidegger's response to this worry led him to undertake an analysis of the phenomenon of conscience that would provide testimony to a kind of resoluteness that is prepared to accept itself as guilty for its own 'being-the-basis-of-a-nullity' (283/329). The outcome is the notion of 'anticipatory resoluteness', 'a resoluteness that runs towards [death]', in which Heidegger effectively combines the existential–ontological freedom of running towards death with the existentiell comportment of resoluteness. But has he done enough to allay his own worry concerning the existentiell deficit in his account?

The charge that Heidegger's interest in pursuing a fundamental ontology does indeed blind him to the problems of concrete existence has been made by a number of critics, including, e.g., K.E. Løgstrup, whose views we shall examine later in this chapter. Løgstrup's criticism also highlights a further questionable feature of Heidegger's argument, namely, its implications for human relationships, that is, for moral or ethical life. But already in Chapters 2 and 3 several distinct critical points have been raised regarding the basic aims of Heidegger's programme. Following Kierkegaard and Rosenzweig, I suggested that, theologically, the religious relationship of Creator–creature already undermines Heidegger's basic project of wanting to understand Dasein as a whole. Then, with the help of Dostoevsky, I questioned the plausibility of the notion of anticipatory resoluteness at the level of concrete existentiell life. In this chapter I move towards endorsing the kind of criticism we find in Løgstrup, albeit with some qualifications. However, preparatory to addressing the question as to the absence (or otherwise) of genuine ethical possibilities in *Being and Time*, I want next to examine further aspects of Heiddegger's turn to the phenomena of conscience and guilt as a way of addressing the question of death and to tease out the connection between these at first sight rather disparate topics.

In what way 'disparate'? The question, we recall, is about finding an existentiell attestation to an authentic comportment vis-à-vis death. The solution that Heidegger seems to be offering is derived from the analysis of conscience. But how can *conscience* help us in relation to death? Isn't the *Sitz-im-Leben* or form of life to which conscience most naturally relates that of moral life and the discernment of right and wrong as they bear upon moral conduct? Isn't conscience about our capacity for knowing the good? And isn't that essentially independent from the question of death? Don't these two phenomena, conscience and death, belong to essentially different language games? How is knowing about right and wrong going to help us with regard to death? And, equally, how might awareness of mortality make us more morally discerning, i.e., conscientious? And what is no less striking is that, although Heidegger has led us to this surprising juxtaposition of conscience and death, death itself is never explicitly thematized in the entire chapter on conscience, except insofar as Dasein's being is characterized in terms of nullity (*Nichtigkeit*), which invites being read as an implicit reference to its annihilation in death. Nor is Heidegger himself unaware that some readers will find this odd. As I noted in Chapter 1, he himself asks, 'What can death and the "concrete Situation" of taking action have in common?' (302/349) and even invites us to consider whether the joining together of 'resoluteness' and 'anticipation' might not be 'an intolerable and quite unphenomenological construction, for which we can no longer claim that it has the character of an ontological projection, based upon the phenomena' (302/349). His response – as we have also seen – is suggested by two further rhetorical questions, to which (I believe) he implies a positive response: 'What if it is only in the anticipation of death that resoluteness, as Dasein's *authentic* truth, has reached the *authentic certainty* which *belongs* to it? What if it is only in the anticipation of death that all the factical "*anticipatoriness*" of resolving would be authentically understood ...?' (302/350). Following Heidegger's argument further, we saw that it leads him to an account of ontological guilt that extends to the entirety of our existence as finite beings who find themselves 'born to die'. We are guilty, that is, of our mortality.

But this, I suggest, is strange. Accepting Heidegger's basic premise that neither Dasein nor, in this case, Dasein's mortality is to be viewed as if it were some kind of entity present-to-hand (i.e., 'mortality' is not an attribute of the 'substance' humanity but a certain 'how' of its manner of existing), it is surely strange that a secular philosopher might wish to portray Dasein's being towards death in terms of *guilt*. The association of death and guilt may, as we shall see, be a basic element of traditional Christian teaching, but how has it crept into Heidegger's argument? Even if Heidegger has removed all forensic associations from the term 'guilt' and glosses it in terms of our 'owing' existence to something beyond ourselves or having to be responsible for our existence, in what way could we possibly be *responsible* for our having to die? Why not just acknowledge death as sheer, meaningless contingency, 'an accident', as Simone de Beauvoir put it.[1]

In terms of Heidegger's project, such an acknowledgement would be an act of surrender, an admission that we simply can't get a grasp on our being as a whole. Even if we are ready to run towards our death, unless or until we are able to see ourselves as guilty, i.e., responsible, for our having to die our death will always, as it were, elude us and we will never, quite, catch up with who we really are.

---

[1]   S. de Beauvoir, *A Very Easy Death*, trans. P. O'Brian (Harmondsworth: Penguin, 1969), p. 92.

Of course, phrases such as 'impossible possibility' and the expressed doubt that he is making a 'fantastical exaction' in requiring a truly courageous and clear-sighted being towards death as the ground of existential authenticity indicate Heidegger's own awareness that he is pushing at the boundaries of what can meaningfully be said. Yet he does – and, in his own terms, perhaps must – press on and say it.

Must he? Again, why *guilt*? And why be guilty for the fact of my nullity, i.e., my thrownness towards death? Even if Heidegger does not want to go the way of French existentialism and embrace straightforward absurdity, why can he not limit himself to saying something like 'and I am responsible for everything that falls this side of the limit at which I lose all possibility of self-consciousness'? Why not invoke the old adage that where death is, I am not and where I am, death is not? On that basis, death would cease to be definitive of human being. Death would then, as many people do seem to experience it, be a merely extrinsic characteristic of human being that does not really define who I am at all. Death may be the end of my life, but it is not its *telos* and it is a purely illusionary reflection of the assumed forwards movement of time that leads to our conflating end and *telos* in this case. Perhaps this is merely to restate de Beauvoir's position, although it does not necessarily involve what she further says of death: that in every case it is 'an unjustifiable violation' of human existence.[2] No. On the view I am proposing it is too external to existence even to count as a 'violation'. But, as I have indicated, were Heidegger to make such a move he would have to surrender the ambition of grasping the whole, an ambition that is central to the whole project of *Being and Time*. If ceasing to be is a defining feature of the human condition it has somehow to be brought into the circle of self-understanding.

In what follows, I shall suggest that what is going on in *Being and Time* in Division II, Chapter 3 is in significant part to be understood against the background of Christian traditions of *memento mori*, more specifically Heidegger's use of Luther and Kierkegaard. Both these figures are generally seen as having offered particularly radical versions of the *memento mori* tradition and also as having played an especially significant part in the genesis of *Being and Time*, a role which, with the further addition of Augustine, was clearly flagged in Bultmann's 1928 article for *Religion in Geschichte und Gegenwart*. There it was stated that 'Augustine, Luther, and Kierkegaard were influential [Heidegger's own preferred wording was 'philosophically essential'] for H. in the development of the [H.: a more radical] understanding of Dasein ....'[3]

In fact, neither Luther nor Kierkegaard are specifically mentioned in the discussion of death in *Being and Time*, although n. iv on p. 190, where Heidegger is discussing anxiety, does refer to each of them, with particular emphasis on Kierkegaard as 'the one who has gone furthest in analysing the phenomenon

---

[2] Ibid.

[3] T. Kisiel and T. Sheehan (eds), *Becoming Heidegger* (Evanston: Northwestern University Press, 2007), p. 331.

of anxiety' (190/492). Since, as we have seen, there is an intrinsic connection between anxiety and death, we may reasonably suppose that this is therefore not without relevance to the question of death. Strikingly, the notes taken on Heidegger's 1924 seminar on the problem of sin in Luther end with a quote from Kierkegaard that underlines just this connection: 'The principle of Protestantism has a special presupposition: a human being who sits there in *mortal anxiety* [emphasis added] – in fear and trembling and great spiritual trial'.[4]

We have already considered objections to understanding *Being and Time* as a 'philosophy of death' in which authentic existence is found only in the unremittingly anxious eye-to-eye confrontation with death and, as such, a modern rewriting of ancient philosophical and religious traditions of the *memento mori*. However, I have also suggested that, whatever else is going on in Heidegger's discussion, it is also about death and human mortality and that the existentiell concern for death (your death, my death) cannot be stripped out of the argument without undermining the ontological interpretation. But if the remembrance of death may legitimately presuppose a broad swathe of human testimony from Plato to Nietzsche and do so without broaching specifically Christian doctrines, the introduction of guilt is strange – strange, that is, for a secular philosopher. Of course, if we suddenly switch roles and begin to think as Christian theologians there is nothing strange about it at all. One of the most widely testified elements of popular Christian teaching is the claim that the origin of death is to be traced back to human beings' sinful disobedience to God's command not to eat from the tree of the knowledge of good and evil. In Genesis 2.16–17 God warns the first man, Adam, that '"You may freely eat of the every tree in the garden [of Eden]; but of the tree of the knowledge of good and evil you shall not eat, for in the day that you eat of it you shall die"'. Consequent upon the first humans having disobeyed this prohibition, God then condemns them to a life of toil, concluding with the sentence that '"By the sweat of your face you shall eat bread until you return to the ground, for out of it you were taken; you are dust and to dust you shall return"' (Genesis 3.19). The further implications of this are defined by the apostle Paul in Romans 5.12: 'sin came into the world through one man [Adam], and death came through sin, and so death spread to all because all have sinned'. As one well-known Christmas carol puts it, 'and all was for an apple ....'

The Pauline view is especially salient in the Augustinian tradition and, perhaps most vividly, in the articulation of that tradition by Luther and other theologians of the Protestant Reformation. The Augsburg Confession, a normative symbol of the Protestant Reformation, stated in its second article that 'after the fall of Adam, all human beings are born in sin, that is, they are without fear of or trust in God, are full of concupiscence, and that this inborn sickness is truly sin that damns and throws to eternal death all those who are not then reborn through baptism'.[5]

---

[4]   Ibid., p. 195.

[5]   *Die Bekenntnis-Schriften der evangelish-lutherischen Kirche* (Göttingen: Vandenhoeck and Ruprecht, 1930), pp. 52–3.

Death is thus conceived (a) as a total and all-encompassing characteristic of human existence, (b) as a punishment for which each of us is rightly regarded as guilty, and (c) (no less importantly) as inseparable from the fact of our being conceived and born through sexual reproduction. In the Lutheran theological context, then, it is entirely consistent to speak of human beings as guilty of their having to die and also to understand this having to die as an essential and defining feature of all post-Adamic humanity as such and not, *pace* Simone de Beauvoir, a mere absurd excrescence or violation.

Heidegger's strange move, then, seems entirely explicable if we read it against the background of such a theology. This is not to suggest that it is itself really only a piece of covert theologizing. Even on a purely phenomenological basis, why should not the 'theological' texts of Paul, Luther, and others also be read as revealing fundamental truths of the human condition, albeit demythologized and stripped of their extra-worldly significations (as happened, in a theological context, in Bultmann's own programme of demythologization[6])? Indeed, this is how Heidegger himself seems to understand his own use of the existentiell and ontic material he finds in such texts.[7]

Yet Heidegger himself does not make this connection explicit in this case. The notes on his 1924 Luther seminar do not directly mention death, apart from the closing (but not insignificant) reference to 'mortal anxiety', to which I have just alluded. Nevertheless, both they and the Luther texts he is expounding are focussed precisely on the issue of sin that he, following Luther, sees as indicating a radical *corruptio* of human existence leading to horror, despair,[8] and flight from the presence of God and therefore as revealing how fallen human beings 'are shaken and unsettled in their very being'.[9] This flight seems to plunge on into infinity and is compounded by the excuses and lies with which Adam, called to account by God, seeks to avoid responsibility for his fault.[10] As I have just stated, Heidegger does not expressly mention the place of death in all this (nor is it salient in the specific Luther texts he is interpreting), but it is clear that for Luther's theology in general it is death that is the epitome and culmination of this entire situation of alienation from God. As in the previously cited quotation from Kierkegaard with which the seminar notes conclude, it is a cumulative portrait of

---

[6] For the demythologizing debate, including Bultmann's original essay 'New Testament and Mythology' see H. Bartsch and R.H. Fuller (eds), *Kerygma and Myth: A Theological Debate* (London: SPCK, 1972).

[7] For further discussion, see my 'Existence, Anxiety, and the Moment of Vision: Fundamental Ontology and Existentiell Faith Revisited' in A.P. Smith and D. Whistler (eds), *After the Postsecular and the Postmodern: New Essays in Continental Philosophy of Religion* (Newcastle-upon-Tyne: Cambridge Scholars Publishing, 2010), pp. 128–49.

[8] Kisiel and Sheehan, *Becoming Heidegger*, pp. 189–90.

[9] Ibid., p. 193.

[10] Ibid.

human existence as indelibly marked by 'mortal anxiety'. The stage seems well prepared for *Being and Time*.

So is what Heidegger says about the interconnection of death, guilt, and the defining nothingness of human existence simply a secularized version of radical Protestant theology? As I have said, a positive answer to this question would not of itself discredit his procedure, any more than the fact that other aspects of his thought involve transformative interpretations of Aristotle or Plato. I am not therefore interested in unmasking a hidden theological agenda in Heidegger nor am I interested in claiming him for theology as opposed to philosophy. Instead, my argument – my objection – is that although the account of death, conscience, and guilt as a single, existential nexus in the life of 'fallen'(!) Dasein is developed from the ontic material that Heidegger finds in the historical testimony of a particular line of Christian theologians, he uses this material in such a way as to occlude key elements that are present in the theologians – primarily Luther and Kierkegaard – under consideration. This is not solely a matter of his not wanting to say anything about God but rather the omission of what is *anthropologically* decisive in their writings. In other words, Heidegger significantly misreads his sources and, most importantly, this misreading has consequences for the plausibility of the existential structure he offers as the outcome of his interpretation. By using a flawed 'ontic' base his own further 'ontological' investigation is then inevitably and significantly distorted. Another way of putting this is to say, rather bluntly, that whatever we make of him as a philosopher, Heidegger proves not to have been a very good theologian – and this deficiency in theology is not without implications for his philosophy. But, to repeat, the issue is not in the first instance or solely related to his self-limitation to the horizons of a methodological atheism. As well as involving the question of God, it is also about the purely human meaning of the texts in question, principally with regard to the question of the ethical and its absence or presence in *Being and Time*. And this question, I suggest, has a relative independence from the question of God, although it may also be seen as related to the possibility of divine transcendence as a formative power in human life.

I shall begin with some comments on Heidegger's reading of Luther and then go on to say something also about his interpretation of Kierkegaard before seeing how what he omits might be retrieved for existential philosophy and how this might relate to a possible existential theology.

Luther and Kierkegaard

As I have indicated, Heidegger's own Luther seminar emphasizes the mortal anxiety of human existence under the sway of sin. In this regard, he is certainly not untrue to the original texts. He sets out how, for Luther, sin is to be understood as a basic disposition, a fundamental affect rather than an accumulation of particular 'sins',[11] and, as such, is characterized by horror, suffering, presumption, pride, corruption, flight, hatred, despair, impenitence, excuses, and lies. At its root it is a rejection of basic belief in the goodness of God and of God's command. Also – and interesting with regard to the *Religion in Geschichte und Gegewart* article's mention of the role of Aristotle and the scholastics for defining certain ontological problems – Luther (as Heidegger notes) repeatedly polemicizes against both Aristotle and the scholastics. In Luther's own words, 'no one can become a theologian unless he becomes one without Aristotle'.[12] His objection is, in fact, a double one. He both objects to Aristotle himself and also questions whether the scholastics have rightly understood him. At the same time, he commends Plato and Anaxogoras at the expense of Aristotle for privileging the Infinite above form.[13] But against Aristotelian 'virtue' he argues that even human beings' good actions are sinful since belief in our own goodness encourages us in an inappropriate self-confidence (what Luther, following Paul, calls 'boasting'), so that if we are to come into a positive relation to grace we must empty ourselves through suffering: 'To be born anew, one must consequently first die and then be raised up with the Son of Man. To die, I say, means to feel death at hand'.[14]

In relation to all of this, Heidegger seems to be appropriately commenting on Luther's own thinking. But, of course, the seminar is based on a rather small selection of works from a rather large authorship and three of these texts are specifically polemical in intent ('The Question of Man's Capacity and Will without Grace' [1516], the 'Disputation against Scholastic Theology [1517], and 'The Heidelberg Disputation' [1518]), whilst the fourth, the commentary on Genesis, deals only with those passages discussing the Fall). But if we turn to Luther's pastoral and devotional works, we find something more that seems not to have interested Heidegger but that (I suggest) he might have benefited from attending to. Take, for example, the sermon on preparing to die from 1519. Here, and seemingly anticipating Heidegger's own insistence on the need to run towards death with open eyes, Luther writes that 'we should familiarize ourselves with death during our lifetime, inviting death into our presence when it is still at a distance and not on the move'.[15] But what does such a familiarization with death involve? Firstly, it means not allowing ourselves to get obsessed by devils, sin, and punishment. 'The one and only approach is to drop them entirely and have nothing to do with them. But how is that done? It is done in this way: You must look at death while you are alive and see sin in the light of grace and hell in the light of

---

[11] Ibid., p. 190.

[12] M. Luther, 'Disputation against the Scholastics' in J. Pelikan and H. Lehmann (eds), *Luther's Works*, vol. 31: *Career of the Reformer I* (Muhlenberg: Concordia, 1957), p. 12.

[13] M. Luther, 'Heidelberg Disputation' in *Luther's Works*, vol. 31, p. 41.

[14] Ibid., p. 55.

[15] M. Luther, 'A Sermon on Preparing to Die' in M. Dietrich and T. Lehmann (eds), *Luther's Works*, vol. 42: *Devotional Writings I* (Philadelphia: Fortress, 1969), pp. 101–2.

heaven, permitting nothing to divert you from that view.'[16] Or, we should look on death 'only as seen in those who died in God's grace and who have overcome death, particularly in Christ and then also in his saints'.[17] In fact, 'death, sin, and hell will flee with all their might if in the night we but keep our eyes on the glowing picture of Christ and his saints'.[18] This is because, on the cross, Christ humbled himself under his suffering and focussed only on the will of the Father, which we too must emulate when and as we let images slip away and hold only to what the sacraments themselves really point to: 'God's words, promises, and signs'.[19]

Luther's position, then, is paradoxical. We are to meditate on death but a true Christian meditation on death will not be about death at all. Human nothingness is not only or even primarily the nothingness of death, as it is for Heidegger, but a nothingness before God and as such is the possibility also of being raised to life.

In his lectures on the Magnificat (Mary's song of praise to God for having chosen her to be the mother of the Christ; see Luke 1.46–55), Luther draws a strong parallel between God's work in creation and in redemption: as God worked in creating the world, so too does he work in renewing it, and characteristic for every form of divine work is that God works alone and unaided:

> Just as God in the beginning of creation made the world out of nothing, whence he is called the Creator and the Almighty, so His manner of working continues unchanged. Even now and to the end of the world, all His works are such that out of that which is nothing, worthless, despised, wretched and dead, He makes that which is something precious, honourable, blessed and living. On the other hand, whatever is something, precious, honourable and living, he makes to be nothing, worthless, despised, wretched, and dying. In this manner no creature can work, no creature can produce anything out of nothing.[20]

This is precisely what Luther sees exemplified in Mary, of whom he says, 'she boasts with heart leaping for joy and praising God, that He regarded her despite her low estate and nothingness.'[21] But of this aspect of Luther, Heidegger says – and *Being and Time* reflects – nothing.

This interpretation of the thrownness and nothingness of human existence in terms of our being created parallels what we have already heard from Kierkegaard's Assessor Vilhelm in Chapter 2. Kierkegaard's 1846 discourse 'At a Graveside', which we also considered in Chapter 2, together with some of the objections to

---

[16]   Ibid., p. 103.

[17]   Ibid., p. 104.

[18]   Ibid., p. 106.

[19]   Ibid., p. 109.

[20]   M. Luther, *Lectures on the Sermon on the Mount and the Magnificat* in J. Pelikan (ed.), *Luther's Writings:* vol. 21 (St. Louis, MO: Concordia, 1955), p. 299.

[21]   Ibid., p. 301.

Heidegger's reading made by Michael Theunissen,[22] also sets further question marks against Heidegger's account.[23]

A key theme of the discourse is the distinction Kierkegaard draws between what he calls 'mood' (or, as we might translate it, 'whimsy') and 'seriousness'. 'Mood' is, essentially, thinking about death in a thoughtless, sentimental, and non-serious way that fails to take into account another key term of the discourse, death's 'decisiveness'. 'Mood' and 'seriousness' think the same thoughts about death, only they think them differently. For example, both recognize that, in death, 'all is over', but 'mood' pictures this as a 'sleep' and thereby weakens the impression of death's decisiveness. The superficiality of this picture is revealed by Kierkegaard's comment that, as he says, 'the one who sleeps in death does not blush like a sleeping child, he does not renew his energy, like the man who is strengthened by sleep, nor do friendly dreams attend him in his sleep as they do the aged'.[24] Seriousness too understands that in death 'all is over', but its attitude is 'let death then keep its power so that "all is over", but let life too keep its power to work while it is still day'.[25] And, summing up the difference between a 'moody' and a 'serious' view of death Kierkegaard writes that 'Death says: "maybe even today", but then seriousness says that whether or not it is today, I say: even today'.[26] Death's decisiveness is how it turns us around so as to see what is really decisive, namely, what we are doing in and with our lives. Thus, as is often the case in Kierkegaard, what we might take as the immediate or obvious sense of a word or phrase is transformed into its opposite: death's 'decisiveness' is precisely the revelation that death is not decisive. What is decisive is how you are, now – today! – in your life.

---

[22] See the references to and discussion of Theunissen's article 'The Upbuilding in the Thought of Death: Traditional Elements, Innovative Ideas, and Unexhausted Possibilities' in Chapter 2 above.

[23] For a contrary interpretation of the 'ethical' significance of this discourse, see G.D. Marino, 'A Critical Perspective on Kierkegaard's "At a Graveside"' in P. Stokes and A.J. Buben (eds), *Kierkegaard and Death* (Bloomington: Indiana University Press, 2011), pp. 150–59. In another article in this volume, Charles Guignon appears to suggest that the only serious difference between Kierkegaard and Heidegger is that the former (justifiably in Guignon's view) remains at what Heidegger would call the level of the existentiell and does not progress to a fundamental ontological interpretation, although there is no essential difference of content. However, whilst I think it is broadly true to say that Kierkegaard has no interest in fundamental ontology, it is central to my argument here that there is a real difference of content in their interpretation of existentiell death. See C. Guignon, 'Heidegger and Kierkegaard on Death: The Existentiell and the Existential' in *Kierkegaard and Death*, pp. 184–203.

[24] S. Kierkegaard, *Tre Taler ved tænkte Leiligheder. Søren Kierkegaards Skrifter*, vol. 5 (Copenhagen: Gad, 1998), p. 451; *Three Discourses on Imagined Occasions*, trans. H.V. Hong and E.H. Hong, (Princeton: Princeton University Press, 1993), p. 81.

[25] Kierkegaard, *Tre Taler*, p. 454; *Three Discourses*, p. 84.

[26] Kierkegaard, *Tre Taler*, p. 454; *Three Discourses*, p. 85.

Kierkegaard makes a similar point when he goes on to discuss how 'mood' and 'seriousness' respond differently to death's indeterminateness. By calling death 'indeterminate' he means that it is the same for all and it therefore seems impossible to characterize it in any specific way: death makes no distinction with regard to whether one is rich, poor, a leader of many, a world historical personality, or just one of the crowd – and no one can be more or less dead when they're dead than anyone else. Reflecting on this, 'mood' consoles itself with the thought that all the inequalities and inequities under which we have suffered in life will be done away with in death. But such an attitude is motivated by resentment against life and offers an intrinsically false consolation since those who can be satisfied with it will not be there to enjoy it when they are dead! Seriousness also understands the negation of worldly differences in death, but it understands them in quite another way. For serious persons will not let themselves be envious of others' distinctions but face-to-face with the prospect of annihilation will see in this a reminder of the equality of all human beings before God, an equality grounded in their common likeness to God. Because they are not in the grip of violent images of destruction, serious persons do not wish the ruin of others' wealth or achievements but see the equality of a death as a means of curing themselves from the vice of comparison, from desiring 'this man's gift and that man's scope'.[27]

We see the same pattern a third time, when, faced with the infinite varieties in which death occurs, 'mood' seeks a logic or a meaning in this multiplicity and tries to come up with some explanation as to why one person dies a violent death and another lives to a ripe old age, finding pseudo-scientific reasons for how a certain kind of personality might succumb to cancer, another to dementia. A serious approach to the matter, however, will not waste time on trying to explain the variety and uncertainty of death but focus on the simple fact of death's certainty. This certainty, that the axe is already laid to the root of the tree, inspires the serious person 'to live each day as if it was the last *and at the same time as if it was the first in a long life and to choose how he will live without regard to whether his actions will need a long life in order to be completed or merely a short time in which to have made a good beginning* [emphasis added]'.[28] Again, the thought that 'this day might be your last' is only one half – and the lesser half – of the picture. More important is the possibility given by the fact that I am now alive and able both to be making a beginning in some good work and to nourish the hope that I will be given the time to bring it to a good end.

Finally, and as we have already considered in Chapter 2, Kierkegaard argues that death is inexplicable. Of course, people have explained it in many ways, as 'a transition, a transformation, a suffering, a battle, the final battle, a punishment,

---

[27]   The reference is to T.S. Eliot, 'Ash Wednesday'. 'Comparison' or mimeticism is a major feature of Kierkegaard's teaching on sin. For further discussion, see my *Kierkegaard and the Theology of the Nineteenth Century* (Cambridge: Cambridge University Press, 2012), Chapter 6, 'Sin'.

[28]   Kierkegaard, *Tre Taler*, p. 464; *Three Discourses*, p. 96.

the wages of sin' and each of these, he adds, imply a whole view of life.[29] But, Kierkegaard insists, these explanations do not 'explain' death so much as explain the enquirer's life and the question is not whether they are correct – since this cannot be answered, death being inexplicable – but whether they are able to have retroactive power in relation to how the individual is living. Death and our attitude to death is, in the end, a test of how we are living. This, Kierkegaard concedes, doesn't tell us all that much about death itself, but, as he adds, this very ignorance can remind us that 'knowing much is not an unconditional good'.[30] And if death can indeed be regarded as rest for the weary or comfort for the sufferer, this can only be genuinely said by those who have earned such knowledge over time, who 'wearied themselves in good deeds, who walked courageously on the right path, who were afflicted in a good cause and who were misunderstood when they strove for what is noble'.[31] In short, it is how we are in life that determines our relation to death and not vice versa. Death's inexplicability means that it cannot be incorporated into life, and, for Kierkegaard, it therefore seems inappropriate to speak of the being of the living human individual as a being towards death. Instead, death points us back to life: it is the end, but not the *telos*, of life. This, as we have seen, provided the point of attack for Theunissen's criticism of Heidegger's attempt, as he put it, to interpret 'end' both as process and result. And, once more, Kierkegaard's way of emphasizing death's inexplicability and his view as to the limitations of knowledge in relation to death suggests that using death as a lever by which to bring about a holistic understanding of existence is intrinsically flawed.[32]

Yet for Kierkegaard too, death would seem to be a barrier, marked, as Heidegger might put it, by a 'not'. In the light of death, we must turn back to life but we do so knowing that life has no permanent or abiding substantial being and that to live is to be handed over to nothingness. At the same time, Kierkegaard is in essential agreement with Luther that since this is a nothingness before God it is also a site of potential transformation. This theme incorporates aspects of the basic determination of the human condition in terms of creatureliness along the lines previously discussed both in this chapter, with reference to Luther, and in Chapter 2, with reference to Kierkegaard himself. However, theologically it also as it were 'repeats' or, to use another Kierkegaardian term, 'potentiates' these themes in terms of a theology of redemption. Let us see, briefly, how it does so and what this means for the interpretation of Dasein's existential situation.

---

[29]   Kierkegaard, *Tre Taler*, p. 466; *Three Discourses*, pp. 98–9.

[30]   Kierkegaard, *Tre Taler*, p. 468; *Three Discourses*, p. 101.

[31]   Kierkegaard, *Tre Taler*, p. 468; *Three Discourses*, p. 101.

[32]   A further feature of Kierkegaard's discourse that is especially striking when we read it in the context of Augustinian–Lutheran theology is the extent to which it declines to invoke the notion of death being a punishment for sin and therefore requiring human beings to adopt an attitude of guilt in relation to it. This is congruent with what I take to be his entire rejection of the notion of original sin as 'inherited' in *The Concept of Anxiety*. See my *Kierkegaard and the Theology of the Nineteenth Century*, Chapter 6.

The theme of nothingness and transformation or, to use the religiously charged term 'transfiguration' that more fully reflects Kierkegaard's Danish, is found in many of his upbuilding discourses. In the discourse 'To desire God is a human being's highest perfection', for example, Kierkegaard tells the story of a self that grows dissatisfied with merely being a part of the world or nature rather than becoming a self-directing centre of conscious freedom. As a result, it sets about trying to master itself and to get control of its own life. But this is not so easy. In fact, Kierkegaard seems to think, it is downright impossible, since no one is stronger than their own self. In seeking to get a grip on ourselves and to ground our existence in our own subjective freedom, we put ourselves in a scenario that Kierkegaard likens to a wrestling match between two exactly equal combatants. In such a situation, the self is fated to fight itself to a standstill, an impasse, in which it effectively annihilates itself – yet this 'annihilation is his truth'[33] and to the extent that a person accepts this annihilation as his subjective truth, he acquires the new possibility of the God-relationship, a relationship that restores him to himself but on a new and unshakeable basis. The shipwreck of human will and understanding clears a space for a foundational dependence on God that encompasses and permeates every aspect of the subject's life in the world. 'He who is himself altogether capable of nothing, cannot undertake even the smallest thing without God's help, that is to say, without being aware that there is a God'.[34] To know that he is nothing is his truth, it is 'truth's secret', entrusted to him by God; in the acceptance of his nothingness he comes to know God.

Similarly in another discourse – 'The person who prays aright strives in prayer and triumphs by allowing God to triumph' – Kierkegaard will write,

> At last it seems to him that he has become an utter nothing. Now the moment has come. Who should the one who thus struggles wish to be like if not God? But if he himself is anything [in his own eyes] or wants to be anything, then this something is enough to prevent the likeness [from appearing]. Only when he himself becomes utterly nothing, only then can God shine through him, so that he becomes like God. Whatever he may otherwise amount to, he cannot express God's likeness but God can only impress his likeness in him when he has become nothing. When the sea exerts all its might, then it is precisely impossible for it to reflect the image of the heavens, and even the smallest movement means that the reflection is not quite pure; but when it becomes still and deep, then heaven's image sinks down into its nothingness.[35]

[33]   Kierkegaard, *Opbyggelige Taler* (also in Kierkegaard's Skrifter, vol. 5: see n. 24 above), p. 302; *Eighteen Upbuilding Discourses*, trans. H.V. Hong and E.H. Hong (Princeton: Princeton University Press, 1990), p. 309.

[34]   Kierkegaard, *Opbyggelige Taler*, p. 302; *Eighteen Upbuilding Discourses*, p. 309.

[35]   Kierkegaard, *Opbyggelige Taler*, p. 380; *Eighteen Upbuilding Discourses*, p. 399.

As another discourse from the collection *Upbuilding Discourses in Various Spirits* (1847) will argue, this is the basic structure involved in being able to say that human beings are created out of nothing yet in such a way as also to be the living image of God.[36] As in Luther, the pattern of God's redemptive action vis-à-vis the anguished soul repeats his action in creation, each time creating out of nothing.

But could Heidegger have followed Luther and Kierkegaard in these further steps 'beyond nothingness' without committing himself to their doctrinal beliefs about God's transcendence and, more particularly, about God's action in creation and redemption? I suggest that he could have done so and that there are two routes along which he might have proceeded had he wanted. The first concerns the character of the time-experience itself and whether human time is essentially defined by its being thrown towards nothingness or whether, in and beyond such thrownness, it also manifests an openness towards something 'more'.[37] The second is the transcendence of the other human person. As I hope to show in Chapter 5 by considering our relations to the dead, these questions are intimately connected. Meanwhile, and also reserving a discussion of whether and how our experience of time might be open to, let's say, 'the Eternal', I turn in the remainder of this chapter to the question concerning the relation to the other that is brought into focus by Kierkegaard's expression 'works of love'. As Kierkegaard comments regarding death's decisiveness, 'Death says: "maybe even today", but then seriousness says that whether or not it is today, I say: even today'.[38] In other words, death points us towards our concrete ethical obligations to the neighbour, urging us to do what we should be doing anyway, namely, 'works of love'. What matters is not whether you are going to die today or not (though you may) but how you are actually living today and whether you are committing yourself to the acts of human love that are being asked of you. So too with regard to death's indeterminateness. Here, as we saw, everything depends on whether we understand this idea from the perspective of envy or human solidarity. Not the manner of our going towards death but the manner of our ethical being-with others is what matters. Death may serve to give added urgency or focus towards the demands of ethics, but these do not originate in the relation to death.

---

[36] See S. Kierkegaard, *En literair Anmeldelse/Opbyggelige Taler i forskjellig Aand. Søren Kierkegaards Skrifter*, vol. 8 (Copenhagen: Gad, 2004), pp. 289–90; *Upbuilding Discourses in Various Spirits*, pp. 192–3.

[37] This is, for example, the position of the Catholic theologian Karl Rahner, who famously honoured Heidegger as his most significant teacher. However, Rahner's position also goes a long way to interpreting the God-relationship itself in terms of silence, nothingness, and death as the context for every human 'Yes' to God. See S. Craigo-Snell, *Silence, Love, and Death: Saying 'Yes' to God in the Theology of Karl Rahner* (Milwaukee, WI: Marquette University Press, 2008).

[38] Kierkegaard, *Opbyggelige Taler*, p. 454; *Three Discourses*, p. 85.

But is this in fact contrary to the thought of *Being and Time* or is Heidegger open to the possibility of a fully ethical relation to others as an integral element of authentic existence? Already in Part I, Heidegger had identified 'being-with' as integral to the basic structure of being-in-the-world (see Division I, Chapter 4). Importantly, this is inseparable from the way in which language is construed as a primordial feature of human Dasein, since language is never the mere invention of the individual but a mode of shared existence, even if, as with other modes of average everyday existence, we typically speak only in the 'fallen' manner of 'idle talk'. With specific regard to resoluteness, Heidegger himself asserts that 'Resoluteness brings the Self right into its current concernful Being – alongside what is ready-to-hand, and pushes it into solicitous Being with Others' (298/344). Indeed, he adds, so little is conscience 'individualistic' that 'When Dasein is resolute, it can become the "conscience" of Others. Only by authentically Being-their-Selves in resoluteness can people authentically be with one another' (298/344). However, I suggest that, read in the perspective of Christian ethics, this is problematic. Heidegger criticizes Kant for construing conscience as a kind of inner 'court of justice' and thus in terms of a moral law (293/339), but Kant emphasizes respect for the other as intrinsic to any operation of a genuinely good will even that seems to be lacking in Heidegger. In this regard he not only rejects the view that we can be awakened to conscience by the intervention of a teacher, he also avoids understanding conscience in terms not of my inner comportment but of the need of the other and the cry of the oppressed and, theologically, of the demand of God.[39] If the primary locus of authenticity is my relation to my own thrownness towards death the relation to the other can surely be no more than a secondary source of obligation, whether the other is teacher, neighbour, or God. Where in Heidegger do we find the credo of Dostoevsky's Elder Zosima, that all of us are guilty of everything and before everyone and I more than others – a credo that was seminal for Lévinas's ethical view of life?[40] And perhaps the simplest statement of such a view is the gospel parable of the sheep and the goats (Matthew 25.31–46), which suggests that what is decisive with regard to our ethical and religious status is not our inner self-accounting but whether we have in fact tended the sick, fed the hungry, or visited the prisoners. Far from the truly conscientious person becoming the conscience of others, the sheep (i.e., the saved) are judged

---

[39] The role of the teacher is especially emphasized in the discussion by S. Mulhall in his *Routledge Philosophy Guidebook to Heidegger and* Being and Time (London: Routledge, 1996), pp. 130–36. A provocative recent study on the importance of an actively intervening moral teacher is A. Strhan, *Levinas, Subjectivity, Education: Towards an Ethics of Radical Responsibility* (Chichester: Wiley-Blackwell, 2012). On the lack of what he calls a 'jewgreek' passion for justice in Heidegger, see J.D. Caputo, *Demythologizing Heidegger* (Bloomington: Indiana University Press, 1993), especially Chapter 10 and the conclusion (pp. 186–214).

[40] See A. Toumayan, '"I More Than the Others": Dostoevsky and Levinas' in *Yale French Studies* 104 (Encounters with Levinas [2004]), pp. 55–66.

not just by the sick and the hungry but by those who are themselves morally deficient, i.e., the prisoners.

That Heidegger's early philosopher is not merely neutral with regard to such ethical possibilities but actively excludes them – and does so precisely by the way in which it links conscience and death – was argued by the Danish philosopher of religion K.E. Løgstrup in a comparative study of Kierkegaard and Heidegger and I shall now develop this line of criticism further with specific reference to Løgstrup and his own proposal for an other-oriented 'ethical demand'.

Løgstrup on Kierkegaard, Heidegger, and the Ethical Demand

Løgstrup states at the outset of his study that he is reading Kierkegaard exclusively as a phenomenological philosopher and not with regard to his theology and he sees both Kierkegaard and Heidegger as depicting the modern human condition in terms of the tension between living as one of the crowd and living as an ('authentic') individual.[41] According to both of them, most people resolve this tension by opting out of the struggle and simply living as one of the crowd. In Kierkegaardian terms, this is because they are entirely absorbed in their temporal and worldly interests, relating absolutely to the relative, and are dispersed in a manifold of thoughts and activities that keep them busy enough but which are prescribed for them by the others with whom they are constantly comparing themselves.[42] This not only generates a mood of anxiety[43] (KHE, 11–12), it also inhibits genuine self-knowledge and a tendency to live via our imaginings of what or how others are and so, for example, to practice love in the light of an imaginary rather than a real understanding of what love means (KHE, 12–13). Such a world is deeply ambiguous and spiritless (KHE, 13). When those who live like this speak of the ethical, it is merely in terms of custom and usage, while the idea of 'the good' is applied only to individual acts and not to the person who acts (KHE, 14). Heidegger for his part offers an essentially similar picture. This time the crucial

---

[41]   For further elaboration of Løgstrup's (complex) relation to Kierkegaard, see K.E. Løgstrup, *Opgør med Kierkegaard* (Copenhagen: Gyldendal, 1968). See also references in M.J. Ferreira, *Love's Grateful Striving: A Commentary on Kierkegaard's Works of Love* (Oxford: Oxford University Press, 2001).

[42]   K.E. Løgstrup, *Kierkegaards und Heideggers Existenzanalyse und ihr Verhältnis zur Verkündigung* (Berlin: Erich Bläschker, 1950), pp. 9–11. Further references are given in the text as KHE.

[43]   Løgstrup's German text here uses the term *Bekümmerung*, etymologically cognate with the Danish *Bekmyring*, often translated in works by Kierkegaard as either 'care' or 'anxiety'. In his early lectures on Augustine, Heidegger himself uses the same word in expounding Augustine's *cura* and in a sense that anticipates the idea of care (*Sorge*). See M. Heidegger, *Phänomenologie des religiösen Lebens. Gesamtausgabe*, vol. 60 (Frankfurt am Main: Klostermann, 1995), p. 206–9.

distinction is between authentic and inauthentic existence, the latter being seen in human beings' typical lostness in 'das Man' (KHE, 14) and the 'idle talk' (*Gerede*) that obscures genuine understanding in favour of mere curiosity (KHE, 15–16), which, as in Kierkegaard, leads to a situation of ambiguity and a form of self-understanding that is merely a reflection of others' opinions (KHE, 16–17). This all happens because while the human being is structured so as to live by caring for himself and others (*Sorge*), our preoccupation with the things that make up our world leads us to forget about our responsibility for being who we really are and to focus on what is merely external (KHE, 17).

Thus far, Løgstrup presents Kierkegaard and Heidegger as saying essentially the same. However, he now identifies an important difference. Kierkegaard's thought reveals a 'strong ethical passion' that is lacking in Heidegger (KHE, 18). This can be seen as deriving from his reaction to speculative philosophy and its indifference to questions of good and evil and indifference that ultimately leads to the ethical being reduced to 'what the age requires' (KHE, 18), thus concealing the particular and individual as the site of ethical responsibility.[44] A second source of Kierkegaard's ethical passion is his conviction that Christianity only ever speaks to the individual qua individual, confronting him with the demand to choose between faith and offence (KHE, 20). This is not at all the case for Heidegger, however, for whom the confusion of the individual and the crowd is rooted in the structure of care. When Heidegger uses terms such as 'idle talk', curiosity, ambiguity, and falling, these are not intended to imply any moral or ethical judgement. 'They are purely matter-of-fact expressions applied in a purely philosophical analysis of human existence' (KHE, 21), as we have heard Heidegger himself emphasize.

Having introduced his two interlocutors, Løgstrup next proceeds to look further into their respective accounts of the internal relational structures of selfhood. Again, he commences with Kierkegaard, showing how the latter figures the self as involving two interrelated syntheses. The first is the synthesis of body and soul (KHE, 23), which, in turn, depends on or is grounded in the synthesis of finitude and the Infinite which Løgstrup also speaks of as the synthesis of time and the Eternal (KHE, 24). However, whereas the synthesis of body and soul may be understood as, in some sense, observable, a psychological or meta-psychological fact, the synthesis of finite/Infinite and temporal/Eternal can only be known as a *demand*, an exigency of human existence as such and therefore also as indicative of an essentially ethical relationship (KHE, 24–5). The individual is not just what he is (in the way that a cat is simply a cat) but is called upon to become who he is and only in so doing can he become what is demanded of him: to live as an ethical self. This is in turn possible only by virtue of his deciding whether to respond

---

[44]   Oddly, Løgstrup sees Kierkegaard's ethical passion as deriving from his reaction to speculative philosophy rather than seeing his reaction to speculative philosophy as an expression of his ethical passion. However, I do not dispute the essential connection Løgstrup is making here, even if I see the 'causal' relationship as running in the opposite direction.

obediently or disobediently to the demand, a decision that has the character of an inward act (KHE, 26). Consequently, the outcome is not so much self-knowledge as an ethical self-affirmation in which the self accepts the self-relation offered by its existential possibilities (KHE, 27). These are not to be understood (as the empirical psychologist might understand them) in terms of possibilities given the self by its genetic, familial, or social inheritance, i.e., by its environment, but as possibilities that arise from within the structure of having to become the self that one is (my paraphrase) (KHE, 28). An important corollary of this is that the human self cannot simply constitute its own being by some kind of self-positing act. Citing Bultmann, Løgstrup suggests that human beings' possibility for speaking of God and their experience of an infinite demand at the heart of their own self-relationship are inter-dependent (KHE, 29). The 'infinite' dimension of human existence cannot therefore be thought of as some kind of essence or attribute but is grounded in a certain lack: called to relate to the infinite demand we have to acknowledge that we are not infinite and our infinitude is always already lost (KHE, 29–30). This leaves the human being in a strange position: on the one hand, the Infinite and the Eternal are integral to human existence as such, on the other, they are experienced only under the rubric of loss (KHE, 30).

Yet there is a further – and dramatic – twist in the tale. A self that simply rested in the immanent infinity of just being what and as it is would scarcely be a self: to be a self in the full sense of the term means becoming a particular self, just this self that I myself am. Consequently, becoming a self means tearing oneself loose from the infinity of innocence and accepting one's guilt, i.e., that one's existing means existing under an infinite debt (KHE, 32). This is the scenario developed in Kierkegaard's account of anxiety (KHE, 32–3) and what it means is that the human being exists as movement, becoming, striving, and passion and these, in turn, are also essentially religious categories (KHE, 33–5), even if, in Jamesian terms (not used by Løgstrup himself) this doesn't involve any specific 'over-beliefs'.

Turning once more to Heidegger, Løgstrup sees the German philosopher as also recognizing not that the self is a substance but that 'existence is movement' (KHE, 37). But where Kierkegaard derives this insight from the relation to the infinite demand, Heidegger derives it from the analysis of *Sorge* and the self's always being-in-advance of itself in caring for its existence in the world. As previously indicated, the founding nature of *Sorge* means that we are always at risk of losing ourselves in the life of '*das Man*' and failing to discern our real possibilities (KHE, 38). Nevertheless, conscience continually calls us back to recognizing that truly to be who we are is down to each of us, as individuals. In conscience we are both caller and called, and what we are called to is to look our own existence in the eye, a demand that we find extremely anxiety generating (KHE, 39). No more than Kierkegaard does Heidegger imagine that human beings are the foundation of their own existence, but neither is there any infinite or eternal power to demand anything of us. The task of becoming who we are is a task to be undertaken in the face of – nothing at all, or, in other words, in the face of the sheer and simple fact that we were 'born to die'. Existence is only 'existence towards death' – and nothing more (KHE, 40–41). And just as the relational structure of the self described by Kierkegaard pointed beyond the limits of self-knowledge in terms of psychology or phenomenology, so too we can only 'know' the possibility of the entire cessation of our existence in death in the mode of anxiety. Facing up to death in this way and realizing that it is what Heidegger calls one's 'ownmost possibility' reveals the finitude of all our existential possibilities, breaks the spell of the illusions spread by 'idle talk' and 'das Man' and gives us a freedom for death (KHE, 43).[45]

Both Heidegger and Kierkegaard address the question as to how we are to live authentically and not as one of the crowd, but whereas for Heidegger becoming and remaining authentic is possible solely on the basis of confronting and accepting our own individual mortality in a radical and unflinching way, Kierkegaard makes the experience of the infinite demand absolutely central (KHE, 44–5). This undoubtedly leaves considerable common ground. Neither sees authenticity in terms of external achievements or what we do or the results of our actions, and both – as we have seen – insist on the dynamic character of existence and emphasize the ineluctable role of decision (KHE, 45–8). Both may also be said to have an essentially negative view of authenticity – in the case of Heidegger because of the 'nothingness' revealed in anxiety and in the case of Kierkegaard because the infinity to which we are called by the infinite demand is an infinity we have always already lost. Yet the fact that Kierkegaard construes the negative relation at the heart of existence in terms of demand means that, as opposed to Heidegger, his thought has a fundamentally ethical character. On the one side, we have care and death – on the other, the demand. In many ways, they seem to say the same, but the content is essentially different (KHE, 48).

But what does this mean in relation to actual human beings? How does it work out concretely? In the case of Heidegger, Løgstrup says, not at all! For Heidegger is not a philosopher of *Existenz* (like Jaspers perhaps?) but an ontologist for whom the analysis of existence is only preliminary to a fundamental ontological interpretation and is not a means of clarifying actual, existentiell issues (KHE, 51). Kierkegaard, by way of contrast, does have an interest in the concrete situation of real-life individuals, and his analysis aims at feeding back into awakening and edifying living human beings. *The Sickness unto Death* especially shows how the self can only become itself by virtue of a double-movement between finite and infinite, temporal and eternal, so that, optimally, it learns to relate to itself in its finitude – but infinitely. But, for Kierkegaard, it is also the case that we first name the Infinite and the Eternal properly when we name them as God, and to say that the individual exists by virtue of striving towards an infinite and eternal horizon that it does not possess within itself in the manner of an essential attribute is therefore to say that the individual stands under the demand of God.

---

[45] In Løgstrup's account we can see an important implicit difference between Kierkegaard and Heidegger that I have also previously noted, namely, that Kierkegaard associates anxiety with freedom, whilst Heidegger associates it primarily with death and only secondarily, via 'freedom towards death', with freedom itself.

The negativity of Kierkegaardian anthropology is therefore that the individual is nothing and can do nothing before God – and to be who we are by virtue of a relation to the demand of an infinitely and qualitatively different God is not at all the same as striving for an infinite ideal (KHE, 58). Such a God-relationship is, for Kierkegaard, fulfilled in worship, in dying to immediacy, and in renunciation and suffering. In short, Kierkegaardian religiousness demands the annihilation of the self before God and, despite his principled commitment to the concrete, the outcome is that such a religious requirement involves an 'infinite abstraction from everything external' (Kierkegaard, quoted by Løgstrup, KHE, 60). Yet – as Kierkegaard's own fictional ethicist saw – if one does not love and honour the concrete life one is to renounce, a total submission to such an infinitely abstract demand must end in pride and inhumanity (KHE, 60). However, although Kierkegaard sometimes indicates awareness of the need for greater attention to human ethical relationships, Løgstrup's view is that Kierkegaard's conception of the infinite demand has no specific content, i.e., it is essentially empty. Kierkegaard himself emphasizes the difficulty of living up to God's demands, but Løgstrup comments that on Kierkegaard's own premises it is downright impossible! The abyss between the abstractness of the absolute demand and the reality of concrete existence can only result in lives of wretchedness and powerlessness for those who try to understand themselves in these terms. The Kierkegaardian infinite demand is exclusively religious and has no relation to the kinds of concrete demands with which ethics or law have to concern themselves. Such concrete or finite demands involve relationships between two persons, and in this context guilt means having wronged the concrete other – whereas Kierkegaardian religious guilt is experienced solely on the basis of abstracting from concrete existence and therefore cannot involve any specific obligation towards the other (KHE, 83).

Does this then mean that we must give up the idea of an infinite demand, or is it possible to understand it in some other way (KHE, 84)? Here Løgstrup begins to develop his own conception of an 'ethical demand' that he would state more fully in his later work.[46] As a matter of fact, he says, we every day experience demands in our common life together that are shaped by the norms and criteria of that life (KHE, 85). At the same time, and beyond or before these, we stand under a demand that is made to us simply by virtue of the existence of the other (KHE, 85–6). I may learn as a child to offer my seat on a bus to women, the elderly, and the incapacitated or to give a certain percentage of my income to charity and I may continue to live by these rules, but if I am really to mature ethically I must also realize that the reason why I am committed to these or similar ethical practices (or, it may be, committed to revising them) is because I am even more fundamentally committed to living in the service of others. And this demand – to live in the service of others – can only be heard in concrete responsibility for the other (KHE, 86).

---

[46] See K.E. Løgstrup, *Den etiske fordring* (Copenhagen: Gyldendal, 1956, 1991); English translation: ed. H. Fink, *The Ethical Demand* (Notre Dame: University of Notre Dame Press, 1997).

A further aspect of this situation is that whereas the juridical approach sees responsibility in terms of a relationship between two parties and whereas Kierkegaardian religiosity replaces this twofold human relationship with the twofold human–God relationship, real responsibility is in fact threefold: I am responsible for another, to a third (KHE, 87). This may (inauthentically) be understood in terms of the responsibility that I have for my neighbour being grounded in the laws or conventions of my society – but this would be to replace a human relationship with an objective relationship and to measure human life by objective and inhuman criteria (KHE, 87–8). Løgstrup is Kierkegaardian and Heideggerian enough to reject such a move. Neither the individual nor the collective other can impose the absolute demand on me since this is a demand that I can only ever make on myself – and if I do not, then I cease to be an individual (KHE, 88–9). The insight on which I base a genuinely responsible action is and can only be mine and not anybody else's – a view for which Løgstrup finds support in Kierkegaard's *Works of Love* (KHE, 89). The demand of absolute responsibility and ethical individuation are mutually defining (KHE, 90). Thus understood, it is universal, like Kantian goodwill but with concrete content, and it is infinite, like the Kierkegaardian religious demand but not limited to the abstraction of the religious relationship (KHE, 91) (i.e., the relation to God). Whereas Kierkegaard and Heidegger could only totalize the individual's guilt-consciousness by abstracting from the concrete content of guilt (e.g., the guilt of shamelessly mistreating one's fiancée or supporting a criminal and murderous government), the understanding of guilt and obligation that necessarily accompanies Løgstrup's version of the absolute demand is total with regard to its content: I am totally responsible for having done this and not done that. Again, Løgstrup is existentialist enough to insist that whilst human beings are born into a definite order of things that brings with it a certain responsibility, the absolute and infinite demand is not founded in this order but has 'a purely personal character' (KHE, 98) and involves acts of judgement of a purely personal nature (KHE, 100). Therefore (and once more in agreement with Kierkegaard), it can never be a fact to be observed or fulfilled to the point of identification with any observable action or series of actions (KHE, 101). If it is unlike the Kierkegaardian demand in demanding attention to the real content of the neighbour's need, it is nevertheless like the Kierkegaardian demand in being essentially characterized by inwardness (KHE, 103).

My previous comments regarding the implications of Kierkegaard's discussion of the decisiveness, indeterminateness, and inexplicability of death should make it clear that I do not accept Løgstrup's argument that Kierkegaard's theocentric interpretation of the infinite demand short-circuits the presence of that demand in the claim of the human other. On the contrary, I believe that Kierkegaard's position is much closer to Løgstrup's own than he may have been prepared to admit – an unwillingness that perhaps reflects a certain 'anxiety of influence'![47]

---

[47]   However, see the discussion in my *The Philosophy of Kierkegaard* (Chesham: Acumen, 2005), pp. 115–26, where I also discuss similar criticisms from Buber and Adorno.

Fully to defend my reading of Kierkegaard on this point would be to digress too far from the question at issue, which concerns the ethical consequences of Heidegger's focus on anticipatory resoluteness as the eminent form of human authenticity. What Løgstrup contributes to this discussion is not only his direct criticism of Heidegger but, more importantly, the adumbration of an alternative perspective in which the specific limitations of Heidegger's conflation of ethical resoluteness with existential running towards death emerge all the more clearly.

Løgstrup's position, we may add, significantly converges with the perhaps more familiar line of criticism developed by E. Lévinas in a variety of works.[48] Lévinas, of course, had his own theological commitments, and although they were not those of Luther or Kierkegaard he too criticized Heidegger for seeing human beings' ultimate future solely under the rubric of being towards death. Insisting on the priority of the infinite appeal presented in the face of the other – an appeal condensed into the commandment 'You shall not kill' – he comments that, for Heidegger, the fear of becoming a murderer would have less force than the fear of being inauthentic in relation to one's own death.[49] Axiomatic for Lévinas is, again, Zosima's injunction that we are all guilty for everything and before everyone, i.e., that guilt and the ethical obligation consequent upon it are rooted in our relation to the other and not in the fact that we experience ourselves as a 'thrown nullity'. This is not to say that there are no connections between these two very different kinds of guilt. We saw how Kierkegaard's discourse on death illustrated the fairly widespread view that a sense of common mortality might and should serve to deepen our sense of human solidarity and mutual obligation. Nevertheless, each of Løgstrup, Lévinas, and Kierkegaard rank these two kinds of guilt (the guilt that arises from the sense of being a thrown nullity and the guilt that is the reflex of the infinite demand presented by the need of the neighbour) very differently from what we find in Heidegger.

All of this being said, some commentators claim that Heidegger's acknowledgement that *Mit-Sein*, being-with, is a fundamental trait of Dasein's being in the world opens the way to a more 'ethical' reading of his work than that of critics such as Løgstrup can allow. However, Heidegger's own discussion seems to place rather tight restrictions on the scope of what such being-with might comprise. As I have already indicated with regard to conscience, it seems scarcely to allow for the possibility that the self-relationship of conscience might be radically challenged by any external voice. It is therefore unsurprising that attempts to develop a more robust ethical teaching than Heidegger himself offers are likely to

---

[48]   On the relationship between Løgstrup and Lévinas, see comments in S. Andersen, 'In the Eyes of a Lutheran Philosopher. How Løgstrup Treated Moral Thinkers' in S. Andersen and K. van Kooten Niekerk (eds), *Concern for the Other: Perspectives on the Ethics of K.E. Løgstrup* (Notre Dame: Notre Dame University Press, 2007), pp. 29–54. However, it should also be said that much of Løgstrup's thought was devoted to trying to bridge the gap between ontology and ethics – precisely the gap opened up by Lévinas's critique of Heidegger.

[49]   E. Lévinas, *Dieu, la mort et le temps* (Paris: Grasset, 1993), p. 107.

be accompanied by the acknowledgement that this is not what Heidegger himself delivers. Towards the end of his study *Heidegger and the Ground of Ethics: A Study of Mitsein*, Frederick A. Olafson concedes that 'It does not seem to have occurred to Heidegger ... that the chief significance of his conception of being as presence lay in what it implies about our relations with one another'.[50]

Connected to the question of the ethical is the further question of hope. Appealing to all the work that remains to be one in the world for the building up of common human life[51] and also to Ernst Bloch's philosophy of hope, Lévinas suggested that hope might be no less basic to being human than the anxiety of being eye to eye with death. This should not, in the first instance, be equated with hope for some post-mortem existence. Bloch himself consistently stated his position as one of resolute atheism, yet commitment to work for a better future is incoherent unless at the same time there is an understanding of the good that such work is intended to realize.[52] Consequently, the decisive issue lies in the question as to how far human beings' find the ground of existential meaning in their mutual relations – Lévinas's ethics and Bloch's common work. A more recent example of a philosophical discourse on hope that points in a similar direction is Jonathan Lear's account of radical hope as a basic possibility of human existence.[53] Lear locates the issue of hope in the fate of a human community that has been threatened in its most basic values and the responsibility falling to the leader of that community to direct his people to a new future. Only when the ethical relationship has priority over thrownness towards death – whether this relationship is conceived in terms of obedience to the commandment, love, or the obligation of common social work – do we find grounds for hope. In this regard, and despite the criticisms – philosophical, not literary – of Tolstoy's claims to insight into the actual experience of death, we must also affirm his observation that it was a moment of compassion for his son that took Ivan Ilych out of himself and enabled him to embrace his impending death.[54]

---

[50]   F.A. Olafson, *Heidegger and the Ground of Ethics: A Study of Mitsein* (Cambridge: Cambridge University Press, 1998), p. 97 n. 2. That being said, I am not unsympathetic to Olafson's view, shared with a number of other Heidegger scholars, that there are resources within Heidegger for a fresh approach to contemporary ethical thinking. My view is simply that such an application of Heidegger, if we can call it that, goes beyond and to some extent against the direction of his own philosophical thinking. The next chapter will give some illustration as to how I think the deficiencies of his account of our relations to others show up in a Christian theological perspective with specific regard to the deaths of others.

[51]   The lack of an appropriate treatment of work is also flagged by Kojève. See A. Kojève, *Introduction à la lecture de Hegel* (Paris: Gallimard, 1947), p. 353.

[52]   Lévinas, *Dieu, la mort*, pp. 109–11.

[53]   See J. Lear, *Radical Hope: Ethics in the Face of Cultural Devastation* (Cambridge, MA: Harvard University Press, 2008).

[54]   I also note how, in the account of the death of Prince Andrei, the dying man's experience of infinite life is glossed as 'Love!'

As we now turn to further aspects of the inter-relationship between love and hope as they impact on our understanding and experience of death with particular reference to our relation to the deaths of others and how we might relate to 'the dead', we may briefly sum up the thrust of this present chapter: death may sharpen and give a certain urgency to our strivings to live according to the will of God or, in secular terms, to live according to the ethical demand of the other, but our obligation to live lives of charity is not ultimately grounded in mortality. Such an obligation is, however, more fundamental to our being or becoming truly human than our being thrown towards death. In a religious perspective, we may make the point by saying that living in love will still be the business of our lives in heaven, when we have sloughed off mortality. There is an obligation that, literally, outlives mortality. A literal understanding of such eschatological hope is obviously not available either to those who do not have a religious faith or to many non-fundamentalist believers, but my point here is not to commend that faith with regard to its dogmatic content but as phenomenologically revelatory of the possible independence of conscience from being towards death. In these terms the comportment it discloses is equally available to those who self-describe as 'religious' and to those who don't. Anxiety in the face of death is a natural human response to ceasing to be, but the ethical and religious way of dealing with this anxiety is precisely to turn away from the vision of death itself to what should be engaging us in our lives. Or, to be more precise, ethical and religious commitment to life yields a perspective in which the natural human fear of death is by no means banished but is given a context that radically re-defines its meaning, downgrading it from the primacy given it by Heidegger. In St Paul's terms it becomes a matter of 'Where, O death, is your victory? Where, O death, is your sting?' (1 Corinthians 15.55). 'Love is strong as death' (Song of Songs 8.6), or perhaps stronger, if 'nothing can separate us from the love of God in Christ Jesus' – including death (Romans 8.38–9). It is in this regard that, as I suggested earlier, I see Heidegger as missing a key element in his own ontic 'religious' sources. That he does so is not an arbitrary or accidental slip of concentration but relates to the fundamental perspective in which he reads these sources and his driving commitment to an existential ontological interpretation that understands Dasein as a whole in the mirror of human mortality. The argument of this chapter has been that it is not death that most urgently and most demandingly calls us to our finitude, however, but the responsibility – Løgstrup's 'demand' – to which we are called in our relations to others.

Chapter 5
The Deaths of Others

Experiencing the Deaths of Others

Heidegger is at his most persuasive in reminding us of the false consolations so frequently offered to the dying, drawing our attention painfully and embarrassedly towards the way in which friends and family (and perhaps even doctors and clergy and, not least, we ourselves) are accustomed to assure the dying person 'that he will escape death and soon return to the tranquillized everydayness of the world of his concern' (253/297) – 'Everything's going to be alright'! Following the cue provided by Kierkegaard's category of 'mood' we may extend such tranquillizing *Gerede* to the kind of talk in which death is formally acknowledged but its reality is softened to the point of falsification, as when we speak of death as 'falling asleep' or 'passing away'. Heidegger's antidote to such evasive talk is, as we have seen, the silent call of conscience summoning us to the sobriety of a serious and exclusively first-person anticipatory resoluteness. But is every kind of talking about death inauthentic? And is Heidegger correct in his view that it is only in relation to our own death and never in relation to the deaths of others that an authentic resoluteness becomes possible? These questions are necessarily interconnected, since discourse, *logos/Rede*, is an integral and basic dimension both of our self-relationship and of our being with others. With regard to this last, how we are with others and the meaning their lives have for us (and vice versa) is manifest in and inseparable from the kind of ways in which we articulate our thoughts about everything under the sun – in this case our common mortality. So, is Heidegger right that talk about death is only ever meaningful within the first-person perspective of seeing death as 'one's own' and nothing but 'one's own' or do we have things to say to one another about one another's death and dying that are not merely evasive? I have been arguing that a Christian response to Heidegger's conception of death might want to turn away from the summons to run towards death and look instead to the obligations we owe one another – submitting ourselves to the law of love (Romans 13.8–10) as the primary locus of a meaningful existence – and this might already indicate the possibility that we might find powerful 'existentiell' attestation to the power of love in the words spoken by and to the dying and in the words and expressive gestures in which we, the living, interpret the meaning their lives have had for us.

Clearly there are several issues here that are hard to separate. Reserving a discussion of the specific place and role of language in Heidegger's interpretation of death for the next chapter, I shall focus here on a question that has clear, if complex, connections to the ethical relationship, namely, the question of the deaths of others. Although, as I have been suggesting, this is not entirely separable in principle from the question as to how we speak about or represent death in language, it is also not the case that everything said about the deaths of others is solely a matter of language. Although we may agree with Heidegger that language is by no means an optional extra grafted onto human beings' experience of themselves and their world, we may also agree with him that the omnipresence of language does not entail a linguistic idealism and that there is a real existential and existentiell stake in what we say about ourselves, with one another.

Few would want to deny that we experience the deaths of others as events of great significance in our lives. It seems to be a matter of fact that whilst the death of a loved one may not take away or (except in pathological cases) ruin the lives of the bereaved, it can and often does change their lives profoundly. And it does so not only because it is arguably the clearest reminder we can have of our own death ('Ask not for whom the bell tolls ....') but also because – as Heidegger himself argues – the very structure of our being in the world includes our being with others. We are not who we are other than in our relations to others, and therefore the death of a loved one (who is likely to also be an actively loving one) has the potential radically to re-orientate our very existence.

As we shall shortly explore further, Heidegger himself seems to come to the brink of such a possibility before rapidly distancing himself from it. He writes,

> The greater the phenomenal appropriateness with which we take the no-longer-Dasein of the deceased, the more plainly is it shown that in such Being-with the dead, the authentic Being-come-to-an-end of the deceased is precisely the sort of thing which we do not experience ... The dying of Others is not something which we experience in a genuine sense; at most we are always just 'there alongside'. (238–9/282)

In other words, we can only ever experience the other's death as an event in the world, and if it means more to us than the felling of a tree it doesn't touch us essentially, in our *being*. We are just 'there alongside'.[1] But is this right?

In his 1929 inaugural lecture 'What Is Metaphysics?' Heidegger revisited themes of being, nothingness, and anxiety familiar from *Being and Time*. In the lecture he makes a sharp distinction between *experience* of all there is[2] and *transcendence* of all there is. In what he calls 'profound boredom' all there is

---

[1]   In what is admittedly a rather dense passage (238–9/282) in which key steps are hinted at rather than made explicit, Heidegger seems to indicate a *tertium quid* between our relation to, e.g., a felled tree and a dead human body. Nevertheless, the conclusion is that, as just cited, we are in the end just 'there alongside' and no more.

[2]   Where the translation in *Pathmarks* (see note 3 below) has 'beings as a whole' for Heidegger's *das Seiende im Ganzen*, I am rendering it as 'all there is' in order to avoid confusion with the rather different idea of Dasein's drive to 'be as a whole' that played such a central part in the argument of *Being and Time*.

becomes manifest, as when we say '*everything*'s so boring'. But, in a somewhat atypical aside, he adds, 'Another possibility of such manifestation is concealed in our joy in the presence of the Dasein – and not simply of the person – of a human being whom we love'.[3] Yet Heidegger does not pursue this thought any further and, turning instead to the idea that there is 'nothing' outside or beyond the totality of all there is, he invites us to consider that this 'nothing' is something we are capable of becoming aware of, namely, in the mood of 'anxiety'. Even if our absorption in the world constituted by and as all there is mostly prevents this awareness from becoming explicit, 'Being held out into the nothing – as Dasein is – on the ground of concealed anxiety is its surpassing of beings as a whole. It is transcendence'.[4]

Here, then, are two ways in which the question of being and of our relation to all there is becomes an issue for us. The first, seemingly equally represented by boredom and love, can only reveal all there is – but it does not reveal us to ourselves in our own first-person existence. The moods operative at this stage reveal our world and reveal our own being to the extent that they reveal that we have a world, whether we relate to it in indifference (boredom) or as fulfilment (love). But this is only a penultimate step, since there is also the further revelation of our own self-projection into and beyond this world – 'beyond' in the sense of *Being and Time*'s analysis of making ourselves its basis through the resolute acceptance of guilt. This is revealed only in anxiety.

Death is no longer explicitly thematized in the lecture, yet the structure of the argument seems congruent with all that we have read in *Being and Time*. Leaving aside the question of boredom, love seems able only to bring us to a proximate revelation of being, namely, to the revelation of beings (*Seiendes*) but not being (*Sein*) and it therefore falls short of making our 'ownmost' freedom manifest to us. Such a revelation is given exclusively in the anxious and individuating revelation of the 'nothing' towards which we and our world as a whole are thrown.

This may seem to open up greater scope for the meaning of the deaths of others than is allowed in *Being and Time* itself. This is because, although Heidegger speaks of the *presence* of the Dasein of the beloved as what evokes a sense of all there is and death might seem to be precisely the disappearance of such presence, everyday experience of the deaths of others might lead us to the view that others are rarely if ever more intensely present to us than in the light of their imminent

---

[3] M. Heidegger, 'What Is Metaphysics?' in idem., ed. W. McNeill, *Pathmarks* (Cambridge: Cambridge University Press, 1998), p. 87; M. Heidegger, *Wegmarken. Gesamtausgabe*, vol. 9 (Frankfurt am Main, Klostermann, 1996), p. 110. Heidegger's point here could be seen as analogous to Schleiermacher's claim that it is only in the feeling of love for another (primarily in the context of heterosexual relationship – Schleiermacher's example is Adam and Eve) that the universe as a whole is revealed to us. See F.D.E. Schleiermacher, *Speeches on Religion*, trans. R. Crouter, (Cambridge: Cambridge University Press, 1988), p. 19.

[4] Heidegger, 'What Is Metaphysics?', p. 93; *Wegmarken*, p. 115.

or actual decease. Yet the lecture essentially draws the same line that was drawn in *Being and Time* and does so still more precisely and therefore all the more definitively. To make a distinction Heidegger does not himself make but which seems congruent with his meaning, the deaths of others can become the occasion for us to see our *lives* but not our *selves* as a whole. At the deathbed of one we love we spontaneously recall all the time that is past and cast our minds forward to how life will be without them, but there is still something external about such retrospective and prospective meditation on 'being as a whole'. Such remembering looks back at life as something represented, as somehow external to my own actual existence here and now – it is, in Heidegger's terms, to see my life in the mode of *Vorhandenheit* or present-to-hand, a mode appropriate to a 'what' but not to a 'who'. Therefore, it is to meditation on our own death that the possibility of a more original and more interior understanding of existence is reserved – all there is in the light of the nothing towards which each of our 'worlds' is thrown. This seems to be Heidegger's point, but, to repeat, is this right?

Paul Tillich, in this respect not so far from Heidegger, spoke of what he called 'the shock of non-being' as what first drives us to raise the question of being, and likewise saw death as an eminent way in which the 'shock of non-being' is manifest in human self-consciousness.[5] But if death can indeed shock us into raising the question of being and what it means for us – for me – to be here at all, why is this shock exclusive to the prospect of my own death? Why should not the deaths of others too impel me to raise the question of my very being, that is, of my being as a whole, my entire being, existence, or life? But then again, and this is Heidegger's point, when the other dies, no matter how close we have been, no matter how much he or she has been a part of my life, *my* life, surely, goes on? As we have heard Heidegger himself say, my world continues and simply incorporates the memory of the departed into it. The death of the other causes a significant adjustment to my world, but my world doesn't come to an end. Only the other's world comes to an end. Therefore, only for the other does the prospect of death call into question his or her being as a whole – just as, for me, only the prospect of my death calls *my* being as a whole into question.

Yet there are reasons for thinking that the distinction Heidegger draws between my 'experience' of the deaths of others and the prospect of my own death is not as sharp as he claims and that the death of the other may be as significant in awaking the question of being as my own. I therefore now turn to exploring some of the ways in which this might be envisaged.

My argument is not without precedent. One contrary view to Heidegger's is that offered by Gabriel Marcel in an essay entitled 'My Death', which is dedicated to contesting some of the basic assumptions of Heidegger's account. In this essay

---

[5]   See, e.g., P. Tillich, *Systematic Theology* ([One vol. edition] Welwyn: James Nisbet, 1968), vol. 1, p. 207, vol. 2, pp. 77ff. See also his sermons 'The Destruction of Death' in *The Shaking of the Foundations* (London: SCM Press, 1949), pp. 169–72 and 'Love Is Stronger than Death' in *The New Being* (New York: Scribner, 1955), pp. 170–74.

Marcel recounts a dispute with Léon Brunschvig, who seems to have interpreted Marcel's own position as somewhat close to Heidegger's. As Marcel writes, 'When Brunschvig remarked that the death of Gabriel Marcel seemed to preoccupy Gabriel Marcel much more than the death of Léon Brunschvig preoccupied Léon Brunschvig, I replied that he had posed the question very badly; the only thing worth preoccupying either of us was the death of someone we loved'.[6] This is because, in what he acknowledges is an excessively simplified counter-move to Heidegger's 'being towards death', Marcel – not unlike Rosenzweig – sees our more primary existential vocation as 'being against death' and such 'being against death' is precisely what is brought home to us by the deaths of those we love. Marcel expands his point by quoting Antoine Sorgue,[7] a character from his play *L'Émissaire*:

> There is one thing I discovered after the death of my parents – that which summons us to survive [*survivre*] is actually what sustains us [*sous-vivre*]. And those whom we have never stopped loving with the best of ourselves become like an immense sky-scape, invisible yet somehow felt, under which we move forward, always more divided from ourselves, toward the instant where everything will be enveloped in love.[8]

The point is argued against Heidegger, yet we could almost equally well say that Heidegger's emphasis on the death of the other being something we do not and cannot *experience* alerts us to the very possibility that Marcel wants to emphasize. Precisely because the moment of the death of the other is a moment in which their being with us finally and definitively *escapes* our consciousness, it reveals the transcendence of their person, their self, over the merely physical conditions of their life. We experience their simple biological decease in the same sense that we experience the tree being felled or the budgerigar falling from its perch. Their death effects a complex of perceptual and emotional psychological states in us. This much is given. But what is shocking in bereavement is not just that a living body has become a corpse but the realization that *he* or *she* is *gone*. A personal centre of existence has ceased to be. This shock makes us realize in a radical and total way that we can never see the wholeness of another life – and just this insight might jerk us into realizing that it is the same with us: that we too, like the one who has just died, live in the world as centres of infinite mystery. Experiencing the death of the other in this way is then more than an experience of loss, and treasuring our relation to the dead may then be more than 'mourning': it may become a way of holding fast to the recognition of our own transcendence and the mystery of our own personality and doing so precisely in and on the ground of a

---

[6]   G. Marcel, *Tragic Wisdom and Beyond*, trans. S. Jolin and P. McCormick (Evanston: Northwestern University Press, 1973), p. 131.

[7]   This is probably not accidentally homophonic with Heidegger's *Sorge* (care).

[8]   Marcel, *Tragic Wisdom*, p. 130.

communion with others that exists beside or around our life in a community of the living. Thinking on the deaths of others in this sense is no longer 'tranquillizing'; rather it is opening out on to a view of life that challenges everyday assumptions about what is good and what is most worth achieving in life. It drives us towards the question as to the meaning of our life *as a whole*. Note how, although the words of Marcel's Antoine Sorgue may seem to offer a somewhat consoling view of death in which, as in Tennyson's *In Memoriam*, we experience ourselves as moving towards a moment when 'everything will be enveloped in love' (cf. Tennyson's 'one far-off divine event,/ To which the whole creation moves'[9]), this experience is accompanied by a contrary sense of being 'always more divided from ourselves'. The 'consolation' of such a vision is won only at the price of accepting an ever-deeper dereliction, to which the words of Johan Arndt, quoted by Kierkegaard, are perhaps apt: how will God wipe away our tears if we have never wept?[10] Against the view that 'everything that consoles is fake', might we not counter the suggestion that the refusal of consolation is also a refusal – or could engender or nourish a refusal – to acknowledge all that is lost in the moment of loss? The refusal of consolation is itself, in this perspective, a kind of defence mechanism and, in its own way, just as 'tranquillizing' as any sentimental funeral notice in the local newspaper.

But this is not yet an adequate response to the doubt as to how the death of the other might ever really raise the question of my being *as a whole* in the way that my own death does. As we have now several times heard Heidegger argue, my life still goes on after the other has died and it is only with regard to my own death that the whole of my world is at stake, including, as we have heard Archimandrite Sophrony suggest, my God, who dies with me when I die. It is only when we meet with death 'under four eyes', as Kierkegaard put it, that the matter becomes genuinely 'serious'. But aren't the kinds of consolatory visions proposed by Marcel precisely a way of masking the total finitude of my existence as revealed in the prospect of *my* death and the knowledge of *my* mortality? Aren't they a way of looking away from the specificity, ineluctability, and totality of death, i.e., (to repeat) *my* death?

I have previously cited – inevitably! – the familiar phrase from Donne's Seventeenth Meditation 'Ask not for whom the bell tolls'. As the meditation continues it seems to make a profoundly Heideggerian point: 'It tolls for thee' (and here we might appreciate the full force of the archaic form of the second-person singular: 'Thou art the man'!). In fact, Donne's own further exposition and prayer accompanying the text develop it in this direction. But this seems to be only one aspect of what the meditation itself argues. Donne writes:

---

[9]   A. Lord Tennyson, 'In Memoriam' in C. Ricks (ed.), *Tennyson. A Selected Edition* (London: Pearson Longman, 2007), epilogue lines, 141–4.

[10]   S. Kierkegaard, *Opbyggelige taler i forskjellig Aand. Søren Kierkegaards Skrifter*, vol. 8 (Copenhagen: Gad, 2004), p. 206; *Upbuilding Discourses in Various Spirits*, trans. H.V. Hong and E. Hong (Princeton: Princeton University Press, 2009), p. 102.

No man is an island, entire of itself; every man is a piece of the continent, a part of the main. If a clod be washed away by the sea, Europe is the less, as well as if a promontory were, as well as if a manor of thy friend's or of thine own were: any man's death diminishes me, because I am involved in mankind, and therefore never send to know for whom the bell tolls, it tolls for thee.[11]

Learning of the death of another is not simply a prompt to meditate on my own mortality. It is already, in and of itself, a diminishment of my own humanity – of my *humanity*; that is to say, it reveals to me that my own singular mortal identity is from the ground up 'involved in mankind' or 'a part of the main'.

It is, of course, true – trivially, I suggest – that my life as a whole could only ever really be grasped in a first-person perspective. There is no one else who ever has a total view of what it means for me to be me. When someone close to me dies, a part of me – perhaps a very large part of me – goes with them, but not the whole. When a parent, a spouse, or a close friend dies a whole stock of experiences and memories shared only with that person disappears from my world. But no matter how close the relationship may have been, it was never total. There are things about my life that are exclusive to my relationship with my mother. These are many and important, perhaps even in certain respects decisive for my being the person that I am. But they are not everything. Even in my childhood there was much my mother didn't know about. Similarly, there are experiences and memories unique to my relationship with my spouse and likewise my relationships with my closest friends. And even if, implausibly, each of these were to sell their story to a newspaper and 'the complete, unexpurgated version' made public, there would inevitably be gaps, errors, and guesswork. The whole would never come into view. It has been said that our friends are the guardians of our story, which is, in its way, an edifying thought,[12] but, ultimately, I am surely the sole guardian of the whole story. Therefore, the death of the other will only ever affect me in part, never as a whole. In terms of Donne's imagery, a promontory may have been torn from the continent, but the continent remains largely intact.

So far, so true – but this is surely to over-simplify the nature of human relationships. Whilst it is true that there are things my parents never knew about me (and some things I actively sought to ensure they would never know), my relationship with them has, in complex and often unconscious ways, affected every aspect of my subsequent life. And the same is true for the key relationships I have formed as an independent adult human being. Moreover, each of these relationships is also connected in once more complex and often unconscious ways to all of the others. Pull one small thread and the whole fabric starts to unwind. The death of any

---

[11] Quoted from J. Donne, *Devotions upon Emergent Occasions Together with Death's Duell* (London: Simpkins, Marshall, Hamilton. Kent and Co. Ltd. [Abbey Classics], 1926), pp. 108–9.

[12] Perhaps especially if we take it in the sense of the obligation we ourselves have to be guardians of our friends' stories.

one of those who have been central to my own life moves the architectonic plates that undergird the construction of my life so as to send shockwaves through the whole of my life, even if, as in any natural earthquake, these will be experienced in different degrees in different areas. Even the deaths of those closest to me may not materially affect how I function in my professional sphere (although, clearly, for some people, they do, and not only in cases of obviously pathological mourning). Yet even here, such a death may affect how I value that professional life as a whole, perhaps weakening, no matter how imperceptibly, my sense that this really is an appropriate focus for the greater part of my energies to the neglect of key relationships (though, equally, in other circumstances, it may reinforce my desire to live up to all the dead expected from me and to recommit with still greater efforts to 'the cause', whatever that is).

Fully to work out such examples would require turning this short essay into something more like a novel or even a sequence of novels – maybe even the entire canon of Western literature – and my point here is merely indicative. And what it is meant to indicate is simply this: in each case the death of the other has the potential to confront me with the question as to the meaning of my life and my being *as a whole*. Clearly, this is more obviously the case with regard to the central relationships of my life – parents, spouses, friends – but, as Donne's poem implies, it is potentially the case with regard to any death, even the death of the person I do not know but 'for whom the bell tolls'.

This may sound as if I have been understanding my being as a whole as if it were a matter of total recall, as when I reflected that there are episodes in my life unknown to my parents or others but only to me. This, of course, is not how Heidegger understands it, and it is not, in fact, central to the point I am making, merely introductory. Like Heidegger, I am seeking testimony from our existentiell and even everyday manner of existing so as to bring to view an aspect of what Heidegger would call our ontological situation, namely, our being as a whole. To the extent that coming into a lived and conscious relation to my being as a whole is a genuine existentiell possibility, there seem to be good reasons why the deaths of others can awaken this possibility just as well as meditating on my own mortality. Therefore they may also be of more significance for the existential–ontological understanding of death than Heidegger is prepared to allow. Yet I have also argued in earlier chapters that the question of our being as a whole is itself problematic, especially with regard to what death reveals about us. And this is as true with regard to the deaths of others as it is with regard to my own death. If – whether with regard to my own death or that of others – death awakens us to the possibility of being as a whole it simultaneously shatters our attempts to realize this possibility and reveals it as an *impossible* possibility.

But can my relation to my own death in fact be separated from my (non-) experience of the deaths of others? Is it not rather the case that the deaths of others are *more* existentially provocative than thinking of my own death, since even when I resolutely understand my life as the life of someone running towards death I am relating myself only to what is 'possible'? I know that it is ineluctable, and there is nothing of which I am more sure than that it will happen. But even though the fact of its future occurrence marks me out from the moment of birth as one who is always dying ('a mortal', to use the parlance of the later Heidegger), thrown towards death from the very beginning of my life, the 'not' of my own death cannot but have a certain abstractness. 'Where it is, I am not; where I am, it is not'. It is a possibility in the Kierkegaardian sense, i.e., an abstraction from and an idealization of the thick and resistant 'stuff' of lived existence. But when it comes to the death of a friend or loved one – or anyone – I cannot escape or deny the sheer present and concrete facticity of death: the person I spoke to just an hour ago no longer moves, no longer opens their eyes, no longer speaks; their body grows cold and will be buried or burned to ashes. I will never speak to them again. The cocoon of I-ness is irrevocably broken open, 'an impossible possibility' has occurred from which I cannot liberate myself by free self-assertion. There is no move I can make to re-establish my own sense of my self as a whole. A bit of who I am has been torn from me. Life will never be the same. I will never be the same. The deaths of others and my consciousness of their having died effects a diremption at the heart of Dasein from which I can flee only by embracing a tactic of denial (and thus far in line with what Heidegger says about our average everyday relation to our own death) but towards which we cannot in any way 'run' and 'for' which I cannot ever become free. If the eminent mode of authentic existence is solely to be found in resolutely running towards death, the deaths of others thus provide a significant problem. But what if, as I have been suggesting, a more truly basic disclosure of being is to be found in the obligation of love – an obligation that, I am suggesting, does more than reveal 'beings as a whole' (my life) but also reveals my fundamental transcendence over being (my self – existing as one who is infinitely indebted to love)?

We shall return to this question, but before doing so I note that a further feature of this shattering impact of the deaths of others is that even our own death is something we discover only in relation to the deaths of others. From the beginning, Heidegger has depicted being with others as a defining feature of Dasein's being-in-the-world. An absolutely autonomous Dasein that, qua self-conscious subjectivity, was the creative centre of its own world à la Fichte would scarcely be capable of envisaging its own death. Heidegger never subscribed to such a view of selfhood. But precisely because he sees Dasein as coming to be the concrete being that it is through its being with others and through the self-understanding that is made possible through a common language shared with others, his approach prompts the question as to what kind of knowledge of its own death Dasein can have that is not, in some way, mediated or, to put it more radically and perhaps even more correctly, *bestowed* by others. That is, it is bestowed in the language that I am given to speak through my participation in common human life and in which alone I can frame whatever thoughts I have about death. Of course, the mediation of our relation to death through language makes us prone to the idle, evasive, and tranquillizing ways in which we 'proximately and for the most part' talk about death – but does it not at the same time give us the possibility of a more authentic possibility of talking about our own death and about the deaths of others? And – as Kierkegaard already saw as constitutive of any *serious* meditation on death – does it not also disclose the commonness of our mortality? And is it not just this – that death is our universal common lot, the one sure thing that all of us human beings have in common – that the deaths of others bring home to us more forcefully and persuasively than meditation on our own individual mortality? If Heidegger's fundamental contention is that each of us must die alone, is it not equally credible to consider that, especially with regard to death, 'we're all in it together'?[13]

Of course, the realization that I myself will one day die and the realization that, qua mortal, I am merely being human, like all other humans, are interconnected. That interconnection, I am suggesting, is just what is effected by my individual experience of the deaths of others. Loss, the loss of what I love, is integral to my self-experience – it is what Heidegger might call an *existentiale*. A good account of what this means is offered by Sharon Krishek in a study of *Kierkegaard on Faith and Love*. 'Being finite and subject to the passage of time, our existence is pervaded by constant loss', she writes. 'Time goes by and seems to take with it everything that gives meaning to our life. Most often this loss is quiet and inconspicuous, but at the same time it is unstoppable'.[14] At any given time we will find ourselves dealing with very particular losses (what Krishek calls 'actual losses'). Bereavement, such as the death of a loved one, is an eminent and defining case of such a loss, but it is also – and often not unrelatedly – experienced with regard to, e.g., moving away from a much-loved home, or the break-up of a relationship. Usually we manage to console ourselves with the thought that we nevertheless still have other good things in our lives: the new home we are moving into, the children with whose welfare we have been entrusted, the possibility of new loves and new friendships. However, as Krishek points out, none of these things are insured against loss of one kind or another. One day we will move out of the new home, one day the children will leave home and perhaps, like the prodigal son, turn their backs on us, and perhaps we will one day be separated from our new friends and lovers by disagreements, indifference, or death. Even when we are not conscious of any actual losses, then, our lives are conditioned in every respect by potential loss, and it is this constant situation of being encompassed by potential loss that Krishek calls the 'essential loss' that she sees as a defining feature of human existence: 'everything that we have, everything that we take to be ours, is in truth *essentially* lost to us' she writes.[15] Essential loss is not just an occasional, perhaps intense, experience. It is an abiding feature of who and how we are. And the more fully we commit ourselves in love, the clearer this is. The Church service for marriage requires the lovers to commit themselves 'till death

---

[13]   For further reflection on language and death, see the following chapter.

[14]   S. Krishek, *Kierkegaard on Faith and Love* (Cambridge: Cambridge University Press, 2009), p. 10.

[15]   Ibid., p. 11. See also my *Kierkegaard's Upbuilding Discourses: Philosophy, Literature and Theology* (London: Routledge, 2002), p. 191.

us do part', whilst reaching out to the need of the other in an ethical sense is also spurred by the recognition that, like us, the other is always in proximate if not immediate danger of death.

Relations with the Dead

But does it follow that in this general situation of 'essential loss' the others – the dead – can truly remain, in some significant sense, present to us – not just a part of our world (as Heidegger suggested) but *with us*? Perhaps the situation of essential loss is just that: a revelation of the essential abandonment and dereliction of the human condition such that mourning and melancholia are properly basic human moods. But if this is so, then any memory of the dead that is not suffused with the sense of abandonment is mere consolation and, as such, 'fake'. The dead are truly lost to us and are 'with' us only in the extremely limited sense that we remember them. They are no more.

This, we saw, was already Heidegger's argument. However, it is also an argument that is used against him by Sartre. To grasp the force of Sartre's argument – not only in relation to Heidegger but also in relation to the theological counter-argument to Heidegger – we must recall that Sartre construes the human subject as (a) irrevocably free, (b) as having its freedom continually threatened by the opposing freedoms of others, and (c) therefore existing in a state of conflict with others, constantly having to wrest its freedom and identity from the attempts of others to coerce, colonize, or otherwise suborn it.[16] In what is perhaps the best-known quote from the entirety of Sartre's work: 'Hell is other people'.

But however successful I may be in resisting the encroachments of others and asserting my own power over them all the days of my life, death is the moment of ultimate defeat since the meaning of my life then passes into the hand of the Other

> like a coat which I leave him after my disappearance .... Richelieu, Louis XV, my grandfather are by no means the simple sum of my memories, nor even the sum of the memories or the pieces of knowledge of all those who have heard of them; they are objective and opaque beings which are reduced to the single dimension of exteriority. In this capacity they will pursue their history in the human world, but they will never be more than transcendences–transcended in the midst of the world.[17]

Death deprives the subject of all its subjective meaning 'in order to hand it over to any objective meaning which the Other is pleased to give to it'. And, as Sartre

---

[16]   For my view of Sartre's account of freedom and its conflicts, see my *God and Being* (Oxford: Oxford University Press, 2011), pp. 207–12.

[17]   J.-P. Sartre, *Being and Nothingness*, trans. H. Barnes (London: Methuen, 1969), p. 544.

adds, since this process of reception is itself unfinished, I am in the end handed over to a contingent and indeterminate future. It is 'the triumph of the Other over me'.[18] What is perhaps worse is that even this does not result in any 'final judgement' on who I am but will always remain revisable. Every new biography can be contested. Thus all the possible meanings of my life remain forever in contingency. I – that is, the historic memory of who I was – could become just about anyone. Sartre sees this as decisively undermining Heidegger's account since it excludes any finality I may hope to give my life by the manner in which I comport myself towards my death. I will always fail in my attempt to authentically ground my own existence by grasping and owning my responsibility for being the thrown nullity that I am, since in every case I will end up being handed over to others and being irredeemably reified in how they remember me. Where Heidegger insists on the 'always my own' quality of an authentic comportment towards death, Sartre sees such 'mineness' as always being wrested away from me and my death – and my life with it – being reduced to just one more event in the world. Where Heidegger believes that I can, as it were, overtake and thus surpass the unsurpassable possibility of my own death, Sartre sees death as always, in the end, overtaking and surpassing me. We recall Simone de Beauvoir's view that no death is natural and every death a violation.

To sum up. If Heidegger allows the possibility of love, this is only with regard to the revelation of my world – not the revelation of my *self*. Love does not and, in principle, cannot outlive death since it is precisely my *world*, all there is, that comes to an end in death. For Sartre the situation is even more hopeless, since death means, invariably, the eclipse of myself, together with all its possibilities, by the other. There is no love beyond the grave. But against both Heidegger and, implicitly, Sartre, Marcel gestures towards an alternative view. For over and above his insistence on the pre-eminence of reflection on the death of the other over reflection on my own death, Marcel also emphasizes a further contrary position, namely, that those whom we have loved – or, to be truer to his own terms, those we still, actively and presently *do* love – accompany us as an 'invisible yet somehow felt' 'sky-scape', 'under which we move forward, always more divided from ourselves, toward the instant where everything will be enveloped in love'.[19] I shall now seek to develop this contrary view more fully – not on the grounds of Christian teaching about the immortality of the soul but on the phenomenological basis of our human experience of the deaths of others and the meaning such deaths can have for our lives and for our being the selves that we are. In doing so I shall place special emphasis on the phenomenon of remembering the dead. In these terms the argument against Heidegger and Sartre is not that they do not represent a Christian or religious point of view (which, of course, they never intended to do) but that their accounts fall short of all that might be said from within the horizon of a purely human, phenomenological interpretation of existence.

---

[18]   Ibid., p. 545.

[19]   Marcel, *Tragic Wisdom*, p. 130.

I have argued against Heidegger that, no less than my own death, the deaths of others can bring us face-to-face with the decisive question as to the meaning of human being as a whole (and my shift from singular to collective here is deliberate). At the same time, I have continued to resist the demand that we *should* be able to *think* our existence as a whole. Perhaps allowing such meaning as our lives might have to depend on, the vast, unmapped, and arguably unmappable continent of our being with others is as good as it gets. They constitute a cloud of witnesses to my life too great to number. Yet I can never really know what they might think of me and I cannot remember them all, every one of them, down to the last detail of all that belonged to them as living. The 'whole' of what this all means is too great, too diffuse to bring into a single, sharp focus. What can it then mean to invoke our relations to the dead as integral to authentic self-experience and self-understanding? Something more is needed than is provided by Marcel's brief evocation of an accompanying 'sky-scape' if we are to resist Sartre's claim that all such remembrance is reificatory. The question, then, is not just about how the deaths of others might awaken us to a decisive concern for our own death or to the meaning of death – and even life – as such, but about what possibilities of human being-with are given in our relationship with the dead.

This potentially invites an encyclopaedic discussion of the manifold forms in which human societies of past and present have remembered their dead, from the simple funerary rites of our Neanderthal kin, through the great public and cosmic rites of Ancient Egypt and the memorial culture of the Middle Ages, down to the minimalist post-liturgical practices of the present, semi-secular West. But that, of course, is another task, and I shall limit my discussion to two examples, both of which belong to the cultural moment that positioned Heidegger's own reflections on death: Søren Kierkegaard and Edwin Muir.

The Work of Love in Remembering the Dead

We have already several times attended to Kierkegaard's discourse 'At a Graveside', but I now want to turn to another discourse, 'The Work of Love in Remembering One Who Is Dead' from the collection *Works of Love*. This discourse, which, as the title suggests, sees remembering the dead as a work of love, has divided readers. Kierkegaard himself wants to maintain that it is the most disinterested kind of love, since there is nothing the dead can do for us; it is the freest kind of love, since there is no way in which the dead can reciprocate our love or feed our egos by their gratitude; and it is the most faithful kind of love, because we can never revise, amend, or re-negotiate the promises we have made to the dead. Of course, even though we may have said, 'I will never forget you' it may equally well be that we do, in time, change and gradually forget. But from the point of view of the departed, there is no possibility of change. Our relation to them thus tests the genuineness of our actual commitment to the love we once professed. However, for a critic such as Adorno, this discourse, which he sees as the 'culmination' of *Works of Love* as a whole, reveals that what Kierkegaard's view of love amounts to is, in fact, a loveless view of life in which the other is merely an empty foil for the 'loving' self's narcissistic obsession with its own motives. That Kierkegaard can see our love for the dead as a pinnacle of love's manifold varieties suggests to Adorno that, on this account, even our love for our living neighbours must practically treat them as if they were dead. Thus, and against his own critical view of the kind of aesthetic love practiced by *Either/Or*'s seducer-figure, Kierkegaard repeats in his own way the Goethean view that 'If I love you, what concern is that of yours?'[20] Kierkegaardian love, in other words, is not love that requires attentiveness or responsiveness to the claim of the other, but, because of Kierkegaard's insistence on right intention on the part of the lover (and specifically the intention to obey the divine command to love), the concrete need of the real-life other is entirely bracketed out of the discussion.[21]

However, there are reasons to demur from Adorno's sweeping condemnation. For a thinker so attentive to the aesthetic, it is perhaps surprising that he overlooks the rhetorical form in which Kierkegaard sets up his argument, namely, as a kind of thought experiment by which to test how a person loves but not as instantiating every aspect of what is involved in loving the living. And it is similarly surprising that he does not note that this is the *pen*ultimate and not the ultimate discourse in the collection. The last discourse, 'The Work of Love in Praising Love', spells out that the whole thrust of *Works of Love* is to provoke us into thinking about how we might speak of love in such a way as to galvanize each other into practicing it, where 'speaking' means engaging in communicative action; testimony and not mere soliloquizing. In other words, *Works of Love* is not to be judged as a

---

[20]   See T.W. Adorno, 'Kierkegaard's Lehre von der Liebe' in idem., *Kierkegaard* (Frankfurt am Main: Suhrkamp, 1974), pp. 271–2.

[21]   For further discussion, see my *The Philosophy of Kierkegaard* (Chesham: Acumen, 2005), pp. 115–26. Peter George sees the problem in similar terms to Adorno, in an article that also considers Dostoevsky's view of remembering the dead, writing that, on their premises, 'any relationship to this dead person cannot be interactive, and hence cannot be social … at the same moment as the reader sees in Kierkegaard's and Dostoevsky's account of remembering the dead a movement away from existential individualism, one is confronted with the most existential experience of all: the experience of death' (P. George, 'Remembering the Dead: Kierkegaard and Dostoevsky' in *Modern Believing* 35.2 [April 1994]: 29–30). A similar view is implied in K.E. Løgstrup's interpretation of Kierkegaard – see Chapter 4 above. For views more sympathetic to what commentators understand Kierkegaard to be saying in this discourse, see M.J. Ferreira, *Love's Grateful Striving: A Commentary on Kierkegaard's* Works of Love (Oxford: Oxford University Press, 2001), Chapter 15, pp. 209–27; H. Pyper, *The Joy of Kierkegaard: Essays on Kierkegaard as a Biblical Reader* (Sheffield: Equinox, 2011), Chapter 6, 'Cities of the Dead', pp. 67–80; and P. Stokes, 'Duties to the Dead? Earnest Imagination and Remembrance' in P. Stokes and A.J. Buben (eds), *Kierkegaard and Death* (Bloomington: Indiana University Press, 2011), pp. 253–73. All of these do, however, acknowledge and address what we might see as the potential 'scandal' of Kierkegaard's view.

description of love but a rhetorical exhortation *to love*. Furthermore, Adorno omits consideration of the 'mood music' with which Kierkegaard opens the discourse. But Kierkegaard's introductions are always rather important, since they are essential (he believes) to getting the reader positioned so as to be able to hear just what is being said in the main text. In this case he – strikingly – urges his readers to go to meditate at the graves of the departed, not, as in the culture of Romantic melancholy, at twilight (as his pseudonym Johannes Climacus does[22]) but on a sunny morning. Why? Because whereas twilight might tempt visitors to solitary reflections on their own mortality, a sunny morning will better serve to open their eyes to the community of the dead that is 'out there' and give them a glimpse into a different kind of society in which, whatever their differences have been in life, each family now has an essentially equal plot of land. Of course, some may have the adornment of a tree (as Kierkegaard's own grave is watched over by a weeping birch), but such variations only serve to underline that, in death, the differences are merely trivial. One family will have at most a metre more of land than another. As in 'At a Graveside', visiting the dead therefore leads to greater insight into the commonality of human life and our essential solidarity one with another. The very opening lines emphasize that the importance of death is that it is 'life's epitome' and that the value of listening to death is that death knows how to speak well about life and direct us to what is most decisive in it. The aim of such a graveyard promenade, then, is not to lose ourselves in debilitating melancholic thoughts, but to learn or re-learn what is essential in life and what is being demanded of us in life, in our relationships with the living.[23]

But it is, surely, true – isn't it? – that the dead don't and can't 'answer back'? And isn't that precisely Kierkegaard's point in speaking of the lack of reciprocity in our relation to the dead – they can't pay us back! And doesn't his exclusive attention to this lack suggest that Adorno is, in the end, right?

As Kierkegaard himself might have said, let us not be over-hasty in rushing towards a conclusion. It is of course and obviously true that in a certain sense the dead don't and can't answer back. It is similarly of course and obviously true that they are not in a position to reward us for taking time to remember them. But such comments fail to attend to the existential stake of the discourse. The deadness of the dead and their lack of physical ability to engage in a normal, average everyday conversation says little or nothing about the quality of our relation to them. And though they can no longer answer back or reward us, Kierkegaard's argument hinges on the fact that we have spoken to them, we have made promises to them, and we have had the experience of a shared future with them. That they have, as it

---

[22]   For a good discussion of the role of 'atmosphere' in Climacus's excursion to the graveyard, see E.F. Mooney, *Excursions with Kierkegaard* (New York: Bloomsbury, 2013), pp. 175–86.

[23]   See S. Kierkegaard, *Kjerlighedens Gerninger. Søren Kierkegaards Skrifter*, vol. 9 (Copenhagen: Gad, 2004), pp. 339–40; idem., *Works of Love*, trans. H.V. Hong and E. Hong (Princeton: Princeton University Press, 1995), pp. 345–6.

were, been removed from temporal flux and what they did and what they said has acquired the permanence of the irrevocable past is only in one respect exemplary for us, still living in time, since the task, as Kierkegaard makes clear, is that we should learn how to be faithful in our relationships in time. He nowhere cites Shakespeare's 'love alters not when it alteration finds' but this could effectively serve as a leitmotif for *Works of Love* as a whole, and nowhere more so than here.[24] Although the dead are no longer physically present in such a way as to be able to constrain us or, for that matter, to appeal to or to charm us, and although they no longer have new words to persuade or enlighten us, it is nevertheless as *living* that we remember them. Whether, as Kierkegaard suggests, it is the matter of something said, or, as is often the case, a look, a gesture, or a tone of voice, our dealings with them after their death extend and repeat our dealings with them in life. It is *they, they living*, that we remember, and not, strictly speaking, 'the dead'.

Naturally, it might immediately be objected that – as in the spirit of Sartre's comments on remembering the dead – this is a relationship in which there is no check to our capacities for falsifying our image of the dead, for good or ill. Consciously or unconsciously, we aggrandize, sacralize, or debunk the dead according to the need of our current life projects. To which the reply must be this: in what way is this essentially different from how we are with the living? As anyone who has been through a course of therapy is likely to be aware, our capacities for projection, transference, and similar psychological manoeuvres is not easily checked in relation to the living, so that – I suggest – the difference between how this works in relation to the dead is more quantitative than qualitative.[25] And if we are indeed human beings living in community, then, as with the living, there will be others' countervailing memories (and in some cases, documentary evidence) to provide a reality check on what we attribute to the dead, calling our misrepresentations to order and reminding us of what we have forgotten.

It may be that, in the particular case of Kierkegaard, some readers read into this discourse and are then troubled by what they see as his morbid obsession with the memory of his dead father, a ponderous super-ego whose unrelenting demands on his son, even after death, were largely contributory to the latter's worldly unhappiness. This is not the place to begin discussions of Kierkegaard's biography, since the point is that even if his own individual way of being faithful to his important dead was, by contemporary standards, morbid, we are by no means obliged to see this as the only way of enacting such remembrance. It is not only to paternal super-egos that Kierkegaard's discourse invites us to be faithful. It is, or may be, equally, to all manner of lessons in laughter, love, and discernment

---

[24]   *Kjerlighedens Gerninger*, pp. 348–51; *Works of Love*, pp. 255–8.

[25]   Kierkegaard himself comments in 'An Occasional Discourse' that our relations to the living are so qualified by the constant calculus of advantage and disadvantage that we are in fact all the more likely to distort or falsify our relationships with them for own maximal benefit than is the case with the dead. See Kierkegaard, *Opbyggelige taler i forskjellig Aand*, pp. 164f.; *Upbuilding Discourses in Various Spirits*, pp. 54f.

that our dead friends – whom we yet remember *as living* – remind us to be faithful. Thus, faithfulness to the dead becomes a way in which we continue, through them, to commit ourselves all the more fully and all the more understandingly to the tasks and pleasures of living with the living.

Echoes Thronging from the Dead

I should now like to turn to further testimony to what this might mean by briefly examining aspects of the poetic vision of Edwin Muir, a Scottish – or, to be exact, Orcadian – poet who flourished in the first half of the twentieth century. Muir shared many cultural horizons with Heidegger, including a constant engagement with both Nietzsche and Hölderlin, and through his translations of Kafka and Hermann Broch was alert to and engaged by the atmosphere of German intellectual life in the inter-war years. I shall focus my reflections on some lines from a short posthumously published poem which begins 'The heart could never speak, but that the Word was spoken'. In the second verse, Muir writes,

> Heart, you would be dumb
> But that your word was said
> In time, and the echoes come
> Thronging from the dead.[26]

In Muir's poetic vision, life in time is inevitably subject to tragedy and loss. And yet time is also the condition of human life, and if we are to be truly human we must each learn to speak our own singular word, our word from the heart, in time. But no human word can be immune from the ravages of time, and a world of timeless ideas or truths would not be our world. Muir is not unmoved by such a possibility, though. In the poem 'The Journey Back' he depicts a self that journeys back into its own archaic past, reliving the lives of each of its ancestors, until it comes at one point to a vision of a world ordered by immortals living in unbroken blessedness:

> They walk high in their mountainland in light
> On winding roads by many a grassy mound
> And paths that wander for their own delight.
> There they like planets pace their tranquil round
> That has no end, whose end is everywhere,
> And tread as to a music underground … (6: 1–6)

---

[26]   E. Muir, *Collected Poems* (London: Faber and Faber, 1984), p. 297. All further references to Muir's poems are given to this edition and are given by title, section (where relevant), and line number in the text. I have footnoted titles only where they are not given in the text. For further discussion see my *'The Heart Could Never Speak': Existentialism and Faith in a Poem of Edwin Muir* (Eugene: Cascade Books, 2013).

This is an order of temporal movement higher than or at least other than that of historical time. It depicts time as a blessed dance, tranquilly progressing through a measured sequence of changes that involve no essential change or break in the luminous silence of the ritual-like movement. But, the poet adds, 'This is the other road, not that we know' (6: 12).

Perhaps we will, one day, come to such a place and see the real or true world stripped of the shadows that, for now, obscure our vision. But while we are in time it is a vision on the very boundary of our existential possibilities, like the vision of the golden harvester of whom Muir speaks elsewhere, a figure sometimes glimpsed in the evening light and portending a harvest that, in time, never arrives. The way to it is precisely 'the other road, not that we know'.

The time of such a world, then, is not the time in which the heart must speak and be spoken to. Our time is the time in which and by which we are thrown beyond ourselves towards the experience of 'essential loss' and the first thing that confronts us on such a road is the encounter with all that we have already and irrevocably lost. As soon as the heart's word is spoken in time, then, it is no surprise that 'the echoes come/ Thronging from the dead'. Whereas for Heidegger the truth of my 'ownmost' relation to my ineluctably solitary death is to be found only in just this quality of exclusive mineness, Muir figures the discovery of our own heart – the core of our inner self-identity – as essentially bound up with our relation to the dead, 'the others'. But in what way 'bound up'?

I have just alluded to the poem 'The Journey Back', which can be connected to the intense psycho-analysis Muir underwent for a period and his consequent 'discovery' of the role his ancestors and their demons still played in shaping his own psychic life.[27] But there is more to such an inner 'journey back' than simply tracking the aetiology of one or another current neurosis. Muir had an intense sense of solidarity with the many generations of poor Orkney farmers from whom he was descended. The ancient dead are remembered not merely that they might be exorcised and leave the present self free to pursue its autonomous devices nor in filial duty, as in a form of 'respectful solicitude'. For Muir the self is what it is as a part of and in solidarity with the larger human community, the tribe, the people, 'all we' (as the opening words of one poem have it). It did not choose this history or this descent, but it is an essential element in its journey to itself that it learns its identity with all who have gone before.

In the first section of *Variations on a Time Theme*, Muir poses a series of questions on behalf – once more – of a 'we', a 'we' that is figured as having reached a point of middle-aged indifference to life, a kind of convalescent self, 'waiting for life,/ Turning away from hope, too dull for speculation' (1: 2–3). So, he asks, 'How did we come here ... Where did the road branch?/ Where did the path turn ... Or did we choose ... Did we come here through darkness or inexplicable light ... Was it truth that lured us here, or falsehood? Virtue itself/

---

[27] On Muir's experience of psycho-analysis, see E. Muir, *An Autobiography* (Edinburgh: Canongate, 1993), pp. 50–58.

Or weakness ...?' (1: 4, 8–9, 12, 17–18, 20–22). In these words, the poem powerfully evokes the sense of having been thrown into a world that we neither designed nor chose and also a world we are fated to lose, thrown as we are towards ultimate annihilation in death. But – here we are! So who are 'we', and what are we to do? 'Can we build a house here', Muir asks; 'Can we sing our songs here,/ Pray, lift a shrine to some god?' (1: 34, 37–8). The questions are left unanswered but are followed by a further specification of who the 'we' he is talking about are. 'We', he says, are 'nameless', 'between the impotent dead/ And the unborn, cut off from both, fateless,/ Yet ruled by fate' (1: 39–41). Implicit here, I suggest, is the following thought: we ourselves will be nameless, unable, as he puts it, to 'till these nameless fields' (1: 38), sing our songs, worship our gods, or build our houses or reconnect to the 'impotent dead/ And the unborn' until we understand ourselves in our deepest solidarity and identity with all our race.

'The Child Dying', written after an accident that Muir believed at the time was going to be fatal for his son Gavin, underlines the point that the terror of death is not simply the terror of annihilation but the breaking of all relationship between the dead and the living. The words of the poem are spoken as if by the dying child, terrified by the onset of 'nothing-filled eternity'. Seeking his father's hand he concludes,

> Hold my hand, oh hold it fast –
> I am changing! – until at last
> My hand in yours no more will change,
> Though yours change on. You here, I there,
> So hand in hand, twin-leafed despair –
> I did not know death was so strange. (25–30)

This 'strangeness' is not the strangeness of the imminent separation of soul and body but is described precisely as having to do with the separation between the living and the dead. Perhaps the most far-reaching expression of this idea is in the poem 'The Absent', in which it is the living who become 'the others'. Why? Because their lives are permeated by the 'great absence' of all those unknown fellow human beings who have preceded them into death, even – perhaps especially – when they are unconscious of missing them: 'And so we sorrow for These that are not with us,/ Not knowing we sorrow or that this is our sorrow ... Sorrow for loss of that which we never possessed,/ The unknown, the nameless ...' (16–17, 19–20). Ignorant of their relation to the dead, they are incapable of being the selves they really are. Nor will they, until they are able to sorrow, 'that sorrow/ And loneliness might bring a blessing upon us' (23–4).

This sorrowing lonely solidarity and community of living and dead seems, then, to offer a dramatic alternative to Heidegger's view that it is only by resolutely running towards our own singular death that we can authentically become ourselves, and it gives flesh to Marcel's belief that 'consideration of one's own death is surpassed by the consideration of the death of a loved one'. Muir would agree but would also go further, claiming, it seems, that it is only when we remake the bonds of love undone by death that we can find a ground on which to learn our own names and to speak our heart's own truth. It is perhaps for this reason that the two poems dedicated to dead friends, 'To J.F.H.' and 'For Ann Scott-Moncrieff', are both addressed in the second person to their dedicatees. Dead, they still belong among the living, to be spoken to and even listened to – 'Yet "the world is a pleasant place"/ I can hear your voice repeat,/ While the summer shone in your face/ last summer in Princes Street' (37–40). We remember the dead not as dead, but as living.

When it is said that the heart that speaks its word in time will be answered by 'echoes' that 'come thronging from the dead', such 'echoes' may therefore reveal the possibility of a new and radical orientation of the self towards the world, towards others, and towards itself. For in such moments the past is, as it were, not past; the dead are, as it were, alive; the absent are, as it were, present (as Muir says to Ann Scott-Moncrieff, you are 'Absent and present so much/ Since out of the world you fell …' [6–7]). In the Christian perspective, this suggests the doctrine of the communion of saints, 'the mystical Body of Christ, that is the blessed company of all faithful people', although in Muir's vision it is not a company that seems to be limited by subscription to a particular creed. On the contrary, it embraces also the long lineage of fathers and fathers' fathers who lived lives of hard and bitter struggle that often warped or broke their personalities. And this line reaches far back into pre-Christian and even prehistoric time. It is the ultimate affirmation of human solidarity and in gesturing towards such solidarity, the poet could well be the voice of which Hermann Broch spoke in his novel *The Sleepwalkers* – as translated here by Muir and his wife Willa: 'the voice that binds our loneliness to all other lonelinesses, and it is not the voice of dread and doom; it falters in the silence of the Logos and yet is borne by it, raised over the clamour of the non-existent. It is the voice of man and of the tribes of men, the voice of comfort and hope and immediate love: "Do thyself no harm! for we are all here!"'[28]

Let us think again about the suggestion that hope is a possibility given by what we experience and learn in the manner of our concrete being with others, especially by virtue of the words in which, together, we articulate how we understand the meaning of death. I am suggesting that these are not only the words we share with the dying and they with us (and Heidegger is right that we are all, in our way, *dying*). They are also the words in which we remain in communication with the dead, hearing their voices speaking to us and in us, and speaking with them, still, as we speak with the living. As we speak with the living? Yes. Not, of course, in the sense that we are to imagine the dead as self-conscious centres of subjectivity articulating their thoughts through the vibrations of their vocal chords. Yet, nevertheless, urgently present in a way that does not require a recording apparatus as providing relevant evidence. 'I can hear your voice …', Muir says of Ann

---

[28]   H. Broch, *The Sleepwalkers*, trans. W. Muir and E. Muir (London: Quartet, 1986), p. 648.

Scott-Moncrieff, giving poetic expression to a common enough experience that in its humble average everydayness testifies to the dead as a continuing presence in our lives, calling to us to be faithful to revelations of truth we have shared and to be hopeful in relation to the new horizons that the love we have shared continues to open up.

For Christian faith, such words of faithfulness and hope also anticipate and are, in their own way, expressive of another Word. Where Heidegger says that 'conscience' speaks by 'keeping silent' and thus reminding us of the silence to which our entire chattering existence will one day be reduced, a religious conscience will understand itself as called, addressed, claimed by a Word that both grants and summons us to be faithful to all our experienced possibilities of hope and love, summing up the promise and claim of all the actual human words that have, as it were, come down to us in our lives. 'The heart could never speak/ But that the Word was spoken', wrote Muir in the opening lines of his poem, the capitalization of 'Word' implying a reference to the Word of St John's prologue – the Word that was in the beginning with God (John 1.1–2). There is probably no argument that might protect what has been said here from being taken as mere wish fulfilment. But what is at issue is not the speculative question of 'life after death'. It is whether and how, in and through the words by which we learn to understand ourselves, we might find meaning in the face of our being ineluctably thrown towards death and to do so other than by silently embracing this thrownness in a kind of hyper-individualized anxiety.

In these last paragraphs (as earlier in this chapter) we have been broaching questions of language that will become the theme of the next chapter, and I shall conclude this present discussion with words from the Russian religious philosopher Nicholas Berdyaev that articulate something of what I am attempting to argue here. Like much that we find in Berdyaev, the thought doubtless lacks analytic rigour and may be described as expressionistic rather than philosophical. Nevertheless, in his own way, Berdyaev points towards a constructive possibility that, I am suggesting, provides a significant alternative to Heidegger and that can be grounded in a closer phenomenological reading of our relations to the dead than Heidegger himself in fact offers. Berdyaev writes,

> Memory of the past is spiritual; it conquers historical time. This ... [is] a creatively transfiguring memory. It carries forward into eternal life not that which is dead in the past but what is alive, not that which is static in the past but what is dynamic. This spiritual memory reminds man, engulfed in his historical time, that in the past there have been great creative movements of the spirit and that they ought to inherit eternity. It reminds him also of the fact that in the past there lived concrete beings, living personalities, with whom we ought in existential time to have a link no less than with those who are living now. Society is always a society not only of the living but also of the dead; and this memory of the dead ... is a creative dynamic memory. The last word belongs not

to death but to resurrection. But resurrection is not a restoration of the past in its evil and untruth, but transfiguration.[29]

The dead who are with us in this resurrection life are co-constitutive of our being. But their being with us is not just a matter of *Mit-Sein*, of just happening to be there. It is a being-with that is possible, that exists and is sustained only as enacted love: as the love that, having been, is irrevocable; the love that is constant in remembrance; the love that trusts itself to the silent abyss of a future that only faith, hope, and love can fathom.[30]

---

[29]   N.A. Berdyaev, *Slavery and Freedom*, trans. R.M. French (London: G. Bles, 1943), p. 111. Some readers may recognize this as a passage I have quoted in several other works. I do so because I believe it is important and worthy of being reflected on. Cf. the saying attributed to the Hasidic master the Ball Shem Tov that 'Remembrance is the secret of redemption; forgetfulness leads to exile'.

[30]   In a recent article, Thomas A. Carlson attributes to Heidegger a view very similar to that which I have here developed *against* Heidegger. The article merits a fuller response than this brief note, although I would comment that with regard to the letters to Hannah Arendt that play an important part in building his case, letters from a professor to a student with whom he is having an affair should be read with a hermeneutics of extreme suspicion. That said, my argument is not that there are no possibilities for developing such a view in Heidegger, but that his work, especially *Being and Time*, also contain elements that, so to speak, suppress it at birth. Moreover, even when, as in other texts, he does speak of love, I am yet to be persuaded that it is love in which the real difference of the other comes decisively to view. See T.A. Carlson, 'Notes on Love and Death in Augustine and Heidegger' in *Medieval Mystical Theology* 21.1 (2012): 9–33.

Chapter 6
Language, Death, and the Eternal

From well before *Being and Time*, Heidegger had conducted his own 'linguistic turn', consistently emphasizing that the character of human being was indissociable from the phenomenon of language. The Aristotelian definition of human being as the *zōon logon echon* ('the living being having *logos*') accompanies his thought in almost the entirety of his paths of thinking. As he put it in his 1923–24 lectures on phenomenological research, 'Language (*Sprache*) is the being and becoming of human beings as such'.[1] 'Language' does not here carry the more restrictive sense it has in some twentieth-century philosophy and linguistics, merely what it means in 'average everyday' English, in which it also largely overlaps with 'language as it is spoke', i.e., 'speech' or 'discourse'. Thus, in lecturing in 1924 on the basic concepts of Aristotelian philosophy, Heidegger starts out from a rather straightforward interpretation of the Greek *logos* as, simply, 'speaking' (*sprechen*) or, more precisely, 'speaking about something', which is both a matter of speaking with others and self-expression (*Sich-selbst-aussprechen*). As such, 'Speaking out as "speaking about" is the basic manner of the being of life, i.e., of being-in-a-world'.[2] In speaking about something with others in this way, one also effects a kind of disclosure, letting what is at issue in the conversation be seen as it is (Heidegger references both *apophainesthai* and *dēloun*).

This interpretation of the Greek sense of *logos* is subsequently incorporated into *Being and Time*, where it becomes basic to his understanding of phenomenological method. How? Because, on the one hand, the term *phainomenon* derives from a root meaning 'that which is bright [i.e., luminous or shining] – in other words, that wherein something can become manifest, visible in itself' (28/51). Thus, 'phenomenon' 'signifies that which shows itself in itself, the manifest' (28/51). On the other hand, he says again that 'Logos as "discourse" means rather the same as *dēloun*: to make manifest what one is "talking about" in one's discourse'.[3] 'The logos lets something be seen' (32/56) – which, as Heidegger emphasizes, once more puts in play the verb *phainesthai*, from which the word 'phenomenon' itself is derived. Genuine discourse is itself therefore 'apophantic', a phenomenologization in which we are enabled to see *what* is being said from the very process of talking

---

[1] M. Heidegger, *Einführung in die phänomenologische Forschung. Gesamtausgabe*, vol. 17 (Frankfurt am Main: Klostermann, 1994), p. 16.

[2] M. Heidegger, *Grundbegriffe der aristotelischen Philosophie. Gesamtausgabe*, vol. 18 (Frankfurt am Main: Klostermann, 2006), p. 21.

[3] Heidegger notes but does not dwell on other kinds of *logos* that do not have this apophantic function, e.g., 'requesting'.

and in such a way that what one person says is disclosed or made accessible to others. This is, of course, very close to everyday usage in English and many other languages, where we speak of 'seeing' what has been said.

If, then, the capacity for *logos* is both a defining feature of being human and of the phenomenological method by which Heidegger hopes to make the meaning of being human manifest, while, at the same time, an authentic relation to the being of human being is only possible by virtue of a resolute running towards death, then it seems likely that there will be an 'intrinsic connection' between the themes of language and death, as the sub-title of Joachim Oberst's study *Heidegger on Language and Death* puts it. As Oberst points out, if, for Heidegger, 'to be a human is to speak' and, at the same time, 'only humans die' (as opposed to mere animal perishing or demise), then language and death must be mutually reinforcing elements in any Heideggerian understanding of being human, an understanding that Oberst finds summed up in another Heideggerian dictum: 'Mortals are, in that there is language'.[4] The interconnection is further spelled out in a key passage from the lecture 'On the Essence of Language', cited by Oberst, where Heidegger says that 'Mortals are those who are able to experience death as death. Animals cannot do this. Neither can animals speak. The essential connection between death and language flashes before us, but it as yet unthought'.[5] The adoption of the term 'mortals' for those 'able to experience death as death' (i.e., capable of running towards death) reflects the usage of the later Heidegger, to which we shall shortly return, but it could as well express the basic view of *Being and Time*. There, it will be recalled, Heidegger made clear that thrownness towards death was not just a matter of having to die at some future point in time but a defining feature of human existence from the moment of birth.

Despite Heidegger's own comment that 'the essential connection between death and language' is 'as yet unthought', he had himself been thinking about it for some considerable time, as is evidenced both by *Being and Time* and by several subsequent writings. This is no less true if it is addressed implicitly rather than explicitly – recall what *Being and Time* says about the reticence of those who, through attending to the silent call of conscience, have become resolute in running towards death. If there is a deliberate act of withholding going on here, we must therefore be chary of trying to say more than Heidegger says and doing so in such a way as to falsify his essential thought. As it will also be the aim of this chapter not only to interpret Heidegger but also to identify a critical disjunction between his view and that of Christian theology this is no mere rhetorical worry, since hearing what Heidegger says only slightly differently might well qualify this disjunction in important ways. But whether or not the understanding of language and death that emerges from the reading of Heidegger being offered here is a faithful statement

---

[4]   J. Oberst, *Heidegger on Language and Death: The Intrinsic Connection in Human Existence* (London: Continuum, 2009), pp. 97–8.

[5]   See Oberst, *Language and Death*, p. 4; M. Heidegger, *Unterwegs zur Sprache. Gesamtausgabe*, vol. 12 (Frankfurt am Main: Klostermann, 1985), p. 203.

of Heidegger's own 'last word' on the subject, it is an interpretation that is made possible by Heidegger's own writings and, in that sense at least, is 'Heideggerian'.

To arrive at the point at issue between the 'Heideggerian' view I shall present and the Christian theological view, I shall begin by going back to the theme of the silent call of conscience. We shall see that this in fact develops an understanding of the self as *called* that pre-dates *Being and Time* by at least 10 years. But, as we shall also see, it also continues to resonate (taking that word in its full sense) through many of his later writings, most explicitly in connection with his treatment of poetic calling, especially prominent in his writings on the poet Friedrich Hölderlin. These writings take us into a complex of issues that can be indicated in a preliminary way by reference to such themes as the gods, nature, silence, and the distinction between animal and human death. The outcome is a Heideggerian version of the classical question concerning 'the origin of language' as relating intimately to the specifically human way of experiencing death. However, this will also bring us back to the critical distinction between Heidegger's ontological question and the nature of human beings' mutual ethical obligations. And, as was the case with regard to ethics, we shall see that the Heideggerian account of the origin of language occludes what is an essentially threefold relationship, in that speech – like the ethical relationship – has a structure of answerability and other-relatedness that Heidegger does not sufficiently address, even though, as we have just seen, he was from an early point on aware that speaking was always speaking with one another and not mere soliloquizing.

This discussion, then, leads via the themes of language, death, and remembrance of the dead to the question as to what it might or could mean to speak of 'the eternal' in human life: can there be an 'eternal memory' of the lives of mortals, and what might such an 'eternal memory' be? This question, however, marks the beginning of a further enquiry and the limit point of this critical essay.

Who Shall I Say Is Calling?

In describing how Dasein can come into an authentic relation to its own distinctive way of being, Heidegger laid particular emphasis on the 'call of conscience' in which Dasein is called away from its lostness in the 'they–self' of '*das Man*' and towards its own anxious thrownness towards death. Yet, as we have seen, although this call is a form of discourse and therefore occurs as articulated speech, it calls precisely by being silent and its effect on those who hear its silent call is to imbue them with a certain reticence vis-à-vis the idle talk of average everyday discourse. As was noted in introducing Heidegger's treatment of conscience, there are several remarkable features to this account, not least the way in which Heidegger introduces it at just this point in his argument. For why or how might conscience – normally a concept associated with morality and the sense of right and wrong – help elucidate what it means for me to be thrown towards death? Surely this is a case of confusing essentially distinct spheres of discourse or language games?

However, this is no arbitrary move on Heidegger's part. Quite apart from the issue as to whether or in what way it reflects the association of guilt and death present in Christian teaching about the Fall,[6] the notion of *call* or *calling* is a persistent theme in Heidegger's thinking, from long before *Being and Time* and on into his later, post–World War II thinking. Let us hear again a passage from one of the letters to Elfride, from 1918, cited in connection with his reading of Dostoevsky:

> Instead of leading to a pure, empty 'I' the whole problem of the 'I' leads to the fulfilled and primordially living ['I'] and its constituent elements – the fulfilling of values grounded in essential openness to value, pointing back to the essence of personal Spirit that I have apprehended as 'Vocation' (*Berufung*) – only so do the eternal properties of the Spirit and their absolute confusion become conceivable – it is along these lines that the problems upon which I have hit while out here are moving, the carrying through of the principle of the historical consciousness – ...[7]

In the following years phrases such as 'the essence of eternal Spirit' and 'the eternal properties of the Spirit' disappear from Heidegger's vocabulary and have no role in *Being and Time*. Yet the notion of vocation, of the 'I' as primordially 'called' remains and comes to play a central and abiding role, most obviously in the discussion of conscience in *Being and Time* as well as in his later development.

But, as Heidegger himself asks, *who* exactly is it that calls when we feel ourselves called by conscience? On some theological and philosophical accounts it might be the voice of God or of reason, my 'true self' that invisibly presides over my every action. For Heidegger, however, God has been methodologically ruled out and, insofar as he might be prepared to talk of a 'true self' at all in *Being and Time*, this could only be the self that I am called, in conscience, to become – not an 'essential' self that somehow already exists in some ideal or metaphysical dimension of my being. That is to say, it is not so much the self that I *am* (present tense) but more the self that I am not-yet but must first become through resolutely running towards death. So who or what calls? His answer: '"It" calls, against our expectations and even against our will .... The call comes from me and yet from beyond me' (275/320). And, as he elaborates,

> The caller is Dasein in its state of homelessness: primordial, thrown Being-in-the-world as the "not-at-home" – the bare 'that-it-is' in the 'nothing' of the world. The caller is unfamiliar to the everyday they–self; it is something like an *alien* voice. What could be more alien to the "they", lost in the manifold 'world' of its concern, than the self which has been individualized down to itself in its state of homelessness and thrown into the "nothing"? (277/321–2 [adapted])

---

6   See Chapter 4 above.

7   G. Heidegger (ed.), *"Mein liebes Seelchen!" Briefe Martin Heideggers an seine Frau Elfride 1915–1970* (Munich: Deutsche-Verlags-Anstalt, 2005), p. 87.

What 'calls' is the bare realization of the utter destitution, ontological homelessness, and solitude of the self as thrown towards death. What calls, in other words, is, simply, the truth of the human condition, when all the pleasant or terrifying masks of average everydayness have been stripped away. This is what we are called to see and it is in the light of this truth that we are 'called' to live.

This analysis also provides Heidegger with a critical perspective on the kind of promotion of the 'I' (the 'egology') that he saw in German Idealism from Fichte through to Schelling. Fichte's 'I' is the epitome of an 'I' that has no sense of being called or commanded: it is in and of itself sovereign, productive of both its self and its world. Even what it experiences in the mode of passivity or affection is, on Fichte's analysis, posited by the 'I' itself, an 'I' that, like the scholastic God, is pure activity. But, as we have seen, it was precisely this that Heidegger – following Kierkegaard, amongst others – saw as deeply problematic, a mere assertion (or *Machtanspruch*) on the part of subjective reason. For Heidegger – and this is essential to the whole notion of the self as thrown towards death – the 'I' is bound to a situation that it has not itself produced and that renders its entire existence ineluctably finite. I have already registered the critical comment that this misidentifies the primary source of our being beholden to a Not-I and if, as I have argued, we see this primary source in terms of the ethical claim of the other rather than thrownness towards death, then talk of being 'called' seems more appropriate.[8] How can death, how can 'nothing' *call*? With what *voice* could death, could nothing, *call*? But others certainly can, and often do, do just that, calling upon us to help, to care, or to share a joy.

I shall return to the specific relationship between death and calling, but, first, it will be helpful to explore further the idea of calling itself, with particular reference to what, for Heidegger, is the eminent instance of calling: poetic vocation.

It is a widely acknowledged feature of Heidegger's development after *Being and Time* that, from the early 1930s onwards the idea of the poetic and the figure of the poet, above all the poet Friedrich Hölderlin, become recurrent foci in his thinking. Distancing his own understanding of the poetic from contemporary ideas about how the creative artist 'expresses' *deep* inner experiences,[9] Heidegger looks for the essence of the poetic in the nature of the poetic word. And what he sees is closely connected to the account we have already heard him give of *logos*. Referring to the Greek verb *deichnumi* he suggests that the poetic word means 'to point, to make something visible, to reveal it, albeit indeed not in its entirety but according to a way of showing that is one's own (*eigen*)'.[10] In these terms, the figure of the poet emerges in Heidegger's thought as the one in whose word the essence of language (*Sprache*) is pre-eminently manifest. And, given everything we have by now heard about the centrality of language in human Dasein, this

---

[8]   See Chapter 3 above.

[9]   See my *Routledge Philosophy Guidebook to the Later Heidegger* (London: Routledge, 2000), pp. 78–83.

[10]   M. Heidegger, *Hölderlins Hymnen 'Germanien' und 'Der Rhein'. Gesamtausgabe*, vol. 39 (Frankfurt am Main: Klostermann, 1989), p. 29.

means that the poet is also the one in whose word the being of human being is itself revealed in a distinctive and eminent degree.[11] But the capacity for effecting such manifestation is not to be understood as a simple attribute of the 'I' or of some peculiarly gifted 'I's. The poetic revelation is not a subjective way of looking but arises out of the poet being gripped by the encompassing power of beings themselves.[12] It is not a matter of genius but of attentiveness to what language, what the word, is always and everywhere saying to us. The poet is not simply a 'creator' (as in the Fichtean–Romantic concept of poetic genius) but speaks only by virtue of being *called*.

This is especially clearly developed in Heidegger's 1942 lectures on Hölderlin's poem 'The Ister' (from its Greek name *Istros*). The poem opens with the poet's invocation to the rising sun: 'Now come, Fire!/ We are desirous/ Of seeing the day'. Heidegger immediately draws attention to the meaning of the call articulated in these few simple words. '[T]his calling', he says, 'is different from the issuing of any high-handed summons or command'[13] since

> The call simultaneously calls upon that which is called, such invocation attesting to the dignity of that which is called upon. Here that which is to come comes of its own accord. It is not the call that first moves that which is coming to its coming. Yet if 'the fire' comes of its own accord, then why is it called? The call does not effect the coming. Yet it calls something to that which is coming. What does it call to it?[14]

In answer to this question Heidegger directs us to the second and third lines of the poem ('We are desirous/ Of seeing the day'), in which the poet speaks of his and his audience's desire to see the coming day. Heidegger interprets this in the sense of the poet speaking on behalf of or as the voice of those who await the coming of the sun to say that they are now ready. But, he adds, they are ready 'only because [they] are called by the coming fire itself'. That is to say, their readiness to greet the day is not a spontaneous manifestation of their inner life but is possible only because they know themselves *called* to welcome the day, 'called by the coming fire itself'. Consequently, 'the ones calling here are those who are called, those who are called upon ... those summoned to hear because they are of such a vocation'[15] – that is, the vocation of the poetic word itself. 'Only those

---

[11]   This seems to suggest that Heidegger has now shifted his starting point from that of the experience of average everydayness. However, as we shall see, the apparent 'Romantic' elevation of the poet is not incompatible with a celebration of the more humble and 'homely' dialect poet Peter Hebbel.

[12]   Heidegger, *'Germanien'*, p. 89.

[13]   M. Heidegger, *Hölderlin's Hymn 'The Ister'*, trans. W. McNeill and J. Davis (Bloomington: Indiana University Press, 1996), p. 6 (GA53, p. 5).

[14]   Heidegger, *'The Ister'*, p. 6 (GA53, pp. 5–6).

[15]   Ibid., p. 7 (GA53, p. 6).

called to a calling can truly call: "come". And this calling that is called alone has a proper necessity to it'. And, in a comment to which we shall shortly have occasion to return, 'This call remains infinitely distinct from what we name a blindly uttered cry'.[16] Such a poetic calling, in which we are called so as to become capable of calling upon, is paradigmatic for the primordial event of the arising of language as distinct from the utterance of a mere cry. But such an arising of language is in turn is inseparable from the event of the arising of the human: in the moment in which the cry becomes a word, the animal becomes human. As Heidegger's closing pages emphasize, the poet is therefore the one who, through his word, creates a place for human dwelling on earth.[17] But although the poet and the poetic word thus acquire a privileged status in Heidegger's thought, it is important to emphasize again that what is revealed in poetic discourse is the power of the word as such, that is, the power that brings human being itself into the light of self-awareness and, in doing so, makes us truly human – 'us' as in 'all of us' and not just the privileged creator-self of Fichtean Romanticism.

The philosophical point that language demands our being able to listen to what calls to us from beyond our subjective 'I' is developed more formally in the 1957 lecture on 'The Principle of Identity', where Heidegger (once more) rejects the Fichtean formulation of the principle of the identity of thought and being, A=A, whilst arguing that, nevertheless, human thinking *belongs* to being, and belongs to being precisely by virtue of our capacity to listen to being and thus to *hear* it. Heidegger's move here – from identity to belonging – is predicated on the metaphoric (but not merely metaphoric) force of the German word translated here as 'to belong', *gehören*, incorporating the verb *hören*, to hear. Human beings belong to being by hearing it. The following passage from the lecture merits being read against the background of the commentary on poetic vocation in 'The Ister':

> To 'belong' [to be one who listens] here still means to be in the order of Being. But man's distinctive feature lies in this, that he, as one who thinks, is open to Being, face to face with being; thus man remains referred to being and so answers to [literally: 'speaks out from' or 'cor*responds* to': *entspricht*] Being, and he is only this. This 'only' does not mean a limitation, but rather an excess. A belonging to Being prevails within man, a belonging which listens to Being because it is appropriated to Being.[18]

Of course, this passage raises its own further questions, but it enables us to see how Heidegger's meditations on the nature of the poetic word are formative in developing the interconnected themes of being, being human, and language that increasingly shape his later philosophy.

---

[16]   Ibid., p. 8 (GA53, p. 7).

[17]   Ibid., pp. 126ff. (GA53, pp. 182ff.).

[18]   M. Heidegger, *Identity and Difference*, trans. J. Stambaugh ([Dual language edition] New York: Harper and Row, 1969), pp. 31, 94 (GA11, p. 39).

But if the poetic has to do with the basic making-manifest of our human way of being, how does this relate to the question of death?

In *Introduction to Metaphysics* (1935), Heidegger addresses the question of being under a sequence of headings: being and becoming, being and appearance, being and thinking, and being and 'the ought'. In the section on being and thinking, he takes his listeners back to the first chorus from Sophocles' *Antigone*, a poetic reflection on the mystery of human existence. In one widely used English translation this opens with the lines 'Wonders are many on earth, and the greatest of these is man'.[19] Heidegger's own translation strikes a rather different tone: 'Manifold is the uncanny [*Unheimliche*]; yet nothing more uncanny bestirs itself with greater fury than the human'.[20] Heidegger's 'uncanny' echoes what we have already heard from *Being and Time* about the uncanniness of human existence in its thrownness towards death. Existence is uncanny/*unheimlich*, that is, lacking a sense of being at home, in the specific sense that human beings are ontologically homeless in the world and have neither a 'home' nor an abiding dwelling on earth. So too here. It is precisely the *dis*location of human existence that Heidegger hears in Sophocles' poem, as it describes human beings' ability to transcend any purely given environment, subordinating the earth, traversing land and sea, mastering the animal world. But, both in the poem and in Heidegger's interpretation, this 'uncanny' power is exemplified not only in human beings' physical dominion over the earth but also, pre-eminently, in the human capacity for language. Although we may have dominion over ocean, earth, and animal, we would never be conscious of what this dominion meant and we would never know the ocean *as* ocean, the earth *as* earth, or the animal *as* animal without 'the powers of language, understanding, attunement and building'. In other words, these latter powers are themselves the conditions of our wider dominion over the earth. This leads Heidegger to speak of poetic discourse as an 'exercise of force' (*Gewalttätigkeit* – which we could also translate as 'violence'), which he explains as the 'binding and connecting of the forces by means of which beings disclose themselves as such when human beings step forward into their domain'.[21] Human beings' homelessness, their not being bound to any one place or any one environment, is also their power to reach out in action and understanding to any possible earthly environment. Uprooted from their place in 'nature' their 'uncanny' power seems to know no natural boundaries.

'There is just one thing with regard to which their exercise of power is immediately frustrated' however.[22] And that, as Sophocles' poem reminds us and Heidegger repeats, is death. But this is not an accidental feature of our existence nor even just a boundary at which we will arrive one day in the future. 'Human beings

---

[19] Sophocles, *The Theban Plays*, trans. E.F. Watling (Harmondsworth: Penguin, 1947), p. 148.

[20] M. Heidegger, *Einführung in die Metaphysik. Gesamtausgabe*, vol. 40 (Frankfurt am Main: Klostermann, 1983), p. 155.

[21] Heidegger, *Einführung*, p. 166.

[22] Ibid., p. 167.

are not only faced ineluctably by death when the time comes for them to die, but constantly and essentially', Heidegger says.[23] 'Insofar as human beings *are*, they stand in relation to the ineluctability of death. Thus [human] being-there [Da-sein] is the happening of the un-canny [*Un-heimlichkeit*] itself .... In naming this power and this uncanniness the poetic word projects their proper boundaries to being and to the essence of being human'.[24] Human beings, sovereign over everything else, are not sovereign over death. But, when it is uttered in the poetic word (or, perhaps more precisely, *as* a poetic word), death ceases to be a mere contingency affecting us from outside; even the boundary that death sets to life can then become a human 'project'. This is because in the poetic word, which is the Ur-word of human language as such, we can 'speak' death and represent it in and as a human *logos*. And although, *of course* (and as Heidegger repeatedly insists), we are not to understand this in terms of the pure activity and creativity of the Fichtean–Romantic subject, this means that death is no mere passivity to be endured. Even as setting a limit to all human power, death becomes, through the poetic word, a human, humanizing, and humanized event.

Here, in a new key, we encounter again the pattern laid down in *Being and Time*'s account of anticipatory resoluteness and here as there we see again a structure that both repeats and critiques the central tendencies of German Idealism. In as far as it repeats these tendencies, it is also open to analogous criticisms and perhaps not least the criticism that, in the end, it conjures away the ineluctable passivity of death and transmutes it into human action under the guise of 'the word'. However, this is not to say that what Heidegger is saying in his new key is merely 'the same' as what he said in *Being and Time* only differently 'illustrated'. By saying it differently, Heidegger also obliges his readers to formulate their response differently. Consequently, I shall now attempt to develop a critical response to the later Heidegger's 'poetic' account of death that takes seriously his own new idiom. My question, then, is this: what – or who – is calling in the call that calls the poet to speak the word in which even death is 'mastered' and made 'our own'? Is there anything in this calling more than the compelling power of a vision of human being as ontologically destitute in its thrownness towards death? Is death not only what we are given to see in the poetic word but also what originally calls it forth?

As is often the case when it is a matter of the poetic, the question is most readily pursued in relation to Heidegger's reading of Hölderlin. One – of several – passages that he sees as especially focussing the essence of the poetic vocation is from the poem 'As on a Feast-Day' (here in a prose translation): 'Yet to us, Oh poets, is due the task of standing with uncovered heads beneath God's thunder, taking in our hands the Father's own ray, that very one, and offering the heavenly gift to the people, enclosed in song'. As Heidegger comments, 'The poet forces and binds the

---

23   Ibid.
24   Ibid.

divine lightning in a word and places this word, burdened with lightning, into the language of his people'.[25]

This reveals a further dimension of the understanding of poetic vocation that we encountered in 'The Ister'. There it was the rising sun that 'called' the poet to readiness; now it is the divine thunder and lightning. In these, as in other examples, the poetic task is intimately connected with what we might call the human mediation of nature. Nor is it coincidental in this connection that several of Heidegger's lecture series focus on poems invoking the German land and the great rivers, the Rhine and the Danube, that moulded the land so as to make it a place in which the wandering Germanic tribes might dwell. The 'divinity' that speaks in the thunder and lightning is the divinity of the super-human powers that, in the Alpine storms that generate torrents and lakes, originate the rivers that, in turn, form the earth into a habitable land for mortal dwelling – although, as Heidegger consistently emphasizes, it is only in the poetic naming of these powers that mortal dwelling becomes genuinely human. But, this all the more sharpens my initial question: *who* then calls in the calling? If we name thunder, lightning, and sun as divine or semi-divine powers, does that of itself make them a 'who'? And for us moderns, who, as Heidegger also emphasizes (and precisely with reference to Hölderlin), have experienced the flight of the gods, does it really make any difference if we name these powers Zeus or Apollo? Is this not, dare we say, a 'merely poetical' way of speaking of indifferent worldly powers that, in Matthew Arnold's words, have 'really neither joy, nor love, nor light,/ Nor certitude, nor peace, nor help for pain'.[26]

Yet it would be a mistake to imagine that Heidegger's Hölderlinian vision is simply a vision of an enchanted or re-enchanted world. Even when it is 'enclosed in song', the divine gift exceeds all human understanding and to hear the thunder as the voice of God is by no means to succumb naively to the pathetic fallacy. Nor is it an unmixed blessing. It would be all too human if, in receiving this gift, the poet were to flinch from it, since, as Heidegger further comments, 'Thunder and lightning are the language of the gods, and the poet is the one who, without flinching, holds out in this language'.[27] These are vast, terrifying, and superhuman manifestations of power and human beings are scarcely able to bear the sublime terror they induce. And yet, even as he is exposed in all his bare humanity to these awe-inspiring powers, the poet is who he is, a poet, because, at the same time, he *speaks* them forth.

The poet's speech will therefore bear within it the mark of his suffering under the burden of his divine message. But this is not all. He must also suffer in so far as the world to which he must speak his word, the world of his contemporary human beings, is, for Heidegger's Hölderlin, a world from which the old gods have fled.

---

[25]   Heidegger, 'Germanien', p. 30.

[26]   Quoted from M. Arnold, 'Dover Beach' in M. Allott (ed.), *Matthew Arnold* (Oxford: Oxford University Press [Oxford Poetry Library], 1995, lines 33–4.

[27]   Heidegger, *'Germanien'*, p. 31.

It is in fact a disenchanted and de-divinized world, so the poet has to bear not only the contradiction of divine power and human existence but also the anguish of the incomprehensibility of that same divine power. The divine word is not in and for itself a human word and the poet is the one who, in speaking the divine word as a human word lives with the stress of this contradiction.[28] And, in the modern world (as we have seen in Chapter 3), the new form of the novel has, as it were, flooded the landscape of literary discourse and, in so doing, inaugurated a world in which speech is polyphonic, unfinalizable, and dialectically ambiguous. The luminosity of poetic speech is dissolved into the chiaroscuro of manifold shades of grey and, as Hegel predicted, beautiful ideals must yield to the prose of everyday life. In this context the madness of Hölderlin is more than a merely biographical–psychological fact. Poetic vocation can never shake off the accompanying shadow of the impossibility of speech, that is, the impossibility of *its* speech. Because its task is to speak forth what, from a certain angle, cannot be said, poetic speech is therefore also inevitably accompanied by a certain silence.

The intertwining of speech, silence, and suffering is revisited by Heidegger in his 1950 lecture 'Language' (*Die Sprache*). This time, it is not Hölderlin whose work provides Heidegger's focus but another poet whom we have already briefly encountered in connection with Heidegger's reading of *Der Brenner*, namely, Georg Trakl, and the poem in question is 'On a Winter Evening'. The poem evokes a scene in which, on a snowy winter's evening, as the vesper bell rings, a wanderer arrives at a well-lit house in which bread and wine are laid out on the table. Expounding the poem line by line, Heidegger comes to the words 'Pain turned the threshold to stone' ('*Schmerz versteinerte die Schwelle*'), which, he says, enunciate the meaning of the poem as a whole. Why? Because the threshold is the dividing line between outside and inside, between the cold, winter world of the wanderer and the welcoming brightness of the house with its simply yet festally decked table. 'The threshold bears the "between"', Heidegger writes.[29] But what does this mean and what does it have to do with pain? Paraphrasing Heidegger, I suggest that his argument is as follows. Human beings exist in the world as conscious of their distinction from it or, as we have heard Heidegger repeatedly say, as conscious that they are not at home in it. This not-being-at-home in the world is itself an expression of the anxious realization of being thrown towards death and, right from the beginning of their lives, human beings are aware of themselves as being thrown beyond their world into annihilation. The threshold that separates the warmth and luminosity of the home from the cold night outside is thus essentially ambivalent. On the one hand, it offers those wandering in the night the possibility of welcome and it is precisely at the threshold, Heidegger

---

[28] In another perspective this makes Heidegger's poet somewhat analogous to the paradoxical Christ of Kierkegaard's *Philosophical Fragments*. For discussion, see my article 'Heidegger's Hölderlin and Kierkegaard's Christ' in S. Mulhall (ed.), *Martin Heidegger* (Aldershot: Ashgate, 2006), pp. 391–404.

[29] M. Heidegger, *Unterwegs zur Sprache*, p. 24.

says, that the 'pure brightness' of this welcome shines forth. Yet the threshold also marks the fact that the home is only a local and provisional possibility within the encompassing night. For every 'inside' there is also an 'outside'. Recognition of the threshold is thus also recollection of the ultimate limitations of the human situation. To put it at its simplest, no matter how deeply 'at home' we are in our world, the threshold is a constant reminder that a time will come when we will be carried over it for the last time, 'feet first'.[30]

Heidegger also takes up a line of thought suggested by the mention of pain. What is pain? he asks. His answer is that it is 'the tear' (in the sense of 'rip' or 'rending'). Pain rips existence apart but not – at least not when gathered into and articulated in the poetic word – so as to shatter it into innumerable splinters. For even in the experience of pain I still experience myself and my world, but I experience them and their relationship precisely as pain. If I could leave my world behind or if the world would only leave me alone, then there would be no more pain. But that is not possible. I am who and as I am by virtue of my being in the world, tied to the finitude of this mortal body. But having to hold self and world together in their centripetal drive towards separation is, precisely, pain. In this way pain is the condition of there being a complex and articulated world, a world to which I can only relate in a manifold of concrete and particular contingencies. As Heidegger puts it, the pure light of welcome spoken in the word, in *this* poetic word, is what summons our world and the things that compose it into their actual and specific form.[31] Trakl's line 'calls world and things to the midst of their inner relatedness. The conjunction of their [being] towards one another is pain'.[32] Yet the poetic word, as word, speaks the pain that is integral to the existence of a complex world in which we ourselves also exist as radically contingent entities in such a way as to enable us to endure it. It brings the turbulence of our world to rest and gathers its manifold competing elements into articulate speech. It is therefore this play of difference that calls the world to unity even in the moment of its being torn apart into multiplicity.

Such a calling, Heidegger says, 'is sounding forth', but, as word, it sounds forth by calling to presence what is otherwise unspoken, that is, what is essentially silent. So, in a much-quoted statement, Heidegger writes that 'Language speaks as the re-sonance of silence' ('*das Geläut der Stille*').[33] And, in the paragraphs that follow, he further specifies that this is where we are to seek another key concept of his later thought: the *Ereignis* or 'event of appropriation' in which human beings and their world belong together through the listening utterance of the word. But, as this passage also emphasizes, this belonging-together occurs to human beings

---

[30] This is not Heidegger's expression but, I think, suggests his meaning.

[31] The 'light of welcome' can perhaps be glossed as the *lumen naturalis*, that is, human beings' basic capacity for making sense of the world into which they are thrown – cf. *Being and Time* 133/171.

[32] Heidegger, *Unterwegs zur Sprache*, p. 25.

[33] Ibid., p. 27.

precisely as mortals. 'Only in so far as human beings belong within the re-sonance of silence, are mortals capable, in their fashion, of resonant speech'.[34]

But does any of this suggest to us that there is some*one* who calls in this 'calling'? As when considering the silent call of conscience, the question inevitably arises as to whether there really is anything that 'calls' other than the compelling vision of our own mortality. Isn't even poetic speaking – and perhaps especially poetic speaking – therefore also speaking that bears within itself and knows the pain of finitude *and nothing more*? And isn't this still the case even if, qua poetry, it also bestows on that pain a form that enables us to bear it and even, as it is said, 'rise above it'? But no matter how 'poetic', isn't this, in the end, an essentially tragic view of life – even if it can inculcate in those who embrace it a certain quiet reverence for Being?[35] Is it ultimately anything more than an ennobling of the animal fear of death by confronting it and saying 'Yes' to it?[36]

In his *Language and Death*, where he explores the relationship flagged in his title with primary reference to Hegel and Heidegger, Giorgio Agamben cites a remarkable passage in Hegel's *Jena Realphilosophie* in which the German philosopher speaks of how the animal can be said to acquire a voice in the face of death, as when it cries out in terror at its imminent demise.[37] Yet this 'voice' is merely 'a vanishing trace'; it expresses 'the power of the negative' but it is not yet meaningful, articulated speech. Language only becomes meaningful in Hegelian terms when it makes manifest the life of the Spirit that not only confronts the advent of death but 'is maintained in death' and 'converts the negative into being'. In other words, whereas the animal merely cries out, the human being exists as and by virtue of being a spiritual entity that knows its own death and understands itself and its life in the light of this knowledge.[38] The voice is eminently suited to be the organ of such knowledge since it exists only 'in the element of air' and has no abiding substantial being.[39] As pure 'intention to signify' and 'prior to any

---

[34]   Ibid., p. 28.

[35]   As James Demske points out, it is not accidental that Heidegger orientates himself towards a poetic understanding of death by referencing Sophoclean tragedy and that this generates a sense of reverence for Being (J.M. Demske, *Sein, Mensch und Tod. Der Todesproblem bei Martin Heidegger* [Freiburg/Munich: Karl Alber, 1963], pp. 116–17).

[36]   Which we could gloss by saying that if death is the limit of our animal life it is not the limit of our human life but, in the word, its beginning.

[37]   It is unclear from Agamben's quotation whether this refers to, e.g., the cry of the prey fleeing the predator or something more like the 'swansong' in which the animal – here the bird – anticipates its death in a unique vocalization of its inner life and feeling. In this context, however, perhaps either would do equally well.

[38]   G. Agamben, *Language and Death: The Place of Negativity. Theory and History of Literature*, vol. 8, trans. K.E. Pinkus and M. Hardt (Minneapolis: University of Minnesota Press, 1991), pp. 41–6. This closely correlates with Kojève's view of the interrelationship of language, Spirit, and death in Hegel (see Chapter 2, n. 28, above).

[39]   Hegel, cited in Agamben, *Language and Death*, p. 42.

categorical significance' the voice is itself 'nothing'[40] and, as such, it manifests a 'pure will to understand' that gives the freedom also to think death and in this way to enable the human being to *die* and not merely perish as the beasts of the field.[41]

Yet, if we follow Agamben's reading of Heidegger on this point, it surely all the more reinforces the suggestion that what we are being offered is, in the end, a tragic view of life. If giving voice to the consciousness of death in this way coincides with the moment of hominization in which human beings first become fully human and are able truly to be *there* (i.e., to be Da-sein), then it seems that the voice that enables such consciousness to find articulate expression has no ground other than the unmotivated flow of life itself, with 'neither joy, nor love'. It may articulate and in articulating also bestow a certain dignity on our vanishing existence, but to the question 'What am I?' does it really offer any other answer than the answer that Tennyson's 'In Memoriam' sets out to refute: 'An infant crying in the night:/ An infant crying for the light:/ And with no language but a cry'?[42]

A philosophy that neither claims nor calls upon religious faith may be content to humble itself under such self-knowledge and this is certainly not a contemptible position.[43] However, a Christian view of life will also want to speak of another possibility. For if Heidegger is right and we exist by virtue of a certain calling, can this make any sense except on the basis of believing that we are called by one who, no less than we ourselves are, is a personal being and, as such and only as such, is able to call us by name, whether in admonition ('Adam, where art thou?'), in the summons to service ('Samuel! Samuel!'), or the call to worship ('Hear, O Israel')? How can we be *called* unless there is one who *calls*, unless there is a 'who' and not just an 'It'? But whether with regard to the call of conscience or the divine thunder, Heidegger's construal of the source of the call cannot be envisaged as a 'who'. I have argued that Heidegger's 'god' is not a god who speaks but a god who thunders and whose voice must be translated from a realm beyond that of humanity and human speech into the language of articulate discourse. And if the Hebrew Bible also speaks of a God who speaks in the thunder and the whirlwind, it never speaks of the thunder and the whirlwind as constituting the divine voice but only ever as that in which and out of which the divine voice speaks.

We are speaking 'mythologically', of course, and do so in order to respond to Heidegger in the terms set up by his own modelling of poetic vocation. But, of course, simply to pit a Jewish or Christian God who speaks against a pagan Heideggerian god who 'speaks' only in a metaphorical sense is merely to stake out a polemically defined point of opposition. In fact, Christian theology is itself

---

[40]   Ibid., pp. 32–6.

[41]   Ibid., p. 59.

[42]   Quoted from A. Lord Tennyson, 'In Memoriam', Canto 54 in C. Ricks (ed.), *Tennyson: A Selected Edition* (London: Pearson Longman, 2007), p. 396.

[43]   Cf. Demske's comment on 'reverence for being' in n. 35 above. See also the concluding comment of G. Steiner's *Heidegger* (London: Fontana, 1978), p. 150: 'There are meaner metaphors to live by'.

aware – how could it not be – of the difficulties and paradoxes of speaking of God as a God who speaks.[44] Karl Barth's meditations on the transcendence of the Word of God over any human word or any manifold of human words have been paradigmatic for much modern theology. As such they have also been seen as issuing in a position not without analogy to deconstruction. The Word of God cannot 'speak' to us except in the form of human words, yet all human words must confess that they are not the Word of God and do so precisely in the moment of being spoken as the Word of God.[45] Heidegger's sometime colleague Rudolf Bultmann too emphasized that the Word of God qua word can only be spoken as a human word, as a word spoken by one human being to another and, consequently, only as Word Incarnate, unadorned with 'radiant, mysterious, or fascinating' properties.[46] Like Kierkegaard's Christ, such a one is necessarily 'incognito'. Yet, running on to questions concerning revelation and the Incarnation takes us a step beyond the ground on which we are seeking to engage Heidegger, although such a step may indicate the direction in which a further theological *Auseinandersetzung* with his thought might wish to proceed. For now, however, we shall continue to attempt to meet Heidegger, as far as possible, on his own ground, namely, the experience of the poet who, open to the sublime powers of the natural world, hears in them the divine voice and, by making that same divine voice speak his own human, poetic words, brings himself and those for whom and to whom he speaks into a truly human relation to the world.

In this spirit, then, I take as a critical counter to Heidegger's Hölderlin the poet described in Kierkegaard's three late (1849) upbuilding discourses collectively entitled *The Lily of the Field and the Bird of the Air* or, individually, 'Silence', 'Obedience', and 'Joy'.[47] Like the Romantic poets, Kierkegaard too liked to go out into nature, to be alone with the birds and the flowers and, under the guidance of the Sermon on the Mount, he wrote many religious discourses on 'The Lilies of the Field and the Birds of the Air' of which the 1849 discourses are perhaps the most concise. But if talk of 'lilies and birds' already seems to be some way from Heidegger's thunder and lightning, it should be said that Kierkegaard too speaks here of the raging sea and the wind howling in the forest, that is, of the sublime power and not just of the beauty or charm of 'nature'. Pointedly, Kierkegaard's

---

[44] The same, mutatis mutandis, is true for Jewish theology.

[45] See K. Barth, *Church Dogmatics*, vol. 1: *The Doctrine of the Word of God, Part 1*, trans. G.W. Bromiley (London: T. & T. Clark, 2004), especially §5, pp. 125–86. See also G. Ward, *Barth, Derrida, and the Language of Theology* (Cambridge: Cambridge University Press, 1995).

[46] See R. Bultmann, *Das Evangelium des Johannes* (Göttingen: Vandenhoeck and Ruprecht, 1950), p. 40.

[47] However, I would emphasize that it is *Heidegger*'s Hölderlin and not Hölderlin himself that is at issue here. There are certainly more Christian elements in Hölderlin than Heidegger is prepared to acknowledge, although interpreting their force and extent is another matter again. See again my 'Heidegger's Hölderlin and Kierkegaard's Christ'.

theme in these discourses is the contrast between the different ways in which the poet and the gospel speak about nature. The poet goes no further than the desire to be like the lilies and the birds. Entranced by the joy he hears pouring forth from the bird, he too aches to sing such a song. In a Kierkegaardian perspective, however, such a song really is no more than 'an infant crying in the night' and, as in Hölderlin's experience of destitution, it is also a song that is incomprehensible to a world from which the gods have flown. The gospel, by way of contrast, demands that we do indeed become like the lilies and the birds: silent, obedient, and joyful – and it believes we can do so. But, as the discourses on silence and obedience especially emphasize, this is only possible if we learn not only to be silent but also to attend to what is being said to us in silence.[48]

How might we do that? Unlike the lilies and the birds, which merely are what and as they are and which fulfil God's purpose for them by being what and as they are, we human beings are able to choose who we are – or, for that matter, to choose not to be who we are and to try to become something or someone else and to flee from ourselves in bad faith and inauthenticity. The self-relation inherent in our human way of being means that if we are to be more than we are and all that we might be we must want that 'more'. But such 'wanting' (Kierkegaard elsewhere calls it 'needing God') is already, in Kierkegaard's view, a kind of prayer – for what, in the end, is prayer but the articulation of what we really, most deeply, and most passionately want yet cannot give ourselves? But if we conventionally think of prayer as a form of words, Kierkegaard suggests that true prayer, the prayer that we learn from the lilies and the birds, means to fall silent. As he writes,

> May the gospel, helped by the lily and the bird, nevertheless succeed in teaching you seriousness, my listener – and me – so as to make you utterly silent before God. And, in silence, may it lead you to forget yourself, forget what you yourself are called, forget your own name, whether it is a renowned or an ignominious or an insignificant name, in order silently to pray to God, 'hallowed be *Your* name'! And, in silence, may it bring you to forget yourself, your plans, whether they are great schemes that encompass everything or so narrow as only to concern yourself and your future, in order to silently pray to God, '*Your* Kingdom come'. And, in silence, may it bring you to forget your will, your willfulness, in order to silently pray '*Your* will be done'. Yes – if you could learn from the lily and the bird to be utterly silent before God there are no limits to what the gospel can help you achieve, for nothing would then be impossible for you.[49]

---

[48]   On the relationship between these discourses and Romantic poetic ideals, see my article 'The Joy of Birdsong or Dialectical Lyrics' in R.L. Perkins (ed.), *International Kierkegaard Commentary*, vol. 10: *Without Authority* (Macon: Mercer University Press, 2007), pp. 11–26.

[49]   S. Kierkegaard, *Lilien paa Marken og Fuglen under Himlen. Søren Kierkegaards Skrifter*, vol. 11 (Copenhagen: Gad, 2006), p. 24; *Kierkegaard's Spiritual Writings*, trans. G. Pattison (New York: Harper, 2010), pp. 193–4.

But is Kierkegaard's Christian not then in the same situation as the Heideggerian poet whose word is, literally at best, the re-sonance of silence? Isn't such a Christian's prayer an echo, in speech, of a seriousness that is found only in silence, silence such as that of the lily and the bird or of the raging sea or the storm-tossed forest? But Kierkegaard has a further gloss on the silence of nature that casts this in a somewhat different light from what we hear in Heidegger. For Kierkegaard's nature is precisely *creation* and its silence a silence *before God*:

> Out there with the lily and the bird is silence. But what does this silence express? It expresses reverence for God and the fact that He is the One who governs and it is to Him alone that wisdom and understanding belong. And it is precisely because this silence reverences God and, in a manner proper to nature, worships Him, that it is so solemn. And it is because this silence is thus solemn that it is possible to sense God in nature – and so it is no wonder that everything keeps silent out of reverence for Him. Even if *He* does not speak, the fact that everything keeps silent out of reverence for Him affects one as if He were speaking.[50]

No more than Heidegger's god, does Kierkegaard's God speak directly, in human words, and yet this God's basic relation to creation, human and non-human, is describable as speech. Consequently, in falling silent and listening to what speaks in the silence of nature, the Kierkegaardian Christian listens, in faith, to one who may indeed and in the fullest sense of the word, *call* to him or her.

The distinction at issue here has been well stated by Jean-Louis Chrétien in the chapter 'The Hospitality of Silence' in his book *The Ark of Speech*. Here he proposes that only 'a creature of speech' (such as the human being) can fall silent: 'silence cannot manifest itself ... except to someone who is able to speak'. And, he continues, speech itself 'comes from the silence that always precedes it ... it accompanies silence, for while it is being uttered, it needs the noises all around and the lips of the other whom it is addressing to be silent: it tends towards silence, which alone can ratify that it has in truth said something and which allows the other to speak ....'[51] Thus far, thus Heideggerian, we may say. But Chrétien further distinguishes between the kind of mystical silence found in neo-Platonism (in Plotinus, for example), in which the aim of the soul is to accommodate itself to an impersonal divine order and the kind of silence that really involves a *listening to*.[52] It is this quality of silent attentiveness that also distinguishes true speech from what we have heard Heidegger describe as 'idle talk', since 'To listen in silence, with all my silence, such indeed is the preface to every speech that is not mere chatter'.[53] Yet this also means that the one to whom we attend in genuine

---

[50] S. Kierkegaard, *Lilien paa Marken*, p. 22; *Kierkegaard's Spiritual Writings*, p. 191.

[51] J.-L. Chrétien, *The Ark of Speech*, trans. A. Brown (London: Routledge, 2004), p. 39.

[52] Chrétien suggests that these are reflected in two quite distinct Greek words, respectively, *siōpē* and *sigē*.

[53] Chrétien, *The Ark of Speech*, p. 57.

silence must, by the same measure, be one who is capable of speaking and, we may say, *calling*. Prayer, even silent prayer then, is not simply 'contemplation' but 'a silence that is offered ... to the one God who listens and sees, and not to a blind, anonymous Absolute ... [it is] a naked appearance before the Word ... whose grace alone is what has made such dispositions possible in us'.[54] Again, this is contrasted with the silence of Plotinus that, Chrétien suspects, 'is surreptitiously nothing more than the adoration of the negation that suppresses our speech and thereby also our silence'.[55] Christian silence, at least, is not simply a negation practiced upon our cognitive capacities: it is the silence of love, that is, of attention to and waiting upon the speech of the other.

In these terms, the silence of the thunder, the lightning, and the rising sun in which the Heideggerian poet is called to his vocation resembles the Plotinian silence more than the Christian – which is, perhaps, scarcely surprising. But whilst this is not to belittle Heidegger's silence, and whilst such a silence might reveal and instruct us in reverence for being, can it teach us love?

We seem to have arrived at a critical point essentially similar to that which we reached in considering the deficit in Heidegger's account of Dasein's relation to others. Of course, there is the difference that, this time, we are speaking not simply of the ethical relation to the other human being but of the religious relation to God, that is, a relation to the one who alone might transform our cry of desperation at the prospect of death into an ontological affirmation that 'all shall be well'. Yet if at this point we see a clear parting of the ways between Heideggerian philosophy and Christian theology, this does not and cannot of itself validate the Christian claim. If, with Heidegger, we choose to see our path through life in terms of mortal wandering, the notion that there might be a God in whose hands our life and our death are held cannot be more than a possibility that language itself projects. Heidegger would, of course, famously affirm that 'only a god can save us' – yet if his whole later thought can in its own way be read as waiting and listening for such a saving god, it would be something else again to say that we might, here and now and in, with, and under the forms of the created world silently attend to and listen to *and hear* the Word of such a God. As many works of theology and poetry testify (we might think of the tension of waiting and fulfilment in Eliot's *The Four Quartets* or the poetry of R.S. Thomas[56]), there are many degrees of emphasis and many subtleties of nuance to be worked through before we could ever finally draw a line of demarcation between the Kierkegaardian and the Heideggerian views in this regard. Nor would a Christian theology that cared to enter such a conversation in the first place be the kind of theology that would have any interest in 'disproving' Heidegger and claiming some kind of 'triumph' for itself. For the question is, in the end, a question of listening, of how well we listen, and, as

---

54   Ibid., p. 61.

55   Ibid., p. 69.

56   T.S. Eliot, 'East Coker' in *Four Quartets* (London: Faber and Faber, 1944), lines 123–8; for Thomas, see such poems as 'Kneeling', 'Waiting', and 'The Empty Church'.

Kierkegaard and Heidegger certainly both agree, true listening will always be marked by deep silence on the part of the one who listens and an accompanying reticence and modesty in setting out what has been heard.

Yet there is a further point. As we silently wait for the Word that might save us, waiting upon one whose speech we cannot yet hear, then the ensuing dialectic of language and silence will also become significant for the human ethical relationship. For if, in the face of our common mortality, we grow silent and listen, it may not always and in the first instance be the voice of God that we are given to hear – even if we believe ourselves to be hearing more than the 'It' of Heideggerian conscience. It may simply be that recognition of ourselves as mortals urges us to attend more closely to each other. Against the 'pure Voice' of which Agamben speaks, we may say that, as in Løgstrup's account of the threefold structure of responsibility, authentic speech too has a threefold structure: *a* speaks with *b* about *c* (as Heidegger himself knows). But when death is what we are to speak about together, it is only by listening to what each of us is saying and how each mortal individual addresses the prospect of his or her own end that we can learn what can and what can't be said, and we are unwise if we are too swift to rule on just where the boundaries of the unsayable really lie – especially if, as Heidegger warns us, we are habituated to speaking about death in the manner of tranquillizing evasiveness. Speaking truthfully together about death we might learn much of what can and cannot be said – of death, of language, and of ourselves. And in such speaking we will indeed learn (how could we not?) much of what it means to be human – not least that our mortality itself directs us to one another in such a way that, together, in the solidarity of having to die, we might learn the deepest and hardest lessons of love. For Heidegger, we die (as we live) alone, even if all our loved ones are gathered around us. For Christian faith, our death (even if we die alone) is the mark of our involvement with humanity and the possibility of solidarity with all of history's unremembered dead. And perhaps – as has already been mooted in Chapter 5 – this may also mean understanding ourselves in relation to a society that reaches out to include the dead as well as the living. In this connection, then, can it even begin to make sense to talk of 'eternal life' or of human life as open to power of the eternal within a Heideggerian perspective? Or must such talk – even in the revisionist forms discussed in the Introduction[57] – mark a final and definitive leave-taking from the Heideggerian path?

Eternal Life?

If language is the bearer of any possible understanding of human being as the being of mortals, it is also often seen as having power to resist, to rise above, and even to conquer the transience of human life, as in the final lines of Schiller's poem 'The Gods of Greece': 'What lives undyingly in song, in life must pass away'. That is

---

[57]   See pp. 3–6 above.

to say, language, the poetic word, preserves 'undyingly' what is otherwise and in its entirety subject to death. As Oberst comments in introducing his study of *Heidegger on Language and Death*, the simplest epitaph is already testimony to a faith in language as somehow reaching out beyond death and keeping memory alive.[58] But can a word really keep memory alive? Can it be *forever*? Can it be *everlasting*? Can it bear witness for all *eternity*?

In a much commented-on note in *Being and Time*, Heidegger criticizes Kierkegaard on the grounds that '[h]e clings to the ordinary conception of time, and defines the "moment of vision" with the help of "now" and "eternity"' (338/497). Leaving to one side the question of the 'now',[59] Heidegger already makes clear in the Introduction that he does not have much use for any concept of the eternal or eternity that is simply contrasted to the flow of time itself and that does not recognize that '[e]ven the "non-temporal" and the "supra-temporal" are "temporal" with regard to their Being, and not just privatively by contrast with something "temporal" as an entity "in time", but in a positive sense', although, as he immediately adds, this sense 'is one which we must first explain' (18/40). More polemically, he later comments that 'the contention that there are "eternal truths" ... belong[s] to those residues of Christian theology within philosophical problematics which have not as yet been radically extruded' (229/272) – as he himself is now seeking to do. In a similar vein, he dismisses the question concerning 'what there may be after death' and does not even wish to consider '[w]hether such a question is a possible theoretical question at all', insisting that 'The this-worldly ontological Interpretation of death takes precedence over any ontical other-worldly speculation' (248/292). In the lectures on Hölderlin's 'Germanien', Heidegger will also say that both the prevalent ideas of eternity in the Western tradition – that of *sempiternitas* (time continuing infinitely into the future) and that of the *nunc stans* or eternal present – are based on a particular way of understanding time, namely, time as the pure vanishing of one moment (or 'now') after another.[60]

It would seem, then, that attempting to develop a constructive dialogue with Heidegger around the topic of the eternal is doomed to failure. But is this so? We have just heard how, in *Being and Time*, he speaks of a positive sense in which time might be experienced in relation to the non-temporal and supra-temporal, whilst

---

[58]   Oberst, *Language and Death*, p. 5.

[59]   And also leaving aside whether Heidegger's criticism is, in fact, justified. See the discussion of Kierkegaard in my *God and Being* (Oxford: Oxford University Press, 2011), pp. 113ff. See also the discussion and further references in J.D. Caputo, 'Kierkegaard, Heidegger, and the Foundering of Metaphysics' in R.L. Perkins (ed.), *International Kierkegaard Commentary*, vol. 6: *Fear and Trembling and Repetition* (Macon: Mercer University Press, 1993), pp. 201–24; C. Carlisle, 'Kierkegaard and Heidegger' in J. Lippitt and G. Pattison (eds), *The Oxford Handbook of Kierkegaard* (Oxford: Oxford University Press, 2013), pp. 413–31.

[60]   Which, as we have also seen, is the position he ascribes to Hegel and to German Idealism more broadly. See p. 46 above.

the lectures on Hölderlin seek to articulate an experience of time that is other than the experience of a mere vanishing and that, to that extent, might be taken as opening up a way towards a new understanding of the eternal. But, keeping our focus on human existence rather than on God, how far might such a move take us towards restoring meaning to or disclosing the meaning of the religious 'symbol' (as Tillich would put it) of 'eternal life'?

I shall address this question by reference to three short texts from the 1960s, all given as public lectures by Heidegger, two of them in his childhood town of Meßkirch. This location is neither accidental nor irrelevant to the content of the lectures, since one commemorates another famous son of the town, the seventeenth-century Viennese court preacher and spiritual writer Abraham à Sancta Clara, and the other is a meditation on the meaning of home and homecoming. Although these are popular addresses and do not take a directly philosophical approach, they helpfully indicate and arguably epitomize tendencies rising from and running through much of Heidegger's later thought – and, in doing so, take us back to our starting point in *Being and Time* itself.

In the lecture on Abraham à Sancta Clara, Heidegger pays particular attention to his subject's pithy and vivid language, and he acclaims the writer's style as manifesting 'an exalted poetic power'.[61] As we might expect, death plays a significant part in the passages cited by Heidegger, as in the following: '"Whoever dies before he dies, does not die when he dies." This means that: whoever frees himself from earthly things before death comes to him, does not cease to be when the end comes. I repeat: "Whoever dies, before he dies, does not die when he dies"', an 'art' the preacher calls 'the art of dying daily'.[62] Some analogy to Heidegger's own 'anticipatory resoluteness' seems unmissable, although we must also acknowledge a significant dis-analogy and, in any case, Heidegger does not immediately comment on the content of the saying. He does, however, comment on another, briefer apothegm: 'Man – this five foot long nothing'. As he points out, 'This saying contains something rather contradictory, since Nothing has no extension and cannot therefore be "five foot long". But precisely this contradiction between Nothing and the "five foot" expresses the truth: earthly greatness and the nothingness of its meaning belong together'.[63] With regard to this last comment, we might think that it all the more shows up the difference between the two 'poetic' thinkers from Meßkirch, since, for the preacher, the meaninglessness of earthly greatness is compensated for by a life beyond death, whilst, for the philosopher, death reveals the annihilation of our entire world and of the entirety

---

[61] M. Heidegger, *Reden und andere Zeugnisse eines Lebenswegs. Gesamtausgabe*, vol. 19 (Frankfurt am Main: Klostermann, 2000), p. 606. I am taking the two Meßkirch talks in reverse chronological order. The talk on Abraham à Sancta Clara dates from 1964, the talk on 'home' from 1961.

[62] Heidegger, *Reden*, p. 605.

[63] Ibid., p. 603

of the structures in and through which we seek to give it meaning, including whatever is for us our God and our heaven.

Yet the final quotation offered by Heidegger points, however tentatively, towards another possibility. It is a quotation he describes as 'perhaps the most astonishing and beautiful poetic word-picture' left us by Abraham à Sancta Clara: 'Come hither, you silver-white swans, who, with your snow-defying wings, row round and about upon the water', to which he appends the further quotation, 'Do you not know that human life is like snow and clover, neither of which abide?'[64] But what does this juxtaposition of images mean? Heidegger's answer is as follows. We all know, he says, that snow will melt on water, yet, in the snow-white plumage of the swan, the preacher gives us an image of the transience of human life counter-intuitively maintained in being ('snow defying') as it moves on the surface of the water, itself a pure and universal image of temporal flux. In other words, the swan is a 'word-picture' of what abides in the midst of temporal change. In Heidegger's words, 'The movement of the white swans on the water is an image for what does not pass away in the midst of what passes away'.[65] But what does or even could this mean on Heidegger's own premises?

To respond to this question I turn now to the other address, given in the context of the 700th centenary celebrations of the foundation of Meßkirch. Heidegger's thoughts in this address go first to the historical nature of the occasion, and the fact that his audience have gathered to think about the Meßkirch of yesterday and of today. But what, he asks, of '... Meßkirch tomorrow? In the future?'[66] The future is not, of course, something we can know, but there are many signs of what is in store, most conspicuously the radio and television aerials springing from every rooftop. These, Heidegger says, 'show that human beings are, strictly speaking, no longer "at home" [*zu Hause*] where, seen from outside they "live"'.[67] In other words, even when I'm sitting at home in my living room, I'm really in the news studio in Bonn, or on Safari in Africa, or in a Hollywood dream. Television is thus the most immediate, the most visible, sign of the dominion of technology over our lives, a dominion that we have every reason to suppose will grow rather than diminish in the future. In the world represented by telecommunications there is no abiding city, the new is rapidly succeeded by the even newer, modernism by post-modernism, post-modernism by post-secularism and post-secularism, doubtless, by something already waiting in the wings. Spellbound and pulled onward by all this, humanity is, as it were, in a process of emigration. It is emigrating from what is *Heimisch* (or homely) to the *Unheimisch* (the alien, the unfamiliar). There is a danger that what was once called home (*Heimat*) will dissolve and disappear. The power of the *Unheimisch* seems to have so overpowered humanity that it can no longer pit itself against it. How can we defend ourselves against the pressure

---

[64] Ibid., p. 607.
[65] Ibid.
[66] Ibid., p. 574.
[67] Ibid., p. 575.

of the *Unheimisch*? Only by this: that we continually arouse the bestowing and healing and preserving strength of the *Heimisch*, that we enable the strengthening springs of the *Heimisch* to flow and create proper channels in which they can flow and so their exert influence.[68]

In order to effectively 'redeem and care for' the *Heimisch*, we have to know exactly what it is that threatens it. In the first instance we can call this 'technology', with its law of ceaseless innovation, symbolized (for Heidegger) by the advent of television. And, at one level, this is irresistible. Even Meßkirch cannot escape it. Perhaps, then, 'home' in the deepest sense is a thing of the past. 'Perhaps humanity is migrating to a condition of homelessness', Heidegger muses; 'Perhaps the relation to home and the pull of home is disappearing from the Dasein of modern humanity'.[69] Perhaps. Or '[p]erhaps a new relation to the *Heimisch* is preparing itself even in the midst of the pressure exerted by the *Unheimisch*'.[70] But what could this be and how might we find the way to it?

The pull of home, Heidegger goes on, is what we call homesickness, a phenomenon that has far from vanished from our modern experience. On the contrary, homesickness is the true meaning of that most modern of moods, boredom, a mood that pervades the world shaped by technology and the technological consciousness. This boredom is 'hidden homesickness'.[71] But, at this point, Heidegger's talk takes a curious twist. The question is this: how are we to recognize this longed-for 'home'? Heidegger's answer is that we do so by preserving that from which we have come and staying near to the mystery of the origin. But how can we do this or, more specifically, *where* are we to do it? Deploying a consciously archaic form of words, Heidegger says we are to do this in 'God's acre', that is, in the graveyard. This is the place where we are to remember what has been, the parental home, and the time of youth; this is the place where the noise and frenzy of modernity are matched by stillness and restraint. The encounter with the *Unheimisch* thus itself occasions reflective remembrance, *Besinnung*, upon the *Heimisch*, the quiet but festive eventide remembrance that enables us to maintain a counter-movement, a *Heimkehr* (literally: a turning homewards), over against the power of the *Unheimisch*. 'By reflecting upon tomorrow, we arouse the healing power of yesterday, understood correctly and appropriated aright. On such ways we first attain the Today that we must live through [endure] between the past and the future. Such living through helps us to become earnest [*inständig*] in what holds its position against all change'.[72]

All of this may simply reinforce our worst fears about Heidegger's essential conservatism and his penchant for small-town sentimentality. But Heidegger is by no means suggesting that there is any opt-out from the continuing advance of the

---

[68]   Ibid., pp. 575–6.

[69]   Ibid., p. 578.

[70]   Ibid.

[71]   Ibid., p. 580.

[72]   Ibid., p. 581.

age of technology any more than there is any opt-out from the flow of time. Yet in God's acre, the place of remembrance where we remember the dead and all that our time with the dead has meant to us, we find a counter-movement that offers the possibility of continuity in the midst of change. It is not simply a matter of now versus then, but of the interconnectedness of past, present, and future gathered in those acts of festive, reflective remembrance in and through which we call to mind the rock of which we are hewn and thereby 'come home' to who we, even now, are.

But such remembrance and homecoming not only finds its proper place in 'God's Acre'. It is also – and, in the light of everything we have heard from Heidegger about the inter-relationship of language and human Dasein, unsurprisingly – an action (or perhaps, better, a comportment) that occurs in and as language. This is the point Heidegger develops in a lecture of 2nd July, 1960 to the annual meeting of the Hebbel society, commemorating the provincial dialect poet Peter Hebbel. This address was subsequently published twice, under two mutually interpreting titles, both of which relate to our reflections here: 'Persistence in the Midst of Change' and 'Language and Home'. The occasion gives Heidegger an opportunity to air some general comments of a kind to which we are, by now, accustomed. 'Humanity', he says, 'is homeless', adding that the threat posed by this homelessness drives us to seek a saving power, a power that would preserve both language and home in what is most proper to them.[73] Stressing the 'and' of the title 'Language and Home', Heidegger defends the apparent provinciality of the Alemannic dialect. For 'the essence of language is rooted in dialect (*Dialekt*). Here too, if the spoken language (*Mundart*) is the mother tongue, are the roots of the homeliness (*das Heimische*), of being at home (*Zuhaus*), of home (*Heimat*) itself. Our spoken language is not only the language of our mothers but first and foremost the mother of language'.[74] Thus, although home and language are alike threatened by the homelessness of our age, these dialect poems are able to take the most homely of all forms of language in such a way as to lay bare the fourfold, the articulated interconnectedness of earth and heaven, human being, and the 'still spirits' whose silent presence pervades all that is said. Thus 'It is poetic saying that first lets mortals dwell on earth, under heaven and before the divine'. Yet, 'Language, by virtue of its poeticizing essence, is the most hidden and for that reason the most adequate, the earnest, bountiful, bringing forth of home ...', and, Heidegger concludes, we should not so much say, 'Language and Home' but 'Language *as* Home'.[75]

These lectures do not themselves spell out the decisive connection on which they seem to converge: that language, death, and home, each 'equi-primordially' and inter-connectedly, provide the counter-movement to the loss of human meaning in the age of global technology. This may seem like a rather surprising trinity, but

---

[73]   M. Heidegger, *Aus der Erfahrung des Denkens. Gesamtausgabe*, vol. 13 (Frankfurt am Main: Klostermann, 2002), p. 157.

[74]   Ibid., p. 156.

[75]   Ibid., p. 180.

the mutual affinity of its parts is not an arbitrary invention on Heidegger's part. That death might be regarded as home is still a conscious element in some religious traditions and is also manifest in the wishes of many entirely secular persons to be buried or have their ashes scattered at a site associated with their place of origin or in military 'homecoming' rituals. Alongside traditions that see death as the ultimate separation from humanity and from God, the Bible also speaks of death as the human being going to his 'eternal home' (Ecclesiastes 12.5),[76] a phrase repeated in many hymns and prayers.[77] Heidegger's use of such traditions is, of course, transformative. He is not speaking mythologically or scientifically but as interpreting a self-understanding on the part of Dasein that is presented in and as language, that is, in the *logos* and, specifically, the *logos* that is the poetic word. This is in clear continuity with how he already understood the relationship between understanding and language in *Being and Time*. But there is also a difference, since the authentic relation to death is no longer that of freely affirming our thrownness towards death. Instead, it is now a matter of taking to heart the poetic word in which death, correlated with the sheltering earth from which we were made and to which we return, is what calls us *home* so that we can become who we are: mortals, wandering on earth beneath an open sky and in the face of the gods.

To sum up. In an age of planetary technology, as humanity is drawn further and further away from home and becomes ever more profoundly gripped by the anxiety that reveals its state of homelessness and the ever more rapid flow of technologically managed time, its best hope is precisely the remembrance of mortality, a remembrance that, in accordance with the basic structure of human Dasein, can occur only in and as an articulated word and, primarily or most profoundly, in and as a *poetic* word. Such a word, like the word-picture of snow on water, calls us home, that is, *re*calls us to what abides in the midst of temporal flux.[78] And we may add that not only is this word articulated as a constant and

---

[76]   The authorized version has the less philosophical but more evocative 'long home'.

[77]   Assmann traces the idea of death and home back to Egyptian sources and to the maternal imagery of one tradition of funeral rites, including the practice of painting the inside of the coffin as a maternal figure to whose womb, in death, we return home. See J. Assmann, *Der Tod als Thema der Kulturtheorie* (Frankfurt am Main: Suhrkamp, 2000), pp. 27ff.

[78]   That Heidegger sets the question up with specific reference to planetary technology suggests significant consequences for practical life. For the extension of biological life by all possible technical means is not only the avowed aim of post- and trans-humanist utopians, it is also a matter of daily medical practice. This practice, however, generates its own manifold problems, which include not just the ethical questions that new technologies bring in their train but the general crisis of an extended old age that leaves many people wretchedly exposed to protracted lives of poverty, isolation, and exposure to degenerative diseases. Most readers will probably be able to supply examples from their own experience. In this context, rethinking our relation to death either in terms of an existential readiness for death or as a poetic homecoming would, probably, go a long way to weaning us from our addiction to technologies whose 'success' is measured in the quantitative extension of the human lifespan but is too often irrelevant to genuine human happiness.

urgent counter-movement to the technologization of life and language, it is also articulated in a world in which, as we saw in Chapter 3, is disposed to see itself in what it believes to be its 'realistic' self-reflection in the modern novel – open-ended, ambiguous, and written in the prose of everyday life.

Even in its own terms, such a poetic word concerning the eternal does not speak of the eternity of Christian eschatology. Of course not. But it does suggest a view of time that is not mere vanishing. A view of time as allowing, in the word of remembrance, the possibility of something more than simple flux and something subtly other than being thrown towards annihilation. If we agree with Heidegger that our different ideas of eternity will reflect different kinds of time-experience, then the kind of time-experience that this possibility opens up would in turn open up a different way of conceiving of eternity and, possibly, a way that, in all its difference, would not be entirely strange to religion.

In this respect, it is striking that English translations of the two Meßkirch addresses were published together in the journal *The Eastern Buddhist*, with an introductory commentary by the Zen philosopher Keiji Nishitani. Although writing from an avowedly Buddhist perspective, Nishitani's comments are framed with explicit reference to the common tasks of Buddhist and Christian discourse in the contemporary world. In this context, he interprets the notion of seeking what is homely in the midst of the movement towards planetary homelessness developed in the Meßkirch anniversary address in terms of the Buddha's teaching on 'the basis of human existence prior to any sort of "Home"' and the breakthrough to 'the great Repose called Nirvana'.[79] Although it transcends 'home' in any conventional material sense, such an 'awakening' and 'attainment of Repose in the midst of Transitoriness', it is, in Heideggerian terms, 'a way of discovering the Home in the immediate midst of homelessness'.[80] For the Buddhist as for Heidegger this is not an 'escape to some other world' but a way of 'living as an awakened one … in this world, that is to say, to "live" in the true sense. Apart from this "life," the "other world" could be only a world of fancy … it can not be our "Home"'.[81] Nishitani further connects this with the development in Mahayana Buddhism of the Pure Land School, in which Enlightenment is figured as rebirth into the Pure Land of peace and light and, although Nishitani does not develop the point here, as attainable not through ascetic exercise but by virtue of faith in the vow of the Buddha to save all sentient beings. In other words, such 'repose' in the midst of time is both a return to the true home before all homes and also an event of grace, gifted to us by a power beyond our power (and thus, in Pure Land parlance, a matter of 'other-power'[82]). Here the Buddhist perspective draws close to that of more theistic religious views.

---

[79] K. Nishitani, 'Preliminary Remark' to M. Heidegger 'Two Addresses'. *The Eastern Buddhist* (New Series) 2 (1966): 53.

[80] Ibid.

[81] Ibid.

[82] The notion of other-power is especially associated with the philosopher Hajime Tanabe. See my *Agnosis: Theology in the Void* (Basingstoke: Macmillan, 1996), pp. 123–37.

Nishitani's comments on Heidegger's exposition of Abraham à Sancta Clara are more specifically framed with a view to the convergence of Christian and Buddhist perspectives. What especially interests him here is the image of the white swan as a word-picture of snow on water, on which he comments:

> The whiteness of the snow appears here in a truer degree than is found in itself. It appears in its own ultimate reality, that is, as a 'pure' whiteness. This silver-whiteness belongs, however, not only to the snow, as its heightened true color; it is also the color of the swans and also belongs to them. It is they, they preserve, through their very swimming, the snow and prevent it from disappearing in the waters. 'The movement of the white swans on the waters is an image of Permanence in the most transitory things.' Isn't it also an expression of the world-affirmation? Isn't it permissible to view this movement of the white swans as an image of a man who 'dies before he dies and does not die when he dies'?[83]

In these terms, Nishitani sees it as an image that affirms Zen insight into the non-duality of permanence and transience, or of being and becoming. Of the first speech, on home and homelessness, he says that it 'implies a valuable suggestion as to the basic plane on which the encounter of Eastern and Western thought in general ought to occur' and, of the second, the speech culminating in the image of the swans, that it points 'to the true contact between Christianity and Zen Buddhism'.[84] This, as I understand Nishitani's remarks, relates to how these talks open the way towards an experience and understanding of time that allows for a rethinking of the meaning of the eternal that would permit us both to accept, with Heidegger, that time is the constant and all-encompassing horizon of the meaning of being and yet 'at the same time' to find in the religious language of eternity, the Eternal, and 'eternal life' a way of articulating what is of greatest significance in being in time itself. And that is no less true if being in time is also being towards death. Remembering that everything that is said here is said in language and as language and that it is only in and as language that this can be said, we therefore conclude as follows. To be is to die. But to live is to live in the light of the Eternal and to live in the light of the Eternal is to experience time itself as generative of hope and, indissociable from that, of the desire for the good. The further interpretation of what this could mean and just how far a Heideggerian understanding of being in time might re-animate the theological interpretation of the Eternal is, however, a task for another work.

---

[83] Nishitani, 'Preliminary Remark', p. 58.

[84] Ibid.

Bibliography

Works by Martin Heidegger (German)

All works from the *Gesamtausgabe* are published in Frankfurt am Main by Vittorio Klostermann.

Aus der Erfahrung des Denkens. Gesamtausgabe, vol. 13 (2002).
Der Deutsche Idealismus (Fichte, Schelling, Hegel) und die philosophische Grundlage der Gegenwart. Gesamtausgabe, vol. 28 (1997).
Die Metaphysik des deutschen Idealismus. Zur erneuten Auslegung von Schelling: Philosophische Untersuchungen über das Wesen der menschlichen Freiheit und die damit zusammenhängenden Gegenstände (1809). Gesamtausgabe, vol. 49 (1991).
Einführung in die Metaphysik (Tübingen: Niemeyer, 1998).
Einführung in die Metaphysik. Gesamtausgabe, vol. 40 1983.
Einführung in die phänomenologische Forschung. Gesamtausgabe, vol. 17 (1994).
Frühe Schriften. Gesamtausgabe, vol. 1 (1978).
Grundbegriffe der aristotelischen Philosophie. Gesamtausgabe, vol. 18 (2006).
Hegel. Gesamtausgabe, vol. 68 (1993).
Hegels Phänomenologie des Geistes. Gesamtausgabe, vol. 32 (1980).
Hölderlins Hymne 'Der Ister'. Gesamtausgabe, vol. 53 (1993).
Hölderlins Hymnen 'Germanien' und 'Der Rhein'. Gesamtausgabe, vol. 39 (1989).
Identität und Differenze. Gesamtausgabe, vol. 11 (2006).
Nietzsche II. Gesamtausgabe, vol. 6.2 (1997).
Phänomenologie des religiösen Lebens. Gesamtausgabe, vol. 60 (1995).
Reden und andere Zeugnisse eines Lebensweges. Gesamtausgabe, vol. 16 (2000).
Schelling: Vom Wesen der menschlichen Freiheit (1809). Gesamtausgabe, vol. 42 (1988).
Sein und Zeit. Gesamtausgabe, vol. 2 (1977).
Unterwegs zur Sprache. Gesamtausgabe, vol. 12 (1985).
Wegmarken. Gesamtausgabe, vol. 9 (1996).

Works by Martin Heidegger (English)

Being and Time, trans. John Macquarrie and Edward Robinson (Oxford: Blackwell, 1962).
Hegel's Phenomenology of Spirit, trans. Parvis Emad and Kenneth Maly (Bloomington: Indiana University Press, 1994).

Hölderlin's Hymn 'The Ister', trans. William McNeill and Julia Davis (Bloomington: Indiana University Press, 1996).

Identity and Difference, trans. Joan Stambaugh ([Dual language edition] New York: Harper and Row, 1969).

Nietzsche, vol. 4: *Nihilism*, trans. Frank A. Capuzzi, ed. David Farrell Krell (New York: HarperCollins, 1982).

Pathmarks, ed. William McNeill (Cambridge: Cambridge University Press, 1998).

'What Is Metaphysics?' in *Pathmarks*, ed. William McNeill (Cambridge: Cambridge University Press, 1998), pp. 82–96.

Works by Søren Kierkegaard (Danish)

Af en endu Levendes Papirer/Om Begrebet Ironi. Søren Kierkegaards Skrifter, vol. 1 (Copenhagen: Gad, 1997).

Afsluttende uvidenskabelige Efterskrift. Søren Kierkegaards Skrifter, vol. 7 (Copenhagen: Gad, 2002).

Begrebet Angest. Søren Kierkegaards Skrifter, vol. 4 (Copenhagen: Gad, 1997).

Enten-Eller 2. Søren Kierkegaards Skrifter, vol. 3 (Copenhagen: Gad, 1997).

Kjerlighedens Gerninger. Søren Kierkegaards Skrifter, vol. 9 (Copenhagen: Gad, 2004).

Lilien paa Marken og Fuglen under Himlen; Tvende ethisk-religieuse Smaa-Afhandlinger; Sygdommen til Døden; 'Yppersterpræsten' – 'Tolderen' – 'Synderinden'. Søren Kierkegaards Skrifter, vol. 11 (Copenhagen: Gad, 2006).

En literair Anmeldelse; Opbyggelige Taler i forskjelling Aand. Søren Kierkegaards Skrifter, vol. 8 (Copenhagen: Gad, 2004).

Opbyggelige Taler 1843; Opbyggelige Taler 1844; Tre Taler ved tænkte Leiligheder. Søren Kierkegaards Skrifter, vol. 5 (Copenhagen: Gad, 1998).

Works by Søren Kierkegaard (English)

The Concept of Anxiety, trans. Reidar Thomte (Princeton: Princeton University Press, 1980).

The Concept of Irony, trans. H.V. Hong and E.H. Hong (Princeton: Princeton University Press, 1989).

Concluding Unscientific Postscript, vol. 1, trans. H.V. Hong and E.H. Hong (Princeton: Princeton University Press, 1992).

Eighteen Upbuilding Discourses, trans. H.V. Hong and E.H. Hong (Princeton: Princeton University Press, 1990).

Either/Or, Part II, trans. H.V. Hong and E.H. Hong (Princeton: Princeton University Press, 1987).

Kierkegaard's Spiritual Writings, trans. George Pattison, George (New York: Harper, 2010).

The Sickness unto Death, trans. H.V. Hong and E.H. Hong (Princeton: Princeton University Press, 1980).

Three Discourses on Imagined Occasions, trans. H.V. Hong and E.H. Hong (Princeton: Princeton University Press, 1993).

Upbuilding Discourses in Various Spirits, trans. H.V. Hong and E.H. Hong (Princeton: Princeton University Press, 2009).

Works of Love, trans. H.V. Hong and E.H. Hong (Princeton: Princeton University Press, 1995).

Other Works

Adorno, Theodor Wiesengrund, 'Kierkegaard's Lehre von der Liebe' in idem., *Kierkegaard* (Frankfurt am Main: Suhrkamp, 1974).

Agamben, Giorgio, *Language and Death: The Place of Negativity (Theory and History of Literature)*, vol. 8, trans. K.E. Pinkus and Michael Hardt (Minneapolis: University of Minnesota Press, 1991).

Andersen, Svend, 'In the Eyes of a Lutheran Philosopher. How Løgstrup Treated Moral Thinkers' in Svend Andersen and Kees van Kooten Niekerk (eds), *Concern for the Other: Perspectives on the Ethics of K.E. Løgstrup* (Notre Dame: Notre Dame University Press, 2007), pp. 29–54.

Arnold, Matthew, *Matthew Arnold*, ed. Miriam Allott (Oxford: Oxford University Press [Oxford Poetry Library], 1995).

Assmann, Jan, *Der Tod als Thema der Kulturtheorie* (Frankfurt am Main: Suhrkamp, 2000).

Bakhtin, M.M., *The Dialogic Imagination: Four Essays*, trans. Caryl Emerson and Michael Holquist, ed. M. Holquist (Austin: University of Texas Press, 1981).

Bakhtin, M.M., *Problems of Dostoevsky's Poetics*, trans. Caryl Emerson (Minneapolis: University of Minnesota Press, 1984).

Barth, Karl, *Church Dogmatics*, vol. 1: *The Doctrine of the Word of God, Part 1*, trans. G.W. Bromiley (London: T. & T. Clark, 2004).

Barth, Karl, *The Letter to the Romans*, trans. E.C. Hoskyns (Oxford: Oxford University Press, 1933).

Barth, Karl, *The Resurrection of the Dead*, trans. H.J. Stanning (London: Hodder and Stoughton, 1933).

Beauvoir, Simone de, *A Very Easy Death*, trans. Patrick O'Brian (Harmondsworth: Penguin, 1969).

Berdyaev, N.A., *Slavery and Freedom*, trans. R.M. French (London: G. Bles, 1943).

Bishop, Jeffrey, *The Anticipatory Corpse: Medicine, Power, and the Care of the Dying* (Notre Dame: University of Notre Dame Press, 2011).

Blattner, William D., 'The Concept of Death in *Being and Time*' in Hubert L. Dreyfus and Mark Wrathall (eds), *Heidegger Re-Examined* (New York: Routledge, 2002), pp. 307–29.

Broch, Hermann, *The Sleepwalkers*, trans. Willa Muir and Edwin Muir (London: Quartet, 1986).

Bultmann, Rudolf, *Das Evangelium des Johannes* (Göttingen: Vandenhoeck and Ruprecht, 1950).

Bultmann, Rudolf, 'New Testament and Mythology' in Hans-Werner Bartsch and Reginald H. Fuller (eds), *Kerygma and Myth: A Theological Debate* (London: SPCK, 1972), pp. 1–44.

Butler, Joseph, *The Analogy of Religion, Natural and Revealed* (London: Dent Dutton, 1906).

Caputo, John D., *Demythologizing Heidegger* (Bloomington: Indiana University Press, 1993).

Caputo, John D., 'Kierkegaard, Heidegger, and the Foundering of Metaphysics' in Robert L. Perkins (ed.), *International Kierkegaard Commentary*, vol. 6: *Fear and Trembling and Repetition* (Macon: Mercer University Press, 1993), pp. 201–24.

Carel, Havi, *Life and Death in Freud and Heidegger* (Amsterdam: Rodopi, 2006).

Carlisle, Clare, 'Kierkegaard and Heidegger' in John Lippitt and George Pattison (eds), *The Oxford Handbook of Kierkegaard* (Oxford: Oxford University Press, 2013), pp. 413–31.

Carlson, Thomas A., 'Notes on Love and Death in Augustine and Heidegger'. *Medieval Mystical Theology* 21.1 (2012): 9–33.

Carman, Taylor, *Heidegger's Analytic: Interpretation, Discourse and Authenticity in* Being and Time (Cambridge: Cambridge University Press, 2009).

Chochinov, H.M., 'Dying, Dignity and New Horizons in Palliative End-of-Life Care'. *CA: A Cancer Journal for Clinicians*, American Cancer Society (October 2006) 56: 82–103.

Chrétien, Jean-Louis, *The Ark of Speech*, trans. Andrew Brown (London: Routledge, 2004).

Craigo-Snell, Shannon, *Silence, Love, and Death: Saying 'Yes' to God in the Theology of Karl Rahner* (Milwaukee: Marquette University Press, 2008).

Cupitt, Don, *Taking Leave of God* (London: SCM Press, 1980).

Davenport, John, and Rudd, Anthony (eds), *Kierkegaard after MacIntyre: Essays on Freedom, Narrative, and Virtue* (Chicago: Open Court, 2001).

Demske, James M., *Sein, Mensch und Tod. Der Todesproblem bei Martin Heidegger* (Freiburg/Munich: Karl Alber, 1963). (English translation: *Being, Man, and Death: A Key to Heidegger* [Lexington: University of Kentucky Press, 1970]).

Der Deutsche Evangelische Kirchenausschuss, *Die Bekenntnis-Schriften der evangelish-lutherischen Kirche* (Göttingen: Vandenhoeck and Ruprecht, 1930).

Dodd, W.J., 'Ein Gottträgervolk, ein geistiger Führer – Die Dostojewskij-Rezeption von der Jahrhundertwende bis zu den zwanziger Jahren als Paradigma des deutschen Rußlandbilds' [A God-bearing people, a spiritual leader – The reception of Dostoevsky from the turn of the century through to the 1920s as a paradigm of the German image of Russia] in Lew Kopelew (ed.), *West-östliche*

Spiegelungen, Reihe A: Russen und Rußland aus deutscher Sicht, Bd. 4: *Das zwanzigste Jahrhundert* (Munich: Wilhelm Fink, 2000), pp. 853–65.

Donne, John, *Devotions upon Emergent Occasions Together with Death's Duell* (London: Simpkins, Marshall, Hamilton. Kent and Co. Ltd [Abbey Classics], 1926).

Dostoevsky, F.M., *The Brothers Karamazov*, trans. Richard Pevear and Larissa Volokhonsky (London: Vintage, 1992).

Dostoevsky, F.M., *The Idiot*, trans. Richard Pevear and Larissa. Volokhonsky (London: Granta, 2001).

Edwards, Paul, *Heidegger on Death: A Critical Evaluation* (La Salle: The Hegeler Institute, 1979).

Eliot, T.S., *Four Quartets* (London: Faber and Faber, 1944).

Ferreira, M. Jamie, *Love's Grateful Striving: A Commentary on Kierkegaard's Works of Love* (Oxford: Oxford University Press, 2001).

Feuerbach, Ludwig, *The Essence of Christianity*, trans. Marian Evans (New York: Prometheus, 1989).

Feuerbach, Ludwig, *The Essence of Faith According to Luther*, trans. Melvin Cherno (New York: Harper and Row, 1967).

Feuerbach, Ludwig, *Thoughts on Death and Immortality: From the Papers of a Thinker, along with an Appendix of Theological-Satirical Epigrams, Edited by One of His Friends*, ed. and trans. James Massey (Berkeley: University of California Press, 1980).

Frank, Joseph, *Dostoevsky: The Years of Ordeal, 1850–1859* (Princeton: Princeton University Press, 1983).

George, Peter, 'Remembering the Dead: Kierkegaard and Dostoevsky', *Modern Believing* 35.2 (April 1994): 24–31.

Geroulanos, Stefanos. *An Atheism That Is Not Humanist Emerges in French Thought* (Stanford: Stanford University Press, 2010).

Gordon, Peter Eli, *Rosenzweig and Heidegger. Between Judaism and German Philosophy* (Berkeley: University of California Press, 2003).

Guardini, Romano, *Religiöse Gestalten in Dostojewksijs Werk* (Munich: Kösel, 1977).

Guérin, Benjamin, 'Chestov – Kierkegaard: faux ami, étrange fraternité' in Ramona Fotiade and Françoise Schwab (eds), *Léon Chestov – Vladimir Jankélévitch. Du tragique à l'ineffable* (Saarbrücken: Editions Universitaires Européennes, 2011), pp. 113–32.

Guignon, Charles, 'Heidegger and Kierkegaard on Death: The Existentiell and the Existential' in Patrick Stokes and Adam J. Buben (eds), *Kierkegaard and Death* (Bloomington: Indiana University Press, 2011), pp. 184–203.

Harris, Horton, *David Friedrich Strauss and His Theology* (Cambridge: Cambridge University Press, 1973).

Heidegger, Gertrud (ed.), *'Mein liebes Seelchen!' Briefe Martin Heideggers an seine Frau Elfride 1915–1970* (Munich: Deutsche-Verlags-Anstalt, 2005).

Hick, John, *Death and Eternal Life* (London: Collins, 1976).

Hühn, Lore, and Schwab, Philipp, 'Kierkegaard and German Idealism' in J.A. Lippitt and George Pattison (eds), *The Oxford Handbook of Kierkegaard* (Oxford: Oxford University Press, forthcoming), pp. 54–85.

Jakim, Boris, and Bird, Robert (eds), *On Spiritual Unity: A Slavophile Reader* (New York: Lindisfarne Books, 1998).

Janicaud, Dominique, *Heidegger en France. Entretiens*, vol. 2 (Paris: Albin Michel, 2001).

Jankélévitch, Vladimir, *Penser la Mort* (Paris: Liana Levi, 1994).

Krishek, Sharon, *Kierkegaard on Faith and Love* (Cambridge: Cambridge University Press, 2009).

Kisiel, Theodor, *The Genesis of Heidegger's* Being and Time (Berkeley: University of California Press, 1993).

Kisiel, Theodor, and Sheehan, Thomas (eds), *Becoming Heidegger* (Evanston: Northwestern University Press, 2007).

Kojève, Alexandre, *Introduction à la lecture de Hegel; leçons sur la phénoménologie de l'esprit* (Paris: Gallimard, 1947).

Kojève, Alexandre, 'Note inédite sur Hegel et Heidegger', *Rue Descartes* 7, ed. Bernard Hesbois (June 1993): 37–9.

Lear, Jonathan, *Radical Hope: Ethics in the Face of Cultural Devastation* (Cambridge: Harvard University Press, 2008).

Lévinas, Emmanuel, *Dieu, la mort et le temps* (Paris: Grasset, 1993).

Løgstrup, K.E., *Den etiske fordring* (Copenhagen: Gyldendal, 1956, 1991).

Løgstrup, K.E., *The Ethical Demand*, ed. Hans Fink (Notre Dame: University of Notre Dame Press, 1997).

Løgstrup, K.E., *Kierkegaards und Heideggers Existenzanalyse und ihr Verhältnis zur Verkündigung* (Berlin: Erich Bläschker, 1950).

Løgstrup, K.E., *Opgør med Kierkegaard* (Copenhagen: Gyldendal, 1968).

Lukács, Georg, *Dostojewski: Notizen und Entwürfe* (Budapest: Akademia I Kiado, 1985).

Luther, Martin, 'Disputation against the Scholastics' and 'Heidelberg Disputation' in Jaroslav Pelikan and Helmut T. Lehmann (eds), *Luther's Works*, vol. 31: *Career of the Reformer I* (Muhlenberg: Concordia, 1957).

Luther, Martin, *Lectures on the Sermon on the Mount and the Magnificat* in Jaroslav Pelikan (ed.), *Luther's Writings*, vol. 21 (St. Louis: Concordia, 1955).

Luther, Martin, 'A Sermon on Preparing to Die' in Martin Dietrich and Helmut T. Lehmann (eds), *Luther's Works*, vol. 42: *Devotional Writings I* (Philadelphia: Fortress, 1969).

Macquarrie, John, 'Death and Its Existential Significance' in John Macquarrie (ed.), *Studies in Christian Existentialism* (Montreal: McGill University Press, 1965).

Malpas, Jeff, and Solomon, Robert C., *Death and Philosophy* (London: Routledge, 1988).

Marcel, Gabriel, *Tragic Wisdom and Beyond*, trans. Stephen Jolin and Peter McCormick (Evanston: Northwestern University Press, 1973).

Marino, Gordon D., 'A Critical Perspective on Kierkegaard's "At a Graveside"' in Patrick Stokes and Adam J. Buben (eds), *Kierkegaard and Death* (Bloomington: Indiana University Press, 2011), pp. 150–59.

Martensen, Hans Lassen, *Af mit Levnet*, vol. 1 (Copenhagen: Gyldendal, 1882).

Mooney, Edward F., *Excursions with Kierkegaard* (New York: Bloomsbury, 2013).

Muir, Edwin, *An Autobiography* (Edinburgh: Canongate, 1993).

Muir, Edwin, *Collected Poems* (London: Faber and Faber, 1984).

Mulhall, Stephen, *Routledge Philosophy Guidebook to Heidegger and* Being and Time (London: Routledge, 1996).

Nietzsche, Friedrich, *Also Sprach Zarathustra. Werke* II (Frankfurt am Main: Ullstein, 1972).

Nishitani, Keiji, 'Preliminary Remark' to Martin Heidegger 'Two Addresses'. *The Eastern Buddhist* (New Series) 2 (1966): 48–59.

Nussbaum, Martha, *Love's Knowledge: Essays on Philosophy and Literature* (Oxford: Oxford University Press, 1990).

Oberst, Joachim, *Heidegger on Language and Death: The Intrinsic Connection in Human Existence* (London: Continuum, 2009).

Olafson, Frederick A., *Heidegger and the Ground of Ethics: A Study of Mitsein* (Cambridge: Cambridge University Press, 1998).

Pattison, George, *Agnosis: Theology in the Void* (Basingstoke: Macmillan, 1996).

Pattison, George, 'Existence, Anxiety, and the Moment of Vision: Fundamental Ontology and Existentiell Faith Revisited' in Anthony Paul Smith and Daniel Whistler (eds), *After the Postsecular and the Postmodern: New Essays in Continental Philosophy of Religion* (Newcastle-upon-Tyne: Cambridge Scholars Publishing, 2010).

Pattison, George, *God and Being* (Oxford: Oxford University Press, 2011).

Pattison, George, *'The Heart Could Never Speak': Existentialism and Faith in a Poem of Edwin Muir* (Eugene: Cascade Books, 2013).

Pattison, George, 'Heidegger's Hölderlin and Kierkegaard's Christ' in Stephen Mulhall (ed.), *Martin Heidegger* (Aldershot: Ashgate, 2006), pp. 391–404.

Pattison, George, 'The Joy of Birdsong or Dialectical Lyrics' in Robert L. Perkins (ed.), *International Kierkegaard Commentary*, vol. 10: *Without Authority* (Macon: Mercer University Press, 2007).

Pattison, George, *Kierkegaard and the Theology of the Nineteenth Century* (Cambridge: Cambridge University Press, 2012).

Pattison, George, *Kierkegaard's Upbuilding Discourses: Philosophy, Literature and Theology* (London: Routledge, 2002).

Pattison, George, *The Philosophy of Kierkegaard* (Chesham: Acumen, 2005).

Pattison, George, *Routledge Philosophy Guidebook to the Later Heidegger* (London: Routledge, 2000).

Phillips, D.Z., *Death and Immortality* (London: Macmillan, 1970).

Pippin, Robert, *Henry James and Modern Moral Life* (Cambridge: Cambridge University Press, 2001).

Pyper, Hugh, *The Joy of Kierkegaard: Essays on Kierkegaard as a Biblical Reader* (Sheffield: Equinox, 2011).

Raphael, Melissa, *The Female Face of God in Auschwitz: A Jewish Feminist Theology* of the Holocaust (London: Routledge, 2003).

Rosenzweig, Franz, *The Star of Redemption*, trans. W.H. Hallo (Notre Dame: Notre Dame University Press, 1985).

Safranski, Rüdiger, *Martin Heidegger: Between Good and Evil* (Cambridge: Harvard University Press, 1998).

Sakharov, Archimandrite Sophrony, *We Shall See Him as He Is* (Tolleshunt Knights: Stavropegic Monastery of St John the Baptist, 2004).

Sartre, Jean-Paul, *Being and Nothingness*, trans. Hazel E. Barnes (London: Methuen, 1969).

Scanlan, James P., *Dostoevsky the Thinker* (Ithaca: Cornell University Press, 2002).

Schleiermacher, F.D.E., *Speeches on Religion*, trans. Richard Crouter (Cambridge: Cambridge University Press, 1988).

Sophocles, *The Theban Plays*, trans. E.F. Watling (Harmondsworth: Penguin, 1947).

Stein, Edith, *Endliches und Ewiges Sein. Gesamtausgabe*, vols 11/12 (Freiburg: Herder, 2006).

Steiner, George, *Heidegger* (London: Fontana, 1978).

Steiner, George, *Tolstoy or Dostoevsky: An Essay in Contrast* (London: Faber and Faber, 1960).

Stokes, Patrick, 'Duties to the Dead? Earnest Imagination and Remembrance' in Patrick Stokes and A.J. Buben (eds), *Kierkegaard and Death* (Bloomington: Indiana University Press, 2011), pp. 253–73.

Strhan, Anna, Levinas, *Subjectivity, Education: Towards an Ethics of Radical Responsibility* (Chichester: Wiley-Blackwell, 2012).

Tennyson, Alfred Lord, 'In Memoriam' in Christopher Ricks (ed.), *Tennyson: A Selected Edition* (London: Pearson Longman, 2007).

Theunissen, Michael, 'The Upbuilding in the Thought of Death: Traditional Elements, Innovative Ideas, and Unexhausted Possibilities', trans. George Pattison, in Richard L. Perkins (ed.), *International Kierkegaard Commentary*: *Prefaces and Writing Sampler* and *Three Discourses on Imagined Occasions*, vols 9 and 10 combined (Macon: Mercer University Press, 2006).

Thompson, D.O., 'Dostoevsky and Science' in W.J. Leatherbarrow (ed.), *The Cambridge Companion to Dostoevskii* (Cambridge: Cambridge University Press, 2002).

Thompson, D.O., and Pattison, George (ed.), *Dostoevsky and the Christian Tradition* (Cambridge: Cambridge University Press, 2002).

Thomson, Ann, *Bodies of Thought: Science, Religion, and the Soul in the Early Enlightenment* (Oxford: Oxford University Press, 2008).

Thurneysen, Eduard, *Dostoevsky*, trans K.R. Crim (London: Epworth Press, 1961).

Tillich, Paul, *The New Being* (New York: Scribner, 1955).

Tillich, Paul, *The Shaking of the Foundations* (London: SCM Press, 1949).

Tillich, Paul, *Systematic Theology* ([One vol. edition] Welwyn: James Nisbet, 1968).

Tolstoy, Leo, *The Death of Ivan Ilych and Other Stories*, trans. Aylmer Maude (New York: New American Library, 1960).

Tolstoy, Leo, *The Gospel in Brief: The Life of Jesus*, trans. D. Condren (New York: Harper, 2011).

Toumayan, A., "'I More Than the Others": Dostoevsky and Levinas'. *Yale French Studies* 104 (Encounters with Levinas] (2004): 55–66.

Ward, Graham, *Barth, Derrida, and the Language of Theology* (Cambridge: Cambridge University Press, 1995).

Weston, Michael, *Philosophy, Literature and the Human Good* (London: Routledge, 2004).

White, Carol J., *Time and Death: Heidegger's Analysis of Finitude* (Aldershot: Ashgate, 2005).

Williams, Rowan, *Dostoevsky: Language, Faith and Fiction* (London: Continuum, 2008).

Wilson, Colin, *The Outsider* (London: Victor Gollancz, 1956).

Wyschogrod, Edith, *Spirit in Ashes: Hegel, Heidegger, and Man-Made Mass Death* (New Haven: Yale University Press, 1985).

Index